T0330266

International Business under Adversity

To David, Chantal and Caroline

In memory of Wladimir Sachs
co-author, colleague and friend

International Business under Adversity

A Role in Corporate Responsibility, Conflict Prevention and Peace

Edited by

Gabriele G.S. Suder

Associate Dean of Global Management, Professor of International Business, CERAM Business School Nice – Sophia Antipolis, France

Edward Elgar
Cheltenham, UK • Northampton, MA, USA

Published by
Edward Elgar Publishing Limited
The Lypiatts
15 Lansdown Road
Cheltenham
Glos GL50 2JA
UK

Edward Elgar Publishing, Inc.
William Pratt House
9 Dewey Court
Northampton
Massachusetts 01060
USA

A catalogue record for this book
is available from the British Library

Library of Congress Control Number: 2008927954

ISBN 978 1 84720 374 8

Printed and bound in Great Britain by MPG Books Ltd, Bodmin, Cornwall

Contents

List of figures   vii
List of tables   viii
List of contributors   ix
Preface   x
Acknowledgements   xii

PART I   FOUNDATIONS

1. Introduction to the role and responsibilities of international
    business in our contemporary world   3
    Gabriele G.S. Suder
2. Human rights and multinational corporations: the Global
    Compact and continuing evolution   8
    David Atkinson and Richard Pierre Claude
3. Corporate social responsibility: an international law
    perspective   25
    Alice de Jonge

PART II   CRITICAL ISSUES

4. Instruments of peace? How businesses might foster religious
    harmony   47
    Timothy L. Fort
5. Expropriation of minority shareholders or social dividend?
    Beware of good corporate citizens   57
    Wladimir M. Sachs and Marleen Dieleman
6. Information management and communication technology for
    conflict prevention and peace   73
    Jeffrey Soar

PART III   DEALING WITH BEST AND WORST PRACTICE

7. Adversarial allies: the evolving China–India nexus   93
    Nikhilesh Dholakia

  8. Corporate social performance in a post-transition context:
     the case of Polish firms   104
     Renata Kaminska-Labbé and Beata Buchelt
  9. The sustainable peace roles of international extractive
     industries   119
     Duane Windsor

PART IV   THE BIG PICTURE – TOOL KITS

 10. Sustainable enterprise and sustainable futures   139
     Malcolm McIntosh
 11. Corporate social responsibility as a new orientation in
     response to crisis management of sea changes and
     navigational dead reckoning   150
     Ihsen Ketata and John R. McIntyre
 12. Corporate responsibility in peace, conflict reduction and
     crisis prevention: human security for thriving
     markets – a tool kit   168
     Gabriele G.S. Suder and Jonathan Lefevre

Index   191

Figures

1.1   Mitigation focus for business profit and community benefit   6
5.1   Expropriation audit   66
5.2   Social capital audit   67
8.1   Promotion of social responsibility by sector   113
8.2   Promotion of social responsibility by ownership structure   113
12.1 Social dominance orientation (SDO) map: the impact of
       MNE specificities in conflict   185

Tables

6.1	Performance of procurement activities	84
8.1	Aspects of CSR mentioned in the mission statement by sector	111
8.2	Aspects of CSR mentioned in the mission statement by ownership type	112
8.3	Existence of a corporate code of conduct by sector	112
8.4	Existence of a corporate code of conduct by ownership structure	113
8.5	Specific actions by sector	114
8.6	Specific actions by ownership type	115

Contributors

David Atkinson, Helsinki School of Economics at Mikkeli, Finland

Beata Buchelt, Cracow University of Economics, Poland

Richard Pierre Claude, Professor Emeritus, University of Maryland, USA

Alice de Jonge, Monash University, Melbourne, Australia

Nikhilesh Dholakia, University of Rhode Inland, USA

Marleen Dieleman, National University of Singapore Business School, Singapore

Timothy L. Fort, George Washington University School of Business, USA

Renata Kaminska-Labbé, CERAM Business School Nice – Sophia Antipolis, France

Ihsen Ketata, Georgia Tech Center for International Business Education and Research, Georgia, USA

Jonathan Lefevre, Deloitte Mexico, Corporate Governance, Mexico

Malcolm McIntosh, University of Coventry, ARCHS, Coventry University, UK

John R. McIntyre, Executive Director, Georgia Tech Center for International Business Education and Research, Georgia, USA

Wladimir M. Sachs, ESC Rennes School of Business, France

Jeffrey Soar, University of Southern Queensland, Australia

Gabriele G.S. Suder, Associate Dean of Global Management, Professor of International Business, CERAM Business School Nice – Sophia Antipolis, France

Duane Windsor, Rice University, USA

Preface

Gabriele G.S. Suder

International Business under Adversity: A Role in Corporate Responsibility, Conflict Prevention and Peace, analyses the essential issues of a corporate responsibility entailed by firms' international activities. The wide spread of specific sets of values, ways of thinking and living, infrastructures and technologies is commonly associated with the motivations of conflict, crisis and terrorism. What is the true impact of international business on values, what on certainties and uncertainties in host communities? Does international business activity accelerate crisis or peace? How can we conceive the "change agent" role of a corporation in a broad cultural and socio-political context? What is the true purpose of corporate citizenship and corporate social responsibility (CSR)?

The objective of this book is twofold. One, it is to help understand nodes of interconnectivity between business profit and community benefit in responsible activities that respect the larger business environment, communities and the planet as a whole, and that encourage peace. Two, it is to provide a starting point for upstream mitigation, in which collective action allows disruption to be avoided at its very roots.

A diversity of contributions, surrounding the leading argument, shed light on issues covering the role of minority groups in corporate networks, the possible bridges between cultural, corporate and political communities worldwide, the potential roles of international business and industries in promoting peace and conflict prevention in developing countries, the international legal and institutional framework, and the issues that corporations and communities share in this context.[1]

On the basis of a review of theory and practice, and a collection of research studies and case examples, the authors propose vehicles of mitigation and develop a tool kit to help solve goal incompatibility and hierarchy imbalance for the benefit of all.

The reader will discover, ultimately, that returns on conflict prevention investments, CSR and responsible business are part of the intangible assets that constitute the know-how of top management and international business leaders. Similar to other corporate citizenship or CSR initiatives, conflict prevention contributions are only considered appropriate for corporations when they do not affect its core finances or core business, but rather take place at the margin of core activity and are in line with corporate strategy and performance aspirations.

The most accessible starting point for corporate contributions in this field is the establishment of best practices, not by benchmarking on others, but by innovating the way in which corporate contributions can be made – for the benefit of all stakeholders and granting returns on investment in the long run.

The objective of this book is the better understanding of international corporations' options, practices and tools in the area of social responsibility, conflict prevention and sustainable peace keeping.

Thank you to all contributors for their engagement in this book project and for their important contribution to awareness raising in this field.

Finally, I wish to dedicate this volume to the memory of Professor Dr Wladimir Sachs, co-author, former colleague, brilliant academic and friend, who died while this book was being finalised, after a long disease.

NOTE

1. The authors' points of view are self-standing and independent, and do not necessarily reflect the stance of the editor or other authors of this book. All contributions provide essential material for the discussion of international firms' responsibilities in the larger community. The views of Chapter 12 do not reflect those of Deloitte Mexico.

Acknowledgements

The editor would like to express thanks for the patience and never-ending comprehension, love and goodwill of David, Chantal and Caroline during this third edited book project (and fifth book publication) – I hope they feel that it was worth it. Also, the particular support by the editor's parents, Ingrid and Rudolf Schmid, plays a most significant part in her inspirations, research and profound beliefs.

The project for the three books crystallised after 11 September 2001, and, though self-standing, this third volume complements the work undertaken for *Terrorism and the International Business Environment: The Security–Business Nexus* (Suder, 2004, Edward Elgar) and for *Corporate Strategies under International Terrorism and Adversity* (Suder, 2006, Edward Elgar). It took shape in discussions at the Academy of International Business Annual Conferences and at the Academy of Management, and through discussions with international business leaders and the World Economic Forum's Risk Network.

This volume contributes significantly to the understanding of academia and corporations that international business is not a self-standing phenomenon but plays a more and more considerable role in the international community and in geopolitics. The volume evolved into a collective undertaking due to the good match of contributors who came together in a critical effort to undertake a cross-border and cross-disciplinary exercise. As editor, I was helped by a dynamic and very competent group of contributors.

Our gratitude as a team of authors goes to the many colleagues, reviewers, business leaders and institutions whose participation, advice and input to our research and discussions was very welcome and valuable. Further comments, suggestions and discussions in regard to this research, the volume's contribution, and the topic in general are most welcome (gabriele.suder@ceram.fr).

At Edward Elgar Publishing, thanks in particular to Francine O'Sullivan, who was once again of great help and professionalism, and to Edward Elgar.

Gabriele Suder

PART I

Foundations

1. Introduction to the role and responsibilities of international business in our contemporary world

Gabriele G.S. Suder

International Business under Adversity: A Role in Corporate Responsibility, Conflict Prevention and Peace is an edited volume presenting a collection of important original research papers in one field, but from a diversity of perspectives and focuses. It is a logical continuation of two preceding edited works that are each self-standing and yet, together, have a continuum in their objective. It is a thread leading the reader from the analysis of the contemporary state of affairs in international business and its non-traditional challenges, the emergence of global terrorism and the global implications of geopolitical turmoil and societal pressures, to the means and strategies to employ in times of adversity to reduce direct and indirect impacts of conflict and crisis and its hidden business costs. This volume continues by looking at the modes in which these hidden costs can be reduced or removed by preventing adversity.

The book *Terrorism and the International Business Environment: The Business–Security Nexus* (Suder 2004) sets the basis for this research. An analysis of geopolitical, economic and financial structures was completed with insight into post-09/11 developments in selected business sectors. With the intent to develop guidelines for international corporations, the material helped firms adjust to the challenges of the post-09/11 era.

The threat, actions and aftermath of global terrorism have far-reaching implications for international business and internationalization strategies, originating from global network structures of both business and terror. The second volume, *Corporate Strategies under International Terrorism and Adversity* (Suder 2006) explored the firm-level strategies to counteract terrorism in the various fields of international business, to avoid hidden costs through downstream mitigation. The main task for business was found to consist of conceptualizing the possible location of disruptions in a given network and its linkages that may be crucial to the company, and to create just enough flexibility at those points of potential weakness to ensure the proper operation of a given business network, without excessive cost. The solutions to these tremendous network problems were mapped out in useful concept and state-of-the-art insights, and remain ultimately company-specific. This second volume concluded with reflections upon the challenges for the future, an understanding of the enemy concept and Darwinian behaviours, and the call for companies under terrorism and adversity threats to engage in peacemaking.

Let us briefly come back to Nancy Adler's (2006) essential argument in this: The "global citizenship" that Adler encourages is based on some substantial amount of rethinking and realigning resources, implying a shift from the mentality that says the rich will be served by the corporate sector while the poor are the business of governments and NGOs. Better business for the benefit of all, as with the example of successful sustainability with a profit, is not only do-able but ultimately necessary.

The quote of Golda Meir, in this context, "War is an immense stupidity", applies to all forms of geopolitical conflict and violence (Fallaci 1976). It also applies when corporations are, directly or indirectly, responsible for conflict and miss out on the opportunity to reduce risk and uncertainty in the community that they are engaged in, for the benefit of shareholders, stakeholders, international strategy and self-interest as much as the value of community work.

While conflict in its various forms is a very complex matter to analyse, peace can be defined in a rather simplistic manner. Peace is the balance of interests of communities, and their proper communication, dialogue and actions regarding challenges and issues they may have, acting responsibly so as to prevent violence.

One question that arises typically in this type of discussion is whether some corporate activity may well be stirring that violence. But also, one wonders what role international companies are to play in this morality, why and how. "The true nature of the threat remains poorly understood, and previously little research has been done on it", Yves Doz Insead wrote to introduce the works of *Corporate Strategies under International Terrorism and Adversity* (Suder 2006). The threat is part of those core global risks that span from economic, environmental, geopolitical and societal to techno-logical risks that are all interlinked in the international community. Kofi A. Annan pointed out many times during his role as UN Secretary General, that business input is crucial for the reduction and, better, prevention of those risks. For instance, he states for the ICT (Information and Communications Technology) Task Force that

> By promoting access to knowledge, they can promote mutual understanding, an essential factor in conflict prevention and post-conflict reconciliation . . .

offer ways to reveal human rights abuses, promote transparent governance, and give people living under repressive regimes access to uncensored information and an outlet to air their grievances and appeal for help (Stauffacher *et al.* 2005, p. iii).

Risks tend to be idiosyncratic in that they may open opportunities to some and problems to others. However, as a community-based paradigm, if the world is faced with an issue that results in threats in a majority of cases, and hinders the healthy functioning of our ecosystem, then a majority of actors in that community need to do something about that issue. This is the case for global warming, pandemics, global terrorism and geopolitical turmoil, to name the most pertinent.

This book analyses the essential issues of corporate responsibility entailed by firms' international activities: the often worldwide spread of specific sets of values, ways of thinking and living, infrastructures and technologies is commonly associated with the motivations of conflict, crisis and terrorism. What is the impact of international business on community values (and vice versa)? What is its impact on certainties and uncertainties in host communities? Does international business activity accelerate crisis or peace? How can we conceive the "change agent" role of a corporation in a broad cultural and socio-political context? What is the true purpose of corporate citizenship, social responsibility and engagement in community work?

An increasing number of think tanks and academic research encourages this new line of thought:

> Could it be – with the right mix of innovation and entrepreneurship – that the creation of sustainable values could become the business opportunity of the 21st century? Are we actually beginning to recognize the next phase of responsible business and global corporate citizenship – and beyond? Can we anticipate a tipping point in business practice, as well as in management education and research that will redefine the very nature of business's approach to earning profits and to positively influencing society?

This question was asked by the AoM (Academy of Management)/UN Global Forum at Case Western Reserve University in November 2006. Additionally: is this finally a recognition that international business has an essential direct and indirect role to play in conflict prevention and peace keeping – and needs to do something about this?

The objective of this book is twofold. One, it is to help *understand nodes of interconnectivity* between business profit and community benefit in responsible activities that respect and encourage peace. Two, it aims to provide a starting point to what the World Economic Forum Global Risk Network terms "upstream mitigation", in which collective action should

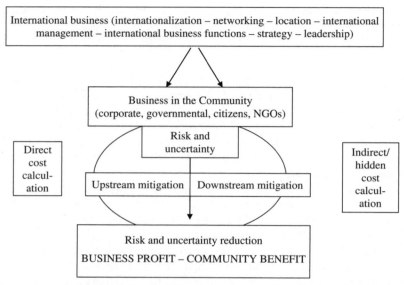

Figure 1.1   Mitigation focus for business profit and community benefit

allow the disruption to be avoided at its very roots. Figure 1.1 presents these concepts in diagrammatic form.

In this line of argument, we now set out to analyse and review the issues of international business: corporations as change agents on a multidisciplinary level, with a role in sustainability that surpasses environmental responsibilities, and plays a role in the legal and technological environment, and in peace and religious harmony, through a focused approach in the field of human rights and corporate citizenship. The volume also includes case studies from China, India and Poland for some country focus, and on the extractive industry and the ICT sector for industry focus. It concludes with a tool kit for international business.

REFERENCES

Adler, N. (2006) "Corporate Global Citizenship: Successfully Partnering with the World", in G. Suder (ed.), *Corporate Strategies under International Terrorism and Adversity*, Cheltenham, UK and Northampton, MA: Edward Elgar, pp. 177–195.

Fallaci, O. (1976) *Interviews with History*, Boston, MA: Houghton Mifflin.

Stauffacher, D., W. Draue, P. Cursion and J. Steinberger (2005) *Information and Communication Technology for Peace. The Role of ICT in Preventing, Responding to and Recovering from Conflict*, UN ICT Task force Series II, New York: UN ICT Task force.

Suder, G.G.S., ed. (2004) *Terrorism and the International Business Environment: The Business–Security Nexus*, Cheltenham, UK and Northampton, MA: Edward Elgar.

Suder, G.G.S., ed. (2006) *Corporate Strategies under International Terrorism and Adversity*, Cheltenham, UK and Northampton, MA: Edward Elgar.

2. Human rights and multinational corporations: the Global Compact and continuing evolution

David Atkinson and Richard Pierre Claude

2.1 INTRODUCTION

The intersection of two important global trends – the advancement of human rights norms with its broad menu of socio-economic and political standard, and the emergence of a globalized economy owing largely to the power and influence of multinational corporations – offers both serious conflict and, at the same time, potential to resolve such conflict. In the context of modern history, the concept of human rights has captured the attention of individuals and groups around the world in the aftermath of World War II. Historian Kenneth Cmiel, who has written extensively on human rights, captures the essence of its modern transition:

> Few political agendas have seen such a rapid and dramatic growth as that of "human rights." Prior to the 1940s, the term was rarely used. There was no sustained international movement in its name. There were no non-governmental organizations (NGOs) with a global reach to defend its principles. There was no international law crafted to protect our human rights. By the 1990s, however, you couldn't escape it (Cmiel, 2004, p. 117).

The adoption of the United Nations *Universal Declaration of Human Rights* in 1948 signaled the modern development of human rights. Since that time, their appeal has reached around the world offering aid, protection and assistance to numerous types of human causes. Traditionally, the struggle over human rights, particularly the effort for their recognition and protection, has been within the political domain defined primarily by the relationship between governments and individuals or groups. Of relatively recent origin, however, concerns over human rights have evolved to include a new domain – the domain of business – defined primarily by the relationship between multinational corporations and individuals and groups.

While the trend toward globalization flows from many sources, its chief impetus is the post-Cold War expansion of international business promoted by multinational corporations (MNCs). Whether driven by new market opportunities new resource opportunities or both, the purpose and the mantra of multinational corporations is the accumulation of wealth and profit. With the help of trade liberalization and the expansion of market economies around the world, MNCs have been quite successful. Unfortunately, the expansion of global corporate activity and the pursuit of increased profits have sometimes exacted painful social costs, risking human rights violations and undermining different aspects of the human condition. Thus, human rights standards have been increasingly directed at the activities of business enterprises and multinational corporations which are not treaty-bound by human rights standards applicable to states. Of course, MNCs have ties to the governments where their headquarters are licensed and to governments of the host countries in which they operate. This milieu of relationships between MNCs and governments at home and abroad tends to create conditions more favorable to MNCs. In other words, the power and influence of MNCs transcends national boundaries and functions in varied circumstances in host countries, where regulations may or may not exist or be enforced.

Sometimes MNCs respond to grassroots criticism for engaging in irresponsible and inhumane practices so as to maximize "the bottom line". When goodwill and corporate reputation are undermined by negative publicity, some multinational corporations accede to international compacts of good behavior. It is good corporate citizenship which matters, whether in fact cooperative behavior is prompted by enlightened leadership or pressured by boycotts, street demonstrations, stockholder caucuses and public criticism. However, the relatively new intersection between human rights and multinational corporate behavior promises to be a long struggle, a view explored with "scenarios analysis" by Rhoda E. Howard-Hassmann. In her view, "globalization is the final assault of capitalism on all those areas of the world that previously escaped it" (Howard-Hassmann, 2005, p. 5). In this light, the reach of MNCs becomes as universal in practice as the application of human rights is universal in theory.

The significance of human rights as a dimension of corporate social responsibility potentially changes the dynamics of corporate direction and governance. Generally and fundamentally, corporate social responsibility rests on the decisions and actions of the corporate body, whether the initiative comes from pressure outside the corporate body or by way of internal corporate initiative. The general assumption of human rights is that they are fundamental and apply to all members of the human race. As stated in the Preamble to the UN *Universal Declaration of Human Rights*, it is the "recognition of the inherent dignity and of the equal and inalienable rights of all members of the human family" and there is a common understanding that "these rights and freedoms are of the greatest importance" (UN, 1948). Moreover, the Preamble also says its internationally defined 30 articles supply a "common standard of achievement for all peoples and nations" critically to assess their own circumstances, and applies not just to governments but should additionally prompt "every individual and every organ of society" "to promote respect for these rights and freedoms". Article 2 reaffirms the breadth and reach of human rights in that "everyone is entitled to all the rights and freedoms set forth in this Declaration, without distinction of any kind, such as race, colour, sex, language, religion, political or other opinion, national or social origin, property, birth or other status". Independent of how rights are recognized, it is clear that human rights are considered fundamental and applicable to all. As Klaus M. Leisinger, Special Advisor to the Secretary-General on the Global Compact, states, "the almost universal recognition of the idea that all people have inalienable rights that are not conferred or granted by a state, a party, or an organization but that are non-negotiable principles is one of the greatest achievements of civilization" (Leisinger, 2006, p. 4).

Thus, human rights are not defined by corporations, nor should the realization of human rights depend on what corporations do. Conceptually, a human rights approach to corporate social responsibility should not rest on the whim or discretion of the corporate body, but rather should address fundamental values and the claims of those seeking recognition and protection. As a matter of practice, however, one acknowledges that even in the sphere of human rights activities vis-à-vis government actions, the realization of human rights is subject to political and legal processes for definition. Nevertheless, the fundamental nature of human rights establishes the validity of seeking confirmation and protection.

By the late 1990s, the role of MNCs – and their behavior toward the needs and claims of people around the world, particularly in the developing areas of the world – had caught the attention of domestic and international bodies. The UK government, for example, published a white paper entitled *Eliminating World Poverty: Making Globalisation Work for the Poor* in 2000 (United Kingdom, 2000). The report noted that, in recent years, a growing public interest in corporate social responsibility had "brought issues such as child labour, corruption, human rights, labour standards, environment and conflict into trade, investment and supply chain relationships" (United Kingdom, 2000, p. 59). The report calls for corporate self-reform, noting that by applying "best practices" in the areas complained of, business can play an increased role in reducing poverty and sustaining development. The white paper concluded that "many companies have also realized important commercial benefits in terms of reputation, risk-management and enhanced productivity" by respecting internationally defined human rights, labor and environmental standards.

The UK study paralleled views that had already prompted action through the Office of the Secretary General of the United Nations. In January 1999 at the World Economic Forum in Davos, Switzerland, Secretary General Kofi Annan challenged business leaders (Annan, 1999, pp. 1–4) to join a "global compact of shared values and principles, which will give a human face to the global market". He argued that unless the global market, like national markets, was held together by shared values, it would be exposed to backlashes from protectionism, populism, nationalism, ethnic chauvinism, fanaticism and terrorism. Calling for a proactive approach, Annan asserted that in addition to the efforts of the UN and other international agencies to promote human rights, the corporate sector must directly tackle issues linking enterprise with internationally defined human rights. Annan urged them to "use these universal values as the cement binding together your global corporations, since they are values people all over the world will recognize as their own". He also cautioned business executives to "make sure that in your own corporate practices you uphold and respect human rights, and that you are not yourselves complicit in human rights abuses".

2.2   THE GLOBAL COMPACT

2.2.1   Principles and Process

Following Kofi Annan's address at the World Economic Forum in 1999, the Global Compact was launched as an operational initiative at the United Nations on 26 July 2000. The development to the Global Compact marks the first significant act by an international body to embrace the values and norms of the UN *Universal Declaration of Human Rights* (UDHR), among other international documents, as norms that apply specifically to multinational corporations. Its creation reflects an increasingly globalized world, with recognition of the consequences of unrestrained behavior by multinational corporations and, at the same time, the need and potential to create a more positive global world.

The Global Compact addresses a wide variety of critical issues related to the conduct of international business around the world by way of its Ten Principles (UN, Global Compact, n.d.a). The original Global Compact included nine principles important in different areas of human rights. A tenth principle was adopted in 2004. To underscore the essential role and conduct of international business, the first two principles of the Compact posit the broad expectations of the business community:

Principle 1:   Businesses should support and respect the protection of internationally proclaimed human rights; and

Principle 2:   Make sure that they are not complicit in human rights abuses.

In the area of protecting labor and the exploitation of labor, global business is expected to respect four specific demands:

Principle 3:   Businesses should uphold the freedom of association and the effective recognition of the right to collective bargaining;

Principle 4:   The elimination of all forms of forced and compulsory labour;

Principle 5:   The effective abolition of child labour; and

Principle 6:   The elimination of discrimination in respect of employment and occupation.

In the area of environmental protection, the expectations for business appear less demanding than other principles but are also supportive of more corporate responsibility:

Principle 7:   Businesses should support a precautionary approach to environmental challenges;

Principle 8:   Undertake initiatives to promote greater environmental responsibility; and

Principle 9:   Encourage the development and diffusion of environmentally friendly technologies.

Principle Ten of the Global Compact was not part of the original document but was adopted later, in 2004. Concern over the role of corruption in the conduct of world business also appeared relevant to the protection and advancement of human rights overall. Hence, an anti-corruption principle was added.

Principle 10: Businesses should work against corruption in all its forms, including extortion and bribery.

What do the principles of the Global Compact mean? And how do they become operational, to be put into practice? It is best here simply to describe the functioning of the Compact as explained by the UN Global

Compact Office itself (www.unglobalcompact.org). Assessments of the Compact and related processes are reserved for later in this chapter. First of all, the Global Compact is a voluntary initiative of the UN, thus, "it does not police or enforce the behavior or actions of companies". Rather, it is "designed to stimulate change and to promote good corporate citizenship and encourage innovative solutions and partnerships". Related to the voluntary nature of the Compact, it "is not a performance or assessment tool". And, "it does not provide a seal of approval, nor does it make judgments on performance". In addition to providing a set of voluntary principles for global corporate behavior, the aim of the Global Compact is to foster and support an engagement mechanism for important stakeholders through policy dialogues, learning networks, local networks and partnership projects. The actors included in the engagement mechanism are "equal partners and important stakeholders", including businesses, civil society (with particular emphasis on non-governmental organizations), labor, academia, the public sector and cities. But while the network spreads a wide net, it is the business enterprise that is the core target of the principles of the Global Compact.

Business participation in the Global Compact is a simple process, initiated by a letter from the Chief Executive Officer of a company (and endorsed by the board) to the Secretary General of the United Nations stating company support for the Global Compact. The business enterprise is also expected to "set in motion changes to business operations so that the Global Compact and its principles become part of strategy, culture and day-to-day operations" (United Nations, Global Compact, 2008). It is also expected to publish in its annual report or similar corporate report a description of the ways in which it is supporting the Global Compact and its ten principles. This function, known as the *Communication on Progress*, is required of business participants. Failure to submit this report can lead to removal of the company as a participant in the Global Compact.

The Global Compact is administered by the Global Compact Office at the UN. The Office also works in collaboration with six other agencies of the UN: the Office of the High Commissioner for Human Rights (OHCHR), the International Labour Organization (ILO), the United Nations Environment Programme (UNEP), the United Nations Office on Drugs and Crime (UNODC), the United Nations Development Programme (UNDP) and the United Nations Industrial Development Organization (UNIDO).

Given the purpose of this book – with its emphasis on conflict prevention and peace – it is appropriate to point out that the Global Compact Office also recognizes the role of global business in conflict prevention and peace building. The Global Compact Office notes that while "governments have the primary responsibility for peace and stability, companies have an important role to play in contributing to security and development" (United Nations, Global Compact, 2008). Company decision making "can exacerbate existing tensions and lead to conflict, or help a country to rebuild after conflict". Companies indeed have a business interest in preventing conflict and maintaining peace. To add support to this function, the Global Compact Office has initiated a number of workshops, papers from network participants, and papers devoted to the business interests in risk management and maintaining peace. In particular, the Office initiated a series of policy dialogues and workshops focusing on "The Role of the Private Sector in Zones of Conflict" (United Nations, Global Compact, 2007).

2.2.2   The Global Compact Network and NGOs

As initially envisioned, the Global Compact (GC) generally defines a process of interaction among corporations, non-governmental organizations, labor organizations, academic partners and public entities. By the end of 2007, there were approximately 4000 GC participants, including approximately 3000 businesses spread among 100 countries. In effect, the network parallels to some extent the very nature of a broad political system, with governing bodies (such as national and local governments) as the core objective of political activity. The essential difference in the network associated with the Global Compact, however, is that its purpose is focused on the behavior and development of multinational corporations and other global business participants, guided of course by the principles of the Global Compact. Two other differences between a general political process and the Global Compact network process are important to point out. One is that, generally, a political process does not define who the actors are, albeit most may be known, whereas actors in the Global Compact network are acknowledged only by application and acceptance into the network. Another difference is that the role of the citizenry in the political process – either as voters or members of the society governed – has no direct counterpart in the Global Compact. Albeit the intent to recognize human rights is an acknowledgment of people generally around the world, citizens are only indirectly represented through organizations involved in the GC network. In other words, there is no direct action or role to be played by citizens or, in a business context, consumers. Nor are they acknowledged. The network associated with the Global Compact is, in effect, an approved network working to apply the GC principles.

At the core of the Global Compact network activity – beyond corporate structures and interests – are the non-governmental organizations. One can argue that NGOs, generally, are important intermediaries between corporate interests and selected interests of individuals and society at large. In short, the Global Compact defined a desired structure for resolving differences and issues addressed by the Compact.

Richard Pierre Claude, who has written extensively on human rights, focuses on the role of human rights NGOs in his book *Science in the Service of Human Rights*. He identifies a wide variety of functions performed by human rights NGOs. These include: the gathering, monitoring and disseminating of information on human rights abuses; organizing advocacy campaigns, including lobbying at all public policy levels; building solidarity with other domestic and international NGOs; providing service functions and humanitarian support; engaging in litigation to protect human rights; and engaging in training and educational activities (Claude, 2002, p. 150). Generally, these functions run the gamut of political activity and strategy, including the important role of information sharing. And while many of these functions may come to bear among NGOs participating in the Global Compact process, the network process itself is not defined in such a way as to capture the full value of the rich diversity of NGO activity. Thus, much of NGO human rights activity is outside the purview of the Global Compact process for developing an actionable agenda for corporate compliance. Collectively, NGO activities and functions offer a comprehensive approach to dealing with human rights issues.

NGO human rights activities – whether those within the Global Compact network or outside it – offer important perspectives and actions vis-à-vis corporate behavior around the world. Human Rights Watch (HRW), an NGO participant in the Global Compact network, notified the Secretary General when the Global Compact was first announced that it approved of the initiative but hopefully only as a first step. Viewed thus, the Compact is arguably comparable to the UDHR presented to the world in 1948 as an educational instrument with a moral rather than legal status. Such "soft moral norm status" should not be trivialized as an unimportant initial step in a complex political process. With no mechanisms to implement new universal standards, the UDHR nevertheless at first held out the prospect that people should critically judge the performance of their government by human rights standards. To the oppressed, soft moral norms are better than none, and the UDHR initially positioned people to confront officials with the proposition: "You promised". Comparably, the Global Compact, while lacking monitoring and enforcement mechanisms, has been sufficient in its early years to confront MNCs politically with moral condemnations by consumers and others but, as noted below, moral condemnation is not sufficient to many observers and activists interested in human rights and corporate social responsibility.

Beyond the "first step" of moral suasion supplied by GC standards, the new UN initiative should eventually establish binding legal standards of corporate conduct requiring institutional oversight or external monitoring. Holding back such progress is the fact that on the international political landscape, there are too few NGOs organized specifically to monitor and report on MNC non-compliance with the Global Compact. The technical expertise needed for such undertakings suggests that cooperative arrangements between university research centers and new specialized NGOs might be a promising strategy to fill an obvious gap in NGO capacity. Expressing fears that NGOs do not have the resources to be the sole monitors of compliance, HRW's Executive Director Kenneth Roth asserted:

> Human Rights Watch has devoted substantial resources to promoting corporate respect for human rights, but our efforts are just a drop in the bucket. Neither we nor other NGOs begin to have sufficient resources to assume an enforcement role that should be the province of governments and the UN (Roth, 2000).

As indicated earlier, the Global Compact is not policed or investigated by the UN but, rather, relies on corporate partnerships with others in the network, including NGOs, for developing and encouraging corporate social responsibility. Implied in this goal, particularly from the point of view of interested NGOs, investigating corporate and government irresponsibility certainly requires more than reading *Communication on Progress* reports as required by the Global Compact. NGOs need to do a great deal more with regard to monitoring and investigating. Clearly such activities are limited by the capacities and resources of NGOs.

As an example of the monitoring function of NGOs, Human Rights Watch's report on a Taiwanese company's toxic waste dumping in Cambodia in 1998 shows how difficult and intricate monitoring in this technical area can be (Human Rights Watch, 1999). It also illustrates the ways in which human rights and environmental issues can be inextricably interwoven. In November 1998, the Formosa Plastics Group of Taiwan shipped nearly 3000 tons of Taiwanese toxic waste to the southern port of Sihanoukville, Cambodia. Even though at the time, there existed no Cambodian law on the subject, Minister of Environment Mok Mareth said publicly and repeatedly that national policy prohibited toxic waste dumping in the country. Nevertheless, mercury-laden refuse was deposited in an open field where impoverished villagers scavenged the poisonous cargo. Soon, many of them complained of sickness, and one quickly died. The Royal Cambodian government, expressing concern, promised a thorough investigation. Thousands of local people panicked and fled the city. Others in Sihanoukville exercised their constitutional rights and through two days of demonstrations, blamed government corruption for the disaster. The demonstrators had failed to obtain permission to protest publicly, and when some of them grew violent and ransacked buildings, the police made several arrests. Two human rights defenders, staff members of the Cambodian League for the Promotion and Defense of Human Rights (LICADHO), were arrested and held for inciting the riots. Although they were released after a month-long detention, attention was diverted from the issue of toxins in the environment. The Cambodian case illustrates the difficult position of those affected by hazardous toxins as well as those attempting to monitor and resolve the issues. Although government officials were finally arrested for permitting the importation and dumping of toxic waste, the two human rights defenders were treated quite harshly. Thus, while trying to protect the right to health, a number of civil and political rights were set aside as well.

The monitoring and "shame and blame" work of Human Rights Watch regarding the Cambodian case points to the positive potential for NGO action directed at human rights abuses by multinational corporations. Such examples have proliferated. In 2007, a British group, the Burma Campaign UK condemned autocratic and brutal suppression of anti-government dissent and street protests in Myanmar/Burma by citing ten Singapore firms named on its "Dirty List" of companies for their business with the Burmese junta, including the Development Bank of Singapore (DBS), the United Overseas Bank (UOB), the Overseas Chinese Banking Corporation (OCBC), and the conglomerate Keppel Corporation (Burma Campaign, 2007).

One of the dynamics of non-governmental organizations focused on human rights abuses is the recognition that more and different efforts are needed to bring about a sense of justice in relation to multinational corporations. While HRW's initiative in the Cambodia case was limited to monitoring and reporting activities and while Burma Campaign UK restricted its action to finger pointing, a few recently formed NGOs offer a more direct "action and enforcement" approach to correcting human rights abuses. A new NGO, International Rights Advocates (IRAdvocates), is an example of a litigation-oriented organization based in the United States committed to the protection of human rights enforcement in different parts of the world. As indicated in its mission statement, IRAdvocates creatively uses "international human rights law in the US court system and those of other nations" to protect and empower "individuals victimized by multinational corporations and other powerful entities that traditionally enjoy impunity or immunity" (International Rights Advocates, n.d.). Further, they "will challenge platitudes about social responsibility and contribute to eliminating the corporate practice of imposing human rights violations on others". As an NGO that stresses litigation, it has focused specifically on developing strategies based on the Alien Tort Claims Act (ACTA) in US law, a statute aimed at protecting the nation's international reputation by enabling non-citizens to use federal courts to hold Americans and others accountable for violations of international law. Using the Alien Tort Claims Act to establish the liability of corporations linked to human rights violations has been a groundbreaking – and successful – legal strategy. The reach of activity by IRAdvocates is considerable in the range of multinational corporations accused and the types of human right abuses. For example, corporate complicity with paramilitary organizations that use a variety of means – including intimidation, abductions, torture, and sometimes murder – as methods to discourage union activity or to stop human rights grievances against the corporation, is vigorously litigated. Some of the multinational corporations that are the object of these charges include companies such as Bridgestone-Firestone, Nestlé, Archer Daniel Midland, Cargill and others. In the area of forced labor, litigation has been pursued against multinational corporations such as Chiquita Brands, Coca-Cola, Drummond Company, DynCorp and Wal-Mart. It is significant to point out, however, that the International Rights Advocates NGO is not a participant in the Global Compact network.

2.3   ASSESSMENT OF THE GLOBAL COMPACT

The Global Compact Office itself describes the value of the Global Compact as a learning network. George Kell, Director of the Office, and David Levin write that the "Global Compact is conceived as a value-based platform designed to promote institutional learning with few formalities and no rigid bureaucratic structures" (Kell and Levin, 2002, p. 2). As a learning network, is learning in fact the outcome? Are there learning outcomes or objects that are identifiable and assessable? Who is in fact assessing the learning? These are not merely rhetorical questions but rather questions in response to how the value of the Global Compact is viewed by the Office responsible for its functioning. In one sense, it is hard not to agree with the value of a learning exercise. However, the value of learning is not necessarily the value that is commonly attributed to the Global Compact; nor, for that matter, is it the ultimate objective of many of the participants. This is not to undermine the value of the network, but when the assessments of the Global Compact by others are stated, few attribute learning as an objective. Objectively stated, there is clearly value to learning with regard to human rights and corporate behavior. But given what is learned, the issue becomes: what should be the next steps in advancing the norms and values of the Global Compact? Other perspectives below may help address that.

Leisinger offers a unique view that attempts to integrate the proposition that corporations need to assume social responsibility with the notion that it is the states that are responsible for holding corporations accountable. He argues that there are a number of good reasons "for assuming corporate responsibility in order to support and respect human rights if national law either is not state of the art or is only a 'paper tiger' that is not consistently implemented." (Leisinger, 2006, p. 17). MNCs, whether working in tandem with national law or not, can rely on no "rational justification for sacrificing other people's human rights to achieve corporate profits". Yet, while it is a moral argument for corporations to assume responsibility – a hierarchy of responsibilities – he states that the duties of providing a legal framework for human rights, enforcing the law and providing sanctions clearly belong to the state and "cannot be delegated to any other organ of society". And while his argument for corporate social responsibility recognizes the value and fundamental nature of human rights, the reasons for corporate responsibility are advanced primarily on business grounds. One perspective is that of a cost-benefit analysis of risk management. In an effort to reduce a company's legal, financial and reputational risks, increased costs due to a "responsible human rights commitment must be seen as an 'insurance premium' against such risks becoming reality". Similar reasons are advanced by recommending a proactive approach with regard to human rights in society, thus having a "social licence" to operate. Companies with a reputation for integrity, it is argued, attract more qualified talent, thus resulting in increased productivity. And, perhaps with a bit of realism in mind, he argues that acceptance of responsibility "is the best argument against political demands for additional regulation". It thus appears that sound business models – developed and applied – may be the enticement for corporations to assume a significant role in social responsibility. It remains the case, however, that any legal accountability comes from the state.

The most persistent and pressing issue with regard to the UN Global Compact relates to the voluntary nature of the Compact itself. While it is reasonable to assume that the voluntary nature of the Global Compact is appealing to multinational corporations, it is also the crux of much of the criticism directed at it. As stated by Mahmood Monshipouri *et al.*, "MNCs will not address specific human rights violations if assigned only to a voluntary set of principles set up in the UN Global Compact" (Monshipouri *et al.*, 2003, p. 967). In sum, "companies cannot be trusted to monitor their own compliance to new human rights standards". This view, as indicated earlier, is also of course shared by many NGOs that would like to see multinationals held directly accountable by the Global Compact. This discussion of voluntary–mandatory compliance raises another issue: if there is to be enforcement, what body should do it – the United Nations or some other quasi-governmental agency? Or the nation-state in which a company resides or engages in business?

Similar to the view of Leisinger – that the state is responsible for protecting human rights – there is a current body of thought about the protection of human rights that is consistent with traditional thinking regarding the political domain of government vis-à-vis human rights. John Gerard Ruggie, the UN Secretary General's Special Representative for Business and Human Rights, argues that any grand strategy for dealing with business and human rights "needs to strengthen and build out from the existing capacity of states and the states system to regulate and adjudicate harmful actions by corporations, not undermine it" (Ruggie, 2007, p. 27). He argues that while "currently, at the domestic level some governments may be unable to take effective action on their own", the imposition of direct obligations on corporations may also have adverse effects on governance capacities. Thus, the more promising approach is "to expand the international regime horizontally, by seeking to clarify and progressively codify the duties of states to protect human rights against corporate violations". Monshipouri *et al.* state a similar perspective: "we argue that in the human rights domain the responsible party is generally the state, and that, especially in the context of neoliberal globalization, the wrongdoers are often the corporations" (Monshipouri *et al.*, 2003, p. 967). The clear implication of this view is that more focused attention needs to be on the state with a keen eye on holding corporations accountable. Hence, one can argue that any network or political process needs to, in effect, draw in the state for a more aggressive role in monitoring and enforcing corporate human rights abuses. Obviously, there are difficulties to overcome there as well. But the state does retain the authority if not always the will or ability – for one reason or another – to hold corporate behavior accountable.

The dilemma that is posed – whether corporations can be directly responsible for human rights abuses through international mechanisms or whether states enhance their ability and willingness to hold corporations accountable – is that corporate strength and influence has to be dealt with in any event. Multinational corporations are most likely to fight to maintain a voluntary approach to corporate social responsibility, not a mandated or enforceable process.

If the responsibility of enforcing actions that violate human rights falls to nation-state authority, what is the value of the Global Compact beyond an exercise in learning or a network approach to resolving human rights issues? For one, as to the value of the Global Compact itself, it is important to view it as a progressive step in the evolution and application of human rights norms. As indicated earlier, the significance of the Global Compact is reflected in the fact that it is the first time that an international body has applied human rights values to multinational corporations. In other words, it can readily be seen as an important step in the evolution of human rights. However, as seen in the political domain, the human rights struggle is long and complex. The business domain is just beginning. Furthermore, if assessed systematically, the Global Compact can be beneficial as a learning network. As with any kind of learning, the outcome may not be clear. But, with new and active partners in the network, what is learned will be known to those outside the corporate body. Does this mean that the Global Compact will become a public relations sanctuary for multinational corporations? Even if that is the case for some, it is not likely to remain long term. Clearly, there are too many NGOs that have the ability to remain diligent and persistent in making known corporate abuse. Along with the fact of enhanced and instantaneous communication around the world, the dissemination by NGOs of information has clearly improved broadened access to information.

Perhaps one of the best critiques of the Global Compact is offered by Surya Deva (2006). Analytically, he provides considerable insight into both the value of, and shortcomings of the Global Compact. In raising the question about the scope and progress of the Global Compact, he asks if it is "still too compact to be global". Here he addresses the simplicity and vagueness of the ten principles themselves and states that, aside from all the tools and guidance from the Global Compact Office itself to explain them, more research and investigation is needed to show "how effective these means would be in providing guidance to corporations in actual, complex business situations" (Deva, 2006, pp. 132–133). Deva also points out that, even with the ever-increasing number of GC participants, now approximately 4000, many of which are corporations, it is still a "drop in the ocean" compared to an estimated 70 000 multinational parent corporations and 900 000 foreign affiliates.

Among the major deficiencies of the Global Compact according to Deva, is its "directional uncertainty", the inadequate nature of the *Communication on Progress* process, the lack of verification and independent monitoring, the misuse of the Compact as a marketing tool, and the amorphous role of nation-states. These are not necessarily new critiques, but they do in fact point to issues and hurdles that the Compact needs to overcome to progress beyond a voluntary and procedural information process to one that addresses the serious nature and challenges to corporate influence and human rights concerns.

2.4 CONCLUSIONS

As globalization spreads, multinational corporations (MNCs) increasingly are involved in human rights violations, because of their operations in countries where there are few constraints. In many developing economies, local governments are desperate for economic growth and are willing to accept corporate investment under almost any terms. Moreover, when a developing country is governed by a corrupt, dictatorial regime willing to inflict economic and human rights abuses on its own people for the sake of enticing foreign investors, there is a greatly increased negative impact. MNCs have been unable to resist the cost savings that result from such "opportunities". The new wave of globalization has brought entirely new challenges, where developing countries compete with each other to attract corporate investment. MNCs can bargain to opt out of national regulations, either explicitly or implicitly. Litigation in the host country is one aspect of the work needed to combat this lawless "development".

For NGOs such as Amnesty International, Human Rights Watch and International Rights Advocates to seriously challenge MNCs' human rights violations, they will need to promote conflict resolution without strife and to eliminate the root causes of conflict and poverty using the methods of monitoring, reporting and litigating in cooperative networks of international and local entities. Opportunities might arise for human rights activists to sit on corporate boards, provided they are not co-opted. Moreover, creative new NGOs are needed to educate people regarding specific MNC human rights shortcomings, to mobilize consumers to use their economic power to show that they expect the companies they patronize to respect human rights, and to organize stockholder voting blocs on behalf of corporate adherence to human rights. Moreover, new NGOs or coalitions of NGOs and university research centers are needed with technological capacities to assess corporate transgressions in terms, for example, of pharmaceutical dumping and environmental pollution viewed as threats to the rights to health and life. In the long term, planning for the implementation of human rights inevitably means changing the culture of MNCs' decision making consistent with their promises under the Global Compact and, most importantly, empowering those who are in a position to support and defend human rights locally. Only when governments, judicial systems, MNCs and other non-state entities in diverse nations commit to promoting respect for the full range of human rights, including economic and social as well as civil and political, will citizens be able to participate fully in development and democracy.

Despite the many critiques of the Global Compact, it has important value in bringing to public light the role of corporations and their relationship to the protection of human rights. The resulting and enlightened attention has also given impetus for more focused inquiry and demands for accountability in civil society, particularly NGOs and nation-states. As a phase in the development of human rights around the world, the evolution in the search for a globalized human rights culture is likely to continue with intensity and visibility.

REFERENCES

Annan, K. (1999) *Secretary-General Proposes Global Compact on Human Rights, Labour, Environment, in Address to World Economic Forum in Davos, Switzerland.* UN, published at www.un.org/News/Press/docs/1999/19990201.sgsm6881.html, accessed 17 January 2008.

Burma Campaign UK (2007) *The Dirty List,* published at www.burmacampaign.org.uk/dirty_list/dirty_list.html, accessed 17 January 2008.

Claude, R.P. (2002) *Science in the Service of Human Rights,* University of Pennsylvania Press, Pennsylvania.

Cmiel, K. (2004) The recent history of human rights, *American Historical Review,* **19**(3), 117–135.

Deva, S. (2006) Global compact: a critique on the U.N.'s "public private" partnership for promoting corporate citizenship, *Syracuse Journal of International Law and Commerce,* **34**, 107–151.

Howard-Hassmann, R.E. (2005) The second great transformation: human rights leap-frogging in the era of globalization, pursuing global justice, *Human Rights Quarterly,* **27**(1), 1–40.

Human Rights Watch (1999) *Toxic Justice: Human Rights, Justice and Toxic Waste,* published at www.hrw.org/reports/1999/cambotox/.

International Rights Advocates (n.d.) *Our Mission,* published at http://iradvocates.org/, accessed 17 January 2008.

Kell, G. and D. Levin (2002) The evolution of the Global Compact Network: an historic experiment in learning and action, paper presented at *The Academy of Management Annual Conference,* Denver, 11–14 August, published at www.unglobalcompact.org/docs/news_events/9.5/denver.pdf, accessed 17 January 2008.

Leisinger, K.M. (2006) *On Corporate Responsibility for Human Rights,* published at www.unglobalcompact.org/docs/news_events/9.6/corpresforhr_kl.pdf, accessed 17 January 2008.

Monshipouri, M., C.E. Welch, Jr. and E.T. Kennedy (2003) Multinational corporations and the ethics of global responsibility: problems and possibilities, *Human Rights Quarterly,* **25**(4), 965–989.

Roth, K. (2000) *Corporate Social Responsibility,* Letter to UN Secretary General Kofi Annan, 28 July, published at www.hrw.org/advocacy/corporations/index.htm, accessed 17 January 2008.

Ruggie, J.G. (2007) *Business and human rights: the evolving international agenda.* Corporate Social Responsibility Initiative, Working Paper No. 38. Cambridge: John F. Kennedy School of Government, Harvard University. Paper is forthcoming in *American Journal of International Law.*

United Kingdom, Department for International Development (2000) *Eliminating World Poverty: Making Globalisation Work for the Poor: White Paper on International Development,* published at www.dfid.gov.uk/Publs/files/whitepaper2000.pdf, accessed 17 January 2008.

United Nations (1948) *Universal Declaration of Human Rights,* published at www.un.org/Overview/rights.html, accessed 17 January 2008.

United Nations, Global Compact (2007) *Conflict Prevention/Peace-Building*, www.unglobalcompact.org/issues/conflict_prevention/index.html, accessed 17 January 2008.

United Nations, Global Compact (2008) *Participation in the Global Compact*, published at http://www.unglobalcompact.org/HowToParticipate/index.html, accessed 17 January 2008.

United Nations, Global Compact (n.d.a) *Participants and Stakeholders*, published at www.unglobalcompact.org/participantsandstakeholders/index.html, accessed 17 January 2008.

United Nations, Global Compact (n.d.b) *The Ten Principles*, published at www.unglobalcompact.org/AboutTheGC/TheTenPrinciples/index.html, accessed October 2007.

3. Corporate social responsibility: an international law perspective

Alice de Jonge

3.1 INTRODUCTION

Multinational corporations (MNCs), are exerting increasing global influence and power. The largest 500 corporations in the world now control 25 per cent of the global economic output (Spisto, 2005, 131). MNCs can and do take their place at global events such as the 1999 WTO forum in Seattle, and exert an important influence when important decisions on trade, investment, law and social policy are made (Burton, 2002). Company managers now have more power than most sovereign governments to determine where people will live, what they will do to earn a living, what they will eat, drink and wear, the information they have access to and the formation of the society their children will inherit (Fraser, 2001).

Rules imposing duties, responsibilities and standards of behaviour on MNCs have not kept up with the expanding reach of their actions. Shareholders, the putative "owners" of the corporation, are shielded from responsibility for the company's actions by the concept of limited liability. The notion of separate legal personhood (in the absence of exceptional circumstances) allows directors also to shield themselves from responsibility for corporate activities (*Salomon v A Salmon & Co Ltd*, 1897). It also allows parent companies to escape responsibility for the activities of subsidiary corporations. The creation of a "shell" corporation with minimal assets has now become a familiar tool to protect directors, officers, shareholders and parent-company assets from liabilities associated with business activities.

Attempts to introduce legislation imposing standards of behaviour on corporations in the name of social responsibility have failed in Australia,[1] the USA,[2] Canada and elsewhere (Klein, 2001). Efforts by courts in America and Canada to make companies accountable for their actions through the concept of (international) enterprise liability have met with only limited success. This concept would treat related corporations as a single juridical unit, and ascribes responsibility for the actions of one corporation to all corporations in that legal unit (Klein, 2001, p. 5).

Attempts to bring corporations and their directors to account in national courts for activities amounting to crimes under international law have also been generally unsuccessful. In the case of *Khulumani et al. v Barclays et al.*, for example, the plaintiffs were unsuccessful in seeking reparation under the US Alien Tort Claims Act for corporate activities in support of the oppressive South African apartheid system during the 1980s and before. Other cases involving corporate names such as Union Carbide,[3] Monsanto,[4] Texaco[5] and James Hardie (Jackson, 2004; Jarron, 2006) provide a constant reminder of the disparity between the harm inflicted and compensation paid by global firms.

Internationally, efforts to impose standards of behaviour on MNCs have centred around the development of voluntary codes of conduct. Examples include:

- *OECD Guidelines for Multinational Enterprises* (2000);
- *UN Global Compact* (United Nations, 2000);
- *Tripartite Declaration of Principles concerning Multilateral Enterprises and Social Policy* (International Labour Organization 1977, revised in 2000);
- *Draft UN Norms on the Responsibilities of Transnational Corporations and Other Business Enterprises with Regard to Human Rights* (United Nations, 2003);
- *UN Environment Program Finance Initiative* (1992, restructured in 2003) (United Nations, Environment Programme, n.d.); and
- UN *Principles for Responsible Investment* (2006).

However well-intentioned, all of these international standard-setting instruments remain subject to three important defects:

- lack of mandatory, effective and verifiable reporting systems;
- lack of effective mechanisms for monitoring corporate activity on an ongoing basis (not just to verify corporate reports); and
- lack of enforcement mechanisms that are effective beyond national boundaries.

Efforts have been made to address each of these defects. So far as reporting mechanisms are concerned, a number of methods have been made available to MNCs that choose to report on the social and environmental aspects of their activities, including the *Global Reporting Initiative* (GRI)

Sustainability Reporting Guidelines (see the website, Global Reporting Initiative, 2007). The GRI Guidelines are supported by other standards issued by the International Auditing and Assurance Standards Board and similar national bodies to regulate the independent verification by auditors of sustainability-type reports (see International Auditing and Assurance Standards Board, 2007).

The *OECD Guidelines for Multinational Enterprises* (2000) encourage voluntary disclosures of non-financial as well as financial performance, while the *UN Global Compact* (2000) asks participants to submit annual *Communication on Progress* using reporting indicators such as the GRI Guidelines. The Carbon Disclosure Project ([2007]) and the *Global Framework for Climate Risk Disclosure* (Climate Risk Disclosure Initiative Steering Committee, 2006) deal with voluntary reporting of matters related to climate change.

In the area of labour relations and social policy, the International Labour Organization's (ILO) *Tripartite Declaration* (1977), adopted by the ILO Governing Body, creates a procedure that requires governments and workers' and employers' organisations to respond at regular intervals to questions relating to its implementation. It also provides for publication of a summary of the replies by the ILO. However, it contains no mechanism for making either reporting or monitoring compulsory, and no mechanism for enforcement (Leary, 2003).

There are various other voluntary reporting standards to which MNCs may subscribe, but none have built into them any mechanism for compulsory, reliable third-party verification and checking. What do perform a similar function, however, are the various indices which have been developed, independently of global firms, to track the actual performance of companies in corporate sustainability and related matters. The main ones are the Dow Jones Sustainability Indexes (Dow Jones, 2006) and the FTSE4Good Index Series (FTSE, 2007), both of which measure the performance of companies identified as meeting globally recognised corporate responsibility standards.

The rest of this chapter argues that at least two things are needed before MNCs can be brought to account for the consequences of their acts and omissions. First, they must be recognised as having legal status (or "personhood") under international law. Second, mechanisms are needed for bringing MNCs before international tribunals able to deliver meaningful and binding judgments. Section 3.2 of this chapter begins by outlining the current unsatisfactory legal position of MNCs under international law, and the need for change. Section 3.3 then looks at a number of mechanisms for bringing MNCs into the international legal system, in the three areas of human rights, labour relations and environmental protection.

3.2   THE CURRENT STATUS OF THE PRIVATE CORPORATION IN INTERNATIONAL LAW

The question of the subjects of international law has been in a state of gradual evolution since the early twentieth century. Both theory and practice have now firmly abandoned the doctrine that states are the exclusive subjects of international law capable of possessing international rights and duties. By the middle of the 20th century, both international organisations and individuals had been brought under the coverage of international law (Harris, 2004, pp. 140–142). So far as individuals are concerned, a number of international instruments have expressly recognised the procedural capacity of the individual as a claimant of rights and as the subject of duties imposed by international law. For example, citizens in those states which have ratified the *First Optional Protocol* can lodge individual complaints with the UN Human Rights Commission (now the Human Rights Council) for breaches of standards contained in the *International Covenant of Civil and Political Rights* (ICCPR) (Harris, 2004, Chapter 9; Anton, Mathew and Morgan, 2005, pp. 703–855).

So far as individual responsibilities are concerned, the 1998 *Rome Statute of the International Criminal Court* (International Criminal Court, 1998) now provides an avenue for bringing individuals to account for "the most serious crimes of concern to the international community as a whole" (article 5).

For the most part, however, the individual's ability to claim rights under international law remains dependent upon her nationality. It is the individual's nationality, for example, that determines which state may protect her against the extravagances of another state. More ominously, it is the individual's nationality which places her within the domestic jurisdiction, and hence the discretionary treatment, of her state of citizenship.

International law treats corporate persons in much the same way as it treats individuals. Thus there is no doubt that treaties can and do provide certain rights for MNCs, as well as imposing certain duties upon private corporate persons. Article III of the *International Convention on Civil Liability for Oil Pollution Damage* (United Nations, 1969, 1976, 1984, 1992a), for example, imposes strict liability for oil pollution on the owner, usually a company, of a ship responsible for such pollution. Even this convention, however, only applies to the extent that states are willing to ratify, implement and enforce its provisions.

In summary, while states and international organisations are subject to mandatory legal requirements established by international law, MNCs, at the global level, are typically subject to nothing stronger than the "motherhood statements" contained in aspirational guidelines. One effect of this situation has been to render the relationship between the nation state and the foreign MNC an extremely unequal one, not just legally, but economically and politically as well.

3.3 BRINGING MNCs UNDER THE JURISDICTION OF INTERNATIONAL LAW

3.3.1 Introduction

Subjecting MNCs to rules of international law is potentially to the benefit of both the global community and the individual firm. If MNCs were given a responsible role in creating and maintaining international laws relating to human rights, labour relations and environmental protection, directors would be able to point to such laws when choosing long-term corporate objectives over short-term gains. This would be to the benefit not only of shareholder value, but of long-term market sustainability as well. The existence of market-based indexes linked to corporate social responsibility (CSR) such as the Dow Jones Sustainability Indexes (Dow Jones, 2006) and the FTSE4Good Index Series (FTSE, 2007) recognises that profit and independently verified standards of corporate social responsibility can coexist.

Clear international requirements in relation to human rights, labour relations and environmental protection would also provide a basis for governments in host states to legislate without fear that foreign investment money would leave in favour of lower standards elsewhere. Subjecting both host states and foreign MNCs to a similar set of obligations arising from global citizenship would unite both in striving for economic development that was both sustainable and respectful of basic human rights.

Subjecting MNCs to international mandatory standards of behaviour need not be in conflict with the voluntary nature of international relations. Just as sovereign states are free to subscribe or not subscribe to international treaties, so also global corporations should be free to subscribe or not subscribe to global standard-setting instruments. Market forces should be left to motivate corporations when deciding whether to participate in such instruments. The only exception to this would be those rules of international law which have gained the status of peremptory norms or *jus cogens* – obligations which are so fundamental that they operate *erga omnes*, that is, they are universally applicable.

3.3.2 Enforcing the Human Rights Responsibilities of MNCs through the United Nations and Regional Human Rights Bodies

A growing number of countries have signed up to international or regional human rights standards, and have provided their citizens with access to regional or international human rights forums as a means of asserting such rights. Regional human rights courts now operate in Europe, America and Africa.[6] Along with other developments, this has made the area of human rights law perhaps the most important example of rules which have now obtained the status of *jus cogens* and have thus become universally binding on all members of the international community.

Given their mandate and expertise, the UN and regional human rights bodies appear to be well placed to implement and enforce MNCs' human rights duties. In addition to hearing individual petitions, the human rights bodies can and do also undertake the public examination of the human rights records of individual states (Kinley and Tadaki, 2004, pp. 997–998). While it would be both conceptually difficult and practically impossible to require *all* MNCs to submit regular human rights reports in the same way that sovereign states do, it would be possible for the various human rights bodies to become more insistent on states providing them with details of measures (including private initiatives) taken to improve the human rights behaviour of corporations operating or established within their territory.

A problem arises, however, in the case of MNCs which are responsible for human rights infringements in countries other than their own home state of original incorporation. In such cases, the MNC's home state can deny responsibility for what goes on in the territory of another state, and can rely on the rule of non-interference in another state's affairs. The state where the alleged human rights infringement occurs can similarly refuse to accept responsibility for the actions of a foreign legal person, and try to pass legal and moral responsibility on to the MNC's home state. A slanging match between two different nations may be the result, while the MNC itself escapes responsibility altogether.

The regional human rights bodies, and even more so the United Nations Human Rights Commission, have in the past regularly been criticised for their lack of effectiveness. Such ineffectiveness stems partly from a lack of adequate status and authority, partly from lack of enforcement powers and mechanisms, partly from a lack of willingness on the part of the human rights bodies to become embroiled in contentious political issues, and partly from lack of adequate financial and human resources. These deficiencies have been recognised, and efforts have been made to improve both the standing and the resourcing of the human rights bodies. On 15 March 2006, for example, the UN General Assembly overwhelmingly voted to establish a new Human Rights Council to replace the ineffective Commission (United Nations, Department of Public Information, News and Media, 2006b).

While the new Human Rights Council is far from perfect, it represents a great improvement on its predecessor. First, the Council is established as a body directly under the UN General Assembly, giving it a higher status than its predecessor the Commission (which reported to the UN Economic and Social Council). Second, the new 47-member Council is generally seen as being more geographically and demographically representative than was the 53-member Commission (United Nations, Department of Public Information, News and Media, 2006a; Annan, 2006). Third, an important provision is that all states sitting on the new Council will be subject to a "universal periodic review mechanism" that examines their human rights records (Lyons, 2006).

Many things will need to change, however, before it becomes politically feasible for the UN community to expand the powers and resources of a UN human rights body to investigate publicly the activities of MNCs as well as states. Likewise, proposals for broadening the monitoring powers and capacities of existing regional human rights bodies remain entirely dependent upon the political will of the state governments concerned – their willingness to cooperate and their ability to commit the significant resources required.

3.3.3 Enforcing the Human Rights Responsibilities of MNCs through World Bank and other International Financial Institutions

By comparison to the UN and regional human rights bodies, global aid institutions such as the World Bank and the Asian Development Bank have fewer problems in terms of adequate resources and institutional technical expertise to enforce their rules effectively. Given their pivotal role in the process of globalisation, and their direct relations with and impact upon corporations, there is some logic in seeking to utilise global financial institutions to ensure MNCs' observance of human rights standards. So far as the World Bank is concerned, its prominent role in global investment flows and its close connection with private businesses makes it a potentially powerful regulator of MNC activities, particularly in developing countries. A key body in this respect is the Bank's private sector arm – the International Finance Corporation (IFC). For further information on this body, see International Finance Corporation (2007).

The IFC provides businesses with loans to implement development projects, usually in partnership with host states. It has a standing policy of carrying out all of its operations in an "environmentally and socially responsible manner", and it requires its business clients to abide by the IFC's environmental, social and disclosure policies. These policies incorporate some of the existing international human rights standards, such as prohibitions on forced labour and child labour, and relating to the rights of indigenous peoples. They are normally incorporated into the investment agreement between the IFC and the corporate client, and the client's failure to comply with the policies can result in suspension or cancellation of an IFC loan. Further, sensitivity to environmental and social issues in the operations of international finance has also been boosted by the recent development and adoption of the "Equator Principles' by a number of international banks (Equator Principles, n.d.). The principles" which are in fact based on the social and environmental policies of the World Bank and the IFC, seek to place certain conditions on the provision of development project finance by the signatory banks.

There are a number of problems, however, with relying on the IFC or any other financial organisation to ensure that corporations involved in development projects respect agreed human rights standards. First there is the reality that such organisations are often unable to monitor their own business clients. In addition, both the IFC and other international financial aid organisations have in the past been accused of violating their own policies, by funding projects that have caused human rights abuses. The desire for economic success provides a disincentive for such organisations to take non-economic issues (such as human rights or environmental externalities) into account. The second problem is that financial institutions, even those motivated by aid and development-promotion agendas, do not have a mandate for protecting human rights. As Kinley and Tadaki have pointed out,

> in the absence of explicit mandates to protect human rights, they cannot be expected to act as general enforcement agencies of the relevant human rights norms that TNCs should respect. The extent to which they are currently willing to enforce human rights obligations of TNCs is limited by their economic objectives. For example, while the World Bank supports the efforts to abolish child and forced labor and to promote gender equality, it is ambivalent about promoting the freedom of association and collective bargaining because the economic effects of those labor standards are apparently unclear. Thus the human rights norms that these institutions are presently prepared to protect would inevitably be selective, based on the market friendliness of the rights rather than on the needs that give rise to the invocation of the rights (Kinley and Tadaki, 2004, p. 1014).

In relation to the international trade forums, a number of writers have explored proposals for linking human rights to trade through the World Trade Organization (WTO) and/or regional trade arrangements (for example, Robinson, 2001; Cottier, 2002; [Dommen, 2002]; and [Marceau, 2002]). This chapter does not seek to revisit the already well-trodden debate over whether or not the WTO can or should play a role in human rights (and/or environmental) protection. Suffice to note that at the heart of the question lies the dilemma of how to bring non-economic consider-ations (such as human rights or the environment) on to the WTO's agenda given the free-market imperative that drives the organisation's culture. There is also the dilemma of the moral double standards that can appear when trade sanctions are used to promote non-economic objectives. The problem is that human rights abuses (like environmental damage) are all too often found in the very nations that need greater access to developed-economy markets simply in order to earn the resources needed for address-ing environmental and social objectives. Imposing trade sanctions on developing nations where human rights and environmental abuses occur may not only impose greater hardship on societies already under strain, but may also serve to make worse the very problem sought to be addressed.

Given these limitations, the WTO, like the World Bank/IFC is only able to provide enforcement mechanisms in specific circumstances and in a piecemeal manner. Although this does not mean that their potential for upholding human rights should be dismissed altogether, it is a potential that is constrained by the economic imperatives that drive their operations.

3.3.4   The Global Firm and the International Criminal Court

The recently created International Criminal Court (ICC) may be ideally placed to take on some significant responsibility for the prevention and punishment of at least some of the most the egregious human rights abuses when private commercial operations are involved.

The first application of the term "international crime" to individuals was,

in 1945 at the conclusion of the Second World War, [when] a number of German government and military leaders were put on trial at Nuremberg for crimes against humanity . . . in subsequent trials, other German leaders, including leaders of industry, were also tried and convicted. The manner in which they conducted their business and led their companies was found to be illegal under international law . . . In 1948, officials from the Krupp company were found guilty of "plunder and spoliation" for their seizure of plant and machinery in conquered France and Holland and sentenced to prison. They were also found guilty of enslavement for Krupp's use of thousands of forced foreign workers, prisoners of war and concentration camp inmates. Other industrialists experi-enced a similar fate, including officials from the massive IG Farbenindustrie AG chemical and synthetics business (Field, 2006).

The Nuremberg Tribunal recognised that "[c]rimes against interna-tional law are committed by men, not by abstract entities, and only by punishing individuals who commit such crimes can the provisions of international law be enforced" (Harris, 2004, p. 141). Most recently, the establishment of the International Criminal Court and the prosecutions (not all of them successful) of Auguste Pinochet, Slobodan Milosevic, Charles Taylor and others, have confirmed the principle that individuals are bound by the obligations of international human rights law, regardless of the law of their state, and regardless of contrary orders received from their superiors.

Sixty years later, the Nuremberg tribunal judgements now provide a precedent for applying the concept of international criminality to legal (corporate) persons in accordance with the principles spelt out in international human rights treaties and the Rome Statute of the International Criminal Court (International Criminal Court, 1998; de Than and Shorts, 2003). At present, the ICC has jurisdiction over "the most serious crimes of concern to the international community as a whole" (Rome Statute, article 5), but this jurisdiction is limited to "natural persons" (Rome Statute, article 25). There is, as yet, no provision for the Court to exercise jurisdiction over corporate persons. But there is historical precedent for creating such a jurisdiction in the Nuremberg tribunal discussions of corporate liability under international criminal law.

The jurisdiction of the ICC should be expanded to cover legal (corporate) persons as well as natural persons. This should be done to facilitate justice for those affected by the criminal behaviour of MNCs. It should also be done as a means of helping to unify the different standards and rules of corporate criminal liability currently found within diverse jurisdictions around the world. Such diversity simply helps to perpetuate forum shopping, as well as creating a hotch-potch of conflicting decisions.

3.3.5   The Global Firm and International Labour Standards

In the area of labour standards, Virginia Leary has convincingly argued that "the focus in international law on state action alone fails to address the influence of the activities of non-state actors, such as multinational enterprises (MNEs), on labor and other social issues" (Leary, 2003, p. 194). International law's preoccupation with the nation state is reflected in the fact that the ILO Tripartite Declaration and other instruments adopted by the ILO Governing Body (where workers' organisations and employer bodies participate alongside governments), have a lesser legal status than instruments adopted by the ILO Annual Conference, which comprises all ILO member states. In addition, it seems that government willingness to participate in ILO surveys and dispute resolution procedures tends to decline in those nations where employer demands for "flexibility" in the workplace have economic influence, and where market forces are given a greater role in regulating labour relations (Leary, 2003).

If MNCs were recognised as having international legal personhood, they could then become an integral part of the Annual Conference and the various sub-committees of the ILO. MNCs would then have greater incentive to subscribe to ILO standards, and to negotiate with recognised worker organisations. Once an individual enterprise had agreed to abide by the standards established in an ILO instrument, that firm would then bring those standards with it wherever it set up business, and in all its business relationships. If compulsory mechanisms for reporting and monitoring were also established for signatory firms, enforcement would also become a possibility. One enforcement mechanism which might be both acceptable to MNCs, and effective in resolving labour disputes, is mandatory ILO arbitration through agreed arbitration procedures.

3.4 THE GLOBAL FIRM AND THE ENVIRONMENT: INTRODUCTION

A similar process could be applied in the area of international environmental law. Just as MNCs should be invited to subscribe to obligations spelt out in key ILO treaties, so also should global corporations be able to participate in the creation and maintenance of relevant environmental treaties. MNCs should also be bound by those tenets of environmental law which have attained the status of *jus cogens*. Customary environmental legal principles which have attained this status include concepts such as the preventative principle, the principle of sustainable development, the precautionary principle, the polluter pays principle and the concept of inter-generational equity (Fitzmaurice, 1995, p. 410).

As Dr Fitzmaurice has noted, issues which arise under international environmental law are undoubtedly "global" in nature – that is, they "cannot ultimately be dealt with at a national or even a regional level". Moreover, the International Court of Justice (ICJ), "because of its dual role in both settlement of disputes and development and elaboration of international law, is especially suited to deal with all aspects of environmental law" (Fitzmaurice, 1995, pp. 400–401).

On the few occasions when the ICJ has been asked to deal with environmental matters, however, it has proven remarkably reluctant and timid in its approach. In the *WHO Nuclear Weapons* case (International Court of Justice, 1993), the Court held that the question put to it by the World Health Organization (WHO) did not fall within the scope of WHO's "activities", as required by Article 96(2) of the Court's Charter. The Court interpreted the WHO Constitution (Article 2) as giving WHO the competence to deal with the effects on health of the use of nuclear weapons and to act preventatively to protect people from these effects. But the question put to the Court concerned the legality of, rather than the effects of, the use of nuclear weapons; which was a matter that did not fall within WHO's remit (Harris, 2004, p. 1081). Two years later, in 1995, the Court again took a cautious approach in Nuclear Test II (International Court of Justice, 1995).

If the Court is to remain relevant as the principal judicial organ involved in the development of international law, it is going to have to find ways to grapple with issues raised by the environment. One way the Court has sought to achieve this is by establishing, in July 1993, a special Chamber for Environmental Matters consisting of the ICJ president and vice-president, and five judges who are elected every three years.[7] Recourse to the Chamber is, however, purely voluntary, and no cases have yet been submitted to it (Bekker, 2006).

The other important feature of contemporary international law relating to the environmental is its fragmented and decentralised nature.

> There are now more than 400 regional and universal multilateral environmental treaties in force, covering a broad range of environmental issues, including biodiversity, climate change and desertification. The sectoral character of these legal instruments and the fragmented machinery for monitoring their implementation make it harder to mount effective responses across the board (United Nations, Secretary-General, 2005, p. 51; Stephens, 2007).

In 2002, the World Summit on Sustainable Development, held in Johannesburg, emphasised the need for a more coherent institutional framework of international environmental governance, with better coordination and monitoring (Department of the Environment, Water, Heritage and the Arts, 2007). As the UN Secretary-General recognised in his 2005 report, *In Larger Freedom*, it is now high time to consider a more integrated structure for environmental standard setting, scientific discussion and monitoring treaty compliance. This should be built on existing institutions, preferably at the UN level (United Nations, Secretary-General, 2005, p. 51). One of the most powerful institutions which could be given a role in protecting the environment is the Security Council.

3.5   A ROLE FOR THE SECURITY COUNCIL IN PROTECTING THE ENVIRONMENT?

It was in 1992 that the Rio Declaration on Environment and Development recognised that "Peace, development and environmental protection are interdependent and indivisible" (United Nations, 1992b). A number of writers and commentators have since shown how scarcity of environmental resources such as energy and water are emerging as major sources of global conflict (for example, Clark, 2005; Ward, 2002). The UN Security Council has also recognised that "The non-military sources of instability in the economic, social, humanitarian and ecological fields have become threats to peace and security" (United Nations, Security Council, 1992). This comment came less than a year after the Council's statement, made during the Gulf War, concerning Iraq's potential liability for environmental harm resulting from its unlawful invasion of Kuwait.

The Security Council's apparently emerging interest in the global environment is at once positive and problematic. It could be a positive development because the state-based international legal system has shown itself to be consistently unable to respond to the global nature of environmental problems through the creation of adequate monitoring and enforcement arrangements. It is, accordingly, tempting to look for a "higher" authority to determine the appropriate course of action in such matters – at least in cases where environmental threats present a "clear and present danger" to international peace and security (Reilly, 1996).

As Reilly recognises, one obvious problem with involving the Security Council in environmental questions is that it would be subject to the veto-wielding powers of the five permanent members. France, for example, would have been able to stymie any attempt by the Council to prevent its resumption of underground nuclear testing at Mururoa Atoll in 1995. Security Council involvement in environmental issues is also problematic for a number of other reasons, not the least of which is the Council's inability to bind non-state actors on the global stage through its statements and decisions.

As new international mechanisms for protecting the environment are developed, there is a need for monitoring and enforcement mechanisms to embrace not only nation states, but non-state actors on the global stage as well. International organisations are already included within the coverage of existing environmental protection measures, but with some few exceptions, MNCs are most notable for their absence in either the creation or binding coverage of international environmental law. This is a major problem given that the vast bulk of environmentally destructive activities are carried out not by nation states, but by corporations, and thus fall outside of the coverage of the international legal system.

From a procedural point of view, the key to solving this problem lies in giving MNCs greater access to international processes. In the same way that many NGOs are now able to take an active part in the deliberations of many UN and regional government organisations, so also could MNCs be welcomed as observers, participants and/or members of global environmental organisations, and invited to participate in standard-setting processes. If private capital is to bear its share of the burden of implementing strategies directed towards environmental ends, then private capital must be brought on board as an essential participant in the evolution of international environmental law.

Given the often intensely political nature of debates and decision making at the UN General Assembly and even more so in the Security Council, there are strong arguments against giving MNCs access to these forums. But the same arguments do not apply when it comes to giving MNCs access to the ICJ in the same way that NGOs are beginning to take part in ICJ proceedings (Chinkin, 1997, p. 53; Clark, 1981).[8] This involves allowing MNCs similarly restricted access to appear before the Environmental Chamber of the ICJ. Especially when company names appear in cases involving environmental issues, natural justice alone requires that the corporation so named has an opportunity to speak.

3.6   THE ICJ AS A GLOBAL COURT OF APPEAL

The ICJ's attempt to take environmental issues more seriously through the establishment of a specialist Chamber for Environmental Matters was noted above. The Chamber, however, is no better equipped to deal effectively with threats to the environment than is the ICJ itself. What is needed are procedural reforms to the ICJ aimed at facilitating access to the Court by NGOs and MNCs. These reforms include allowing greater use of the *amicus curiae* brief in both contentious and advisory cases, and allowing MNCs and NGOs to have access to the advisory jurisdiction of the Court in cases of international importance. This latter proposal in particular would be part of enabling the ICJ to act as a global "court of appeal", able to begin the process of harmonising international jurisprudence in the area of environmental law.

Existing forums to which MNCs already have access – such as the NAFTA Chapter 11 arbitration procedures, and the International Centre for the Settlement of Investment Disputes (ICSID) – should be brought into an integrated global environmental law regime. This could be achieved through relatively simple amendments to their individual charters. These amendments would be aimed at ensuring that for decisions having potentially significant environmental implications, either party to a dispute could appeal on matters of law to the ICJ.

Other international dispute-settlement regimes, such as the WTO's Dispute Settlement Understanding, and the relevant provisions of the UN *Convention on the Law of the Sea*, would require two kinds of amendments – first to allow

NGOs and MNCs to participate in dispute resolution proceedings, and second to facilitate appeals on points of law to the ICJ. This linking of international forums through a common line of appeal should initially be restricted to environmental cases, for which it is most suited, and where it could be of most use.

Nor is this a radical or new idea. Dr Fitzmaurice, speaking in 1995, envisaged a time when organisations, including NGOs and even private organisations, could be permitted to access a global system of courts and tribunals, possibly headed by the ICJ. Her vision was of an international legal system where specialised courts would "exist within a single, or at least linked, system of international courts, within which the ICJ would maintain an appellate position, enabling it to guide the unified development of general rules of international law" (Fitzmaurice, 1997, pp. 413–416).

3.7 CONCLUSION

In this chapter I have outlined the unsatisfactory situation with regard to the position of MNCs under international law, and I have discussed a number of proposals aimed at bringing MNCs within the coverage of binding international standards. Some proposals, such as expanding the work of international human rights tribunals to include scrutinising the activities of MNCs, appear somewhat idealistic in the face of political and resource constraints. Other proposals, such as for giving the UN Security Council a role in regulating the environmentally destructive activities of MNCs, appear politically self-defeating at best. Proposals for leaving the job of monitoring corporate behaviour to the WTO or to the World Bank and/or other financial institutions, are also open to criticism. What might be both politically acceptable and economically feasible, however, is to expand the jurisdiction of the International Criminal Court (ICC) in cases of grievous abuses of human rights to cover not just natural persons but legal persons as well. Similarly hopeful are proposals for continuing the gradual reform of ICJ procedural rules to allow increased access to the Court by NGOs and MNCs in environmental cases. Creating links between the ICJ Environmental Chamber and other international tribunals could also play a part in meeting the need for a more integrated structure for environmental standard setting, monitoring and enforcement.

NOTES

1. In September 2000, a Corporate Code of Conduct Bill was tabled in the Australian Senate, but was never passed into law. Six years later, the Australian Parliamentary Joint

Committee on Corporations and Financial Services (2006) declined to recommend any significant changes to existing legal standards for corporate behaviour.

2. In America, the Sarbanes-Oxley reforms have primarily focussed upon investor and creditor protection, rather than social responsibility. So far as corporate social responsibility is concerned, reliance is still on voluntary guidelines such as the American Law Institute's *Principles of Corporate Governance* (1994) model clauses.

3. See Bhopal Medical Appeal and Sambhavna Trust (n.d.). See also Bhopal Information Centre (2007) and Union Carbide (2007).

4. Pesticide Action Network Updates Service (2006).

5. Klein (2001) p. 5, citing Sherrill (1997).

6. By June 2004, all 191 Member States of the United Nations and one non-Member State were a party to one or more of the 12 international human rights treaties of the United Nations that establish committees of experts to monitor their implementation: Office of the United Nations High Commissioner for Human Rights (2004). See also European Court of Human Rights (n.d.).

   In America, the American Convention on Human Rights, which entered into force on 18 July 1978, created two organs to promote and protect human rights: the Inter-American Commission on Human Rights and the Inter-American Court of Human Rights (University of Minnesota, Human Rights Library, n.d.).

   In Africa, the Protocol to the African Charter on Human and Peoples' Rights Establishing an African Court of Human and Peoples' Rights entered into force on 25 January 2004. The 11 judges of the inaugural African Court on Human and Peoples' Rights were sworn in at the seventh session of the meeting of the African Union Heads of Government in Banjul, Gambia, on 16 July 2006: Amnesty International (2004); Anaba (2006).

7. Article 26, paragraph 1 of the ICJ Statute authorises the Court "to form one or more chambers, composed of three or more judges as the Court may determine, for dealing with particular categories of cases'. The Chamber for Environmental Matters is the only one to have been established by the Court pursuant to this Article (International Court of Justice, 2005).

8. See article 34 (in relation to contentious cases) and article 66 (in relation to advisory opinion requests) of the ICJ Statute. See also article 43 of the Rules of the ICJ (as amended on 29 September 2005).

REFERENCES

AccountAbility (2003) *AA1000 Assurance Standard*, available at www.eldis.org/static/DOC11920.htm; accessed on 11 January 2008.

American Law Institute (1994) *Principles of Corporate Governance: Analysis and Recommendations, Volumes 1 and 2*, American Law Institute Publishers, Philadelphia, PA.

Amnesty International (2004) *Establishing an African Court on Human Rights*, Press Release, 26 January, available at www.scoop.co.nz/stories/WO0401/S00167.htm; accessed on 11 January 2008.

Anaba, I. (2006) *African Human Rights Court Judges Sworn In*, 17 July, available at www.justiceinitiative.org/db/resource2?res_id=103299; accessed on 11 February 2008.

Annan, K. (2006) *True Test of New Human Rights Council will be Use Member States Make of it, Secretary-General Says*, United Nations Press Release, 15 March, available at www.un.org/News/Press/docs/2006/sgsm10376.doc.htm; accessed on 5 December 2006.

Anton, D., Mathew, P. and Morgan, W. (2005) *International Law: Cases and Materials*, Oxford University Press, Oxford.

Bekker, P. (2006) "Argentina-Uruguay Environmental Border Dispute Before the World Court", *ASIL Insight*, 16 May, **10**(11), available at www.asil.org/insights/2006/05/insights 060516.html; accessed on 11 January 2008.

Bhopal Information Centre (2007) website available at www.bhopal.com/; accessed on 18 February 2006.

Bhopal Medical Appeal and Sambhavna Trust (n.d.) *What Happened in Bhopal*, available at www.bhopal.org/whathappened.html; accessed on 15 February 2006.

Burton, B. (2002) "PNG Law Shields BHP from Ok Tedi Liabilities", *Mining Monitor*, **6**(4), 1.

Carbon Disclosure Project ([2007]) *Homepage*, available at www.cdproject.net/; accessed on 11 January 2008.

Chinkin, C. (1997) "Increasing the Use and Appeal of the Court: Presentation", in C. Peck and R.S. Lee (eds) *Increasing the Effectiveness of the International Court of Justice*, Martinus Nijhoff, The Hague.

Clark, R. (1981) "The International League for Human Rights and South West Africa 1947–1957: The Human-Rights NGO as Catalyst in the International Legal Process", *Human Rights Quarterly*, **3**(4), 101–136.

Clark, W.R. (2005) *PetroDollar Warfare: Oil, Iraq and the Future of the Dollar*, New Society Publishers, Gabriola Island, BC.

Climate Risk Disclosure Initiative Steering Committee (2006) *Global Framework for Climate Risk Disclosure: A Statement of Investor Expectations for Comprehensive Corporate Disclosure*, available at www.iigcc.org/docs/PDF/Public/GlobalFramework.pdf; accessed on 8 January 2008.

Cottier, T. (2002) "Trade and Human Rights: A Relationship to Discover", *Journal of International Economic Law*, **5**(1), 111–132.

de Than, C. and Shorts, E. (2003) *International Criminal Law and Human Rights*, Sweet and Maxwell, London.

Department of the Environment, Water, Heritage and the Arts, Australia (2007) *World Summit on Sustainable Development*, available at www.environment.gov.au/commitments/wssd/index.html; accessed on 11 January 2008. Contains links to summit outcome documents.

Dommen, C. (2002) "Raising Human Rights Concerns in the World Trade Organization: Actors, Processes and Possible Strategies', *Human Rights Quarterly*, **24**(1), 1–50.

Dow Jones (2006) *Sustainability Indexes*, available at www.sustainability-index.com/; accessed on 11 January 2008.

Equator Principles (n.d.) website available at www.equator-principles.com/; accessed on 3 August 2007.

European Court of Human Rights (n.d.) website available at www.echr.coe.int/ECHR/EN/; accessed on 11 January 2008.

Field, A. (2006) "Nuremberg Defence Doesn't Make the Grade for Suspect Corporate Citizens', *The Age* (Melbourne) 18 January.

Fitzmaurice, M. (1995) "Presentation", in C. Peck and R.S. Lee (eds) *Increasing the Effectiveness of the International Court of Justice*, Martinus Nijhoff, The Hague, pp. 397–444.

Fraser, M. (2001) *My Country 2050*, Melbourne Festival Deakin Lecture, 20 May; available at www.abc.net.au/rn/deakin/docs/fraser.doc; accessed on 11 January 2008.

FTSE (2007) *FTSE4Good Index Series*, available at www.ftse.com/Indices/ FTSE4Good_Index_Series/index.jsp; accessed on 11 January 2008.

Global Reporting Initiative (2007) website available at www.globalreporting.org/; accessed on 11 January 2008.

Harris, D.J. (2004) *Cases and Materials on International Law*, 6th ed., Sweet and Maxwell, London; Law Book, Sydney.

International Auditing and Assurance Standards Board (2007) website available at www.ifac.org/IAASB/; accessed on 11 January 2008.

International Court of Justice (1993) *Request For Advisory Opinion transmitted to the Court under a World Health Assembly resolution of 14 May 1993: Legality Of The Use By A State Of Nuclear Weapons In Armed Conflict*, available at www.icj-cij.org/docket/index.php?p 1=3&p 2=4&k=e1&case=93&code=anw&p 3=0; accessed on 14 January 2008.

International Court of Justice (1995) *Request for an Examination of the Situation in Accordance with Paragraph 63 of the Court's Judgment of 20 December 1974 in the Nuclear Tests (New Zealand v France) Case*, available at www.icj-cij.org/ docket/index.php?p 1=3&code=nzfr&case=97&k=cd; accessed on 11 January 2008.

International Court of Justice (2005) *Reshuffle of the Court's Chambers and Committees*, Press release 2005/10, available at www.icj-cij.org/presscom/ index.php?pr=2&pt=1&p 1=6&p 2=1; accessed on 14 January 2008.

International Criminal Court (1998) *Rome Statute of the International Criminal Court*, 17 July, available at www.un.org/law/icc/statute/romefra.htm; accessed on 13 February 2008.

International Finance Corporation (2007) website available at www.ifc.org/; accessed on 3 August 2007.

International Labour Organization (1977, revised in 2000) *Tripartite Declaration of Principles Concerning Multinational Enterprises and Social Policy*, Document OB LXXXIII, 2000, Series A, No. 3, available at http://training.itcilo.org/ils/foa/ library/tridecl/text_en.htm; accessed on 11 January 2008.

Jackson, D. (2004) *Report of the Special Commission of Inquiry into the Medical Research Fund and Compensation Foundation*, The Cabinet Office, Sydney.

Jarron, C. (2006) "The Social Control of Business", paper presented at the *Enhancing Corporate Accountability Prospects and Challenges* Conference, Melbourne, 8–9 February 2006. In Acquaah-Gaisie, G. and Clulow, V. (eds), *Enhancing Corporate Accountability Prospects and Challenges Conference Proceedings*, Monash University, Melbourne pp. 155–180.

Khulumani et al. v Barclays et al. 346 F. Supp. 2d 538; 2004 U.S. Dist. LEXIS 23944 (29 November 2004).

Kinley, D. and Tadaki, J. (2004) "From Talk to Walk: The Emergence of Human Rights Responsibilities for Corporations at International Law", *Virginia Journal of International Law*, **44**, 931–1023.

Klein, S. (2001) *Submission to the Canadian Democracy and Corporate Accountability Commission*, 17 June; available at www.aurora.ca/docs/AccountabilityComm Submisssion.pdf; accessed on 29 March 2006.

Leary, V. (2003) "Form Follows Function: Formulation of International Labor Standards – Treaties, Codes, Soft Law, Trade Agreements", in J. Gross (ed.), *Workers Rights as Human Rights*, Cornell University Press, Ithaca, pp. 179–206.

Lyons, S. (2006) "The New United Nations Human Rights Council", *ASIL Insight*, 27 March, **10**(7), available at www.asil.org/insights/2006/03/insights 060327.html; accessed on 11 January 2008.

Marceau, G. (2002) "WTO Dispute Settlement and Human Rights", *European Journal of International Law*, **13**(4), 753–814.

OECD (2000) *Guidelines for Multinational Enterprises*, available at www.oecd. org/document/18/0,3343,en_2649_34889_2397532_1_1_1_1,00.html; accessed on 11 January 2008.

Office of the United Nations High Commissioner for Human Rights (2004) *Status of Ratifications of the Principal International Human Rights Treaties as of 9 June 2004*. Geneva: Office of the UNHCR.

Parliamentary Joint Committee on Corporations and Financial Services, Australia (2006) *Inquiry into corporate responsibility*, available at www.aph.gov.au/Senate/committee/corporations_ctte/corporate_responsibility/; accessed on 14 January 2008.

Pesticide Action Network Updates Service (PANUPS) (2006) "Monsanto Hurts Texas Farmers: Cotton Farmers Sue Monsanto for Crop Loss", 27 March, available at www.panna.org/legacy/panups/panup_20060327.dv.html; accessed on 3 August 2007.

Reilly, B. (1996) " 'Clear and Present Danger': A Role for the United Nations Security Council in Protecting the Global Environment", *Melbourne University Law Review*, **20**, pp. 763–804.

Robinson, M. (2001) "Making the Global Economy Work for Human Rights", in G.P. Sampson (ed.) *The Role of the World Trade Organization in Global Governance*, United Nations University Press, New York.

Salomon v A Salomon and Co Ltd (1897) AC 22. [210 U.S. 206, 1897].

Sherrill, R. (1997) "A Year in Corporate Crime" *The Nation*, 7 April.

Spisto, M. (2005) "Stakeholder Interests in Corporate Governance: Is a New Model of Governance a Change for the Better for South Africa? Part 1", *Australian Journal of Corporate Law*, **18**(2), 129–147.

Stephens, T. (2007) *Multiple International Courts and the "Fragmentation" of International Environmental Law*, Legal Studies Research Paper No. 07/14, University of Sydney, Sydney Law School, abstract available at http://ssrn.com/abstract=969569; accessed on 11 January 2008.

Union Carbide (2007) *Bhopal Information Center*, available at http://unioncarbide.com/bhopal; accessed on 20 February 2006.

United Nations (1969) *International Convention on Civil Liability for Oil Pollution Damage*, available at http://sedac.ciesin.org/entri/texts/civil.liability.oil.pollution.damage.1969.html; accessed on 24 October 2005.

United Nations (1976) *Protocol to the International Convention on Civil Liability for Oil Pollution Damage of 29 November 1969*, available at www.admiralty-lawguide.com/conven/protocivilpol1976.html; accessed on 11 January 2008.

United Nations (1984) *Protocol to amend the International Convention on Civil Liability for Oil Pollution Damage*, available at http://sedac.ciesin.columbia.edu/entri/texts/civil.liability.oil.pollution.damage.protocol1984.html; accessed on 11 January 2008 (no longer in force).

United Nations (1992a) *International Maritime Organization Protocol of 1992 to amend the International Convention on Civil Liability for Oil Pollution Damage of 29 November 1969*, available at www.admiraltylawguide.com/conven/protocivilpol1992.html; accessed on 11 January 2008.

United Nations (1992b) *Report of the United Nations Conference on Environment and Development*, Rio de Janiero, 3–14 June, A/Conf.151/26 (Vol. 1), available at www.un.org/documents/ga/conf151/aconf15126-1annex1.htm; accessed 11 January 2008.

United Nations (2000) *Global Compact Website* available at www.globalcompact.org/; accessed on 13 January 2008.

United Nations (2003) *Draft UN Norms on the Responsibilities of Transnational Corporations and Other Business Enterprises with Regard to Human Rights*, E/CN.4/Sub.2/2003/12 (2003) available at www.law.wits.ac.za/humanrts/links/NormsApril2003.html; accessed on 11 January 2008.

United Nations (2006) *Principles for Responsible Investment*, available at www.unpri.org/; accessed on 11 January 2008.

United Nations, Department of Public Information, News and Media Division (2006a) *Fifth Committee Considers Budget Implications of Proposed Human Rights Council*, GA/AB/3720, 3 June, available at www.un.org/News/Press/docs/2006/gaab3720.doc.htm; accessed on 11 January 2008.

United Nations, Department of Public Information, News and Media Division (2006b), *Press Conference on Human Rights Council by General Assembly President*, Press Release, 15 March, available at www.un.org/News/briefings/docs/2006/060315_Eliasson_PC.doc.htm; accessed on 6 December 2006.

United Nations, Environment Programme (n.d.) *Finance Initiative Website*, available at www.unepfi.org/; accessed 14 January 2008.

United Nations, Secretary-General (2005) *In Larger Freedom: Towards Security, Development and Human Rights for All*, available at www.un.org/largerfreedom/; accessed on 11 January 2008.

United Nations, Security Council (1992) "Summit Statement Concerning the Council's Responsibility in the Maintenance of International Peace and Security, 31 January 1992", *International Legal Materials*, **31**(3),749, 758.

University of Minnesota, Human Rights Library (n.d.) *Basic Documents Relevant to the Inter-American Court of Human Rights*, available at www1.umn.edu/humanrts/iachr/iachr.html; accessed on 11 January 2008.

Ward, D.R. (2002) *Water Wars: Drought, Flood, Folly and the Politics of Thirst*, Riverhead, New York.

PART II

Critical issues

4. Instruments of peace? How businesses might foster religious harmony

Timothy L. Fort

4.1 INTRODUCTION

When I first began to research the topic of what is now in the U.S. called "Peace Through Commerce", I found an odd assortment of resources that had not been put together. Other than Jane Nelson's book, *The Business of Peace* (2000), there was no direct integration of business and peace. There were, of course, the usual concepts of how trade fosters peace and the classic philosophical formulations of philosophers such as Kant and Montesquieu that linked commercial republics and peace, but 21st Century business and peace? That was new.

Yet in the last ten years or so, the topic has surged in academic interests. In the U.S. alone, a half-dozen conferences were held on the topic along with two special issues of journals: *American Business Law Journal* and *Journal of Corporate Citizenship*. In 2007, I hosted my fifth conference on the topic and finished my third book. Governments have begun to take notice.

If there was a group of individuals most likely to be skeptical about the positive role businesses might play to encourage peace however, they may well have been not hard-headed political realists but religious believers. Indeed, when I proudly told my former doctoral adviser that I was pursuing the connection as a new research interest, he was flabbergasted. Trying to get businesses to be more ethical was daunting challenge enough; to suggest that they actually play a constructive role in fostering peace, justice and stability was a bit beyond his imagination.

Yet, as Swiss theologian Hans Küng is fond of saying, there can be no peace without peace among world religions. And if one of the core drivers of global interaction today is business, then it is not completely unreasonable to think that business might have a role to play in gluing religious factions together even if the common goal that unites them is as mundane as making money. Fine in theory, but when one gets to the nuts and bolts of human behavior, religion can be an agent for both great good and great horror. And businesses have their own sordid history, a history that my doctoral adviser took to heart. Putting these two powerhouses together may not be as good an idea as we might think.

But that's exactly what I'd like to suggest that we do. Businesses, I want to argue, could be instruments of peace, perhaps not quite in as holy a way as St Francis thought when he penned his prayer petitioning that the Lord make him an instrument of peace, but still in a way that is a genuine contribution to reduced bloodshed. Let me give a personal example that suggests the possibilities.

In the early 1990s, before Communism fell in Albania, many snuck out of the country into what was then thought to be a safe haven of Belgrade, where they lived in refugee camps. I learned that the U.S. State Department would approve the immigration of these refugees if American families would promise 1) to provide a place for them to live for three months; 2) to help them learn English and 3) to help them to find a job. We applied and brought Petrov (not his real name) to live in our home for three months while we worked with him on the other items.

Petrov told us that practicing of religion had been punishable by death in Albania from the time he was one year old and there was plenty of corroborating evidence to back up his claim. So, although Petrov was raised in a family with a Catholic heritage, he had not had one moment of religious instruction.

One night after dinner, Petrov asked me who God was. I only had my Masters in Theology at the time, but started to plunge into my description of the divine when Petrov interrupted me:

I hate Muslims.

Petrov, a minute ago, you were asking who God was. How can you hate Muslims?

I hate Muslims.

But why?

Because I am Catholic.

What does being Catholic mean?

It means I hate Muslims.

We went around on this for quite awhile before I gave up. There wasn't a shred of theological dispute in doubt – indeed because of the ban on religious practice, there couldn't be a religious difference – but religious affiliation was a marker of identity based on hatred of another.

Oh, and there was one other thing. I asked Petrov about the people he worked with.

Catholics and Muslims.

How did you get along with the Muslims?

They were OK; they worked hard. I liked them.

Now this is an anecdote and it is a slim foundation on which to argue that business provides a way around religious differences. But working together can provide such a way. It can bring people together who might otherwise prefer to kill each other. Given a chance, maybe they would go ahead and fight. But in a world that needs platforms on which to build common ground, it is hard to see why we would not try to take advantage of the opportunities business provides. Business may not finally get a Sisyphean rock on the top of a hill, but it can keep the rock pushed up into higher levels of behavior rather than having it mired at the bottom of the hill in the dark violence of human nature.

4.2   PEACE THROUGH COMMERCE BASICS

Carolyn Woo, the Dean of the Mendoza College of Business at the University of Notre Dame, gets credit for the term "Peace Through Commerce". As one of the originators of the academic renaissance of the topic, I had run three conferences at the University of Michigan under the cumbersome rubric of "Corporate Governance, Stakeholder Accountability, and Sustainable Peace". Peace Through Commerce is far catchier, but there is a danger associated with it as well. Does any kind of commerce promote peace? I don't think that is an avenue we want to travel. Colonialism is commerce. So is sweatshop exploitation, environmentally degrading extraction of minerals and slavery. Such practices aren't likely to produce much peace; they are more likely to build resentments that could lead to the flashpoints of violence.

It is a particular kind of commerce that leads to peace. In a book I co-authored with Cindy Schipani, *The Role of Business in Fostering Peaceful Societies* (2004) and also in a 2007 book of my own, *Business, Integrity, and Peace*, I argued that there is a happy coincidence between anthropological, political and economically determined attributes of relatively non-violent societies and consensus-based recommendations for ethical business behavior. In other words, if businesses follow commonly accepted recommendations for ethical practices, there may be an unexpected impact: those practices may tend to reduce violence.

The first of those practices is, indeed, economic performance. With clear links established by the World Bank and the United Nations between poverty and violence, businesses help countries to the extent that they help to build economic capabilities. That is particularly true if they go beyond extraction and bring added value to the economy.

The second of the practices is adherence to the rule of law. That includes support of independent judiciaries, and contract and property law, but more specifically it means avoiding corruption. There are clear correlative links between those countries that are the most corrupt and those that resolve disputes by violence. Companies which have policies that discourage bribery contribute to a social milieu that seems to lead away from violence and toward non-violent resolution of disputes.

The third of these practices is building a sense of community in two ways. The first way is externally. Are corporations good citizens? Are they culturally sensitive and environmentally responsible? The second way is internal. Do companies build their organizations so that they are communities? This includes empowering employees with voice, respecting rights, and to the extent possible, fostering gender equity.

None of these practices is particularly controversial. They are all within reach of businesses today. Because they are in reach of business, businesses can practice them and make a contribution to sustainable peace.

This is all fine in theory. Identifying similarities between anthropologically determined peaceful societies and engaging in correlative studies showing various linkages is important, but what happens when business runs into that most tricky of social forces: religious belief. That is the topic of my 2008 book: *Prophets, Profits, and Peace*. The next section summarizes the six main points of that book.

4.3   RELIGION: SIX KEY POINTS

The first thing that is important to see is that, like it or not, business bumps into religion. This is important because there can be a temptation to believe that business can simply choose to avoid religious issues. Perhaps that can happen to some extent, but businesses can also find themselves bumping into religious beliefs without intending to. For several years, I taught a course that provided an overview of world religions as a way to see how cultural practices are similar and different. One of the assignments was for students to look in the media for stories about religion and business interacting. From the hundreds of examples they came up with, I narrowed them down to about sixty cases. They ranged from employment issues (engaging in prayer, wearing certain clothing and so on) to banking practices (such as avoiding usury), to marketing practices. The first two are relatively straightforward. The third, however, featured a myriad of examples of business running headlong into religion, mostly negligently.

For example, McDonalds faced protests and even settled a lawsuit because it changed the way it fried its French fries. It had been frying them in vegetable oil, but changed to a formulation that included beef tallow. McDonalds didn't tell anyone it was switching though, so millions of Hindus and other vegetarians unwittingly violated their religious beliefs by consuming beef (*Hinduism Today*, 2003). Other examples include a propensity of some swimwear and lingerie companies to sew religious figures into women's swimwear and lingerie (Lim, 2004). Both Harrods and Roberto Cavalli issued apologies (Priyadarshi, 2004). In another example, a company faced Hindu protests about having the picture of a Hindu god on a toilet seat; the company's response was itself interesting, albeit non-discriminatory: it said that it wasn't singling out Hinduism for ridicule; it also had another toilet seat featuring the Virgin Mary.

The above issues are basically issues of marketing and interface with the general public. Many other issues of religion and business occur in the workplace. They involve freedom to express one's religion, discriminatory practices, inadvertent offensiveness, and accommodation practices and requirements. Still other examples involve specific practices, such as banking, where a religious belief has direct implications for a particular product or service. The rise of the Internet creates still other issues, such as whether a requirement not to conduct business requires Internet businesses to block possible Sabbath sales.

Some of the examples I detail in the book are understandable mistakes, some are knotty dilemmas, and others involve deep issues of serious balancing of faith and business. Others are simply daffy; exactly why does a manufacturer find it constructive to place sacred figures on toilet seats? But there is a simple point. Businesses do bump up against religious sentiments. Religion and business do interact, and if they interact, the question is how they should do so optimally.

That leads to the second point. It concerns why religious believers should be free to speak freely about their religious beliefs. Expression of religious belief does not always engender calm dialogue. In a scientific age, some have argued that non-religious, rational belief has epistemological superiority over that of knowledge derived through religious belief. And so there is a challenge as to whether, if one has a religious belief, it should be expressed in public.

On the other hand, philosophically speaking, believers should have a right to express themselves and there are good reasons for us to encourage them to do so. It is generally better for someone to state honestly the reasons why they are doing what they do, so if a reason for their action is religious, it is better to have them be honest about it. For that matter, some philosophers have questioned whether rationality is really epistemologically superior to faith-based belief because, in the final analysis, confidence in rationality itself requires some leap of faith.

At the same time, while one might justify a right to express one's religious belief in the workplace, it may not be wise to be so explicit about one's faith. Expressing a belief may be so incendiary that it offends others who do not share your belief. And so, it may be strategically wise to soften one's statements. That does not mean being dishonest, nor does it necessarily mean that one should edit one's beliefs. Instead, it means to learn enough about other individuals' religious beliefs so as to be able to find common ground with those faiths. Thus, rather than simply saying that one's beliefs are to love one's neighbor in a Christian way, one could also note that Buddhism's notion of unlimited friendliness offers a similar sentiment. Thus, if one is working in a Buddhist culture, one could be honest about one's Christian beliefs and indeed teach the Buddhist culture more about Christianity, but do so in a way that shows respect, knowledge and common ground with Buddhists. This is a literacy sorely lacking in business today, but if we are to avoid the misunderstandings that can trigger religious hatred, this capability is crucial to a globalized business strategy.

The third question is why businesses might want to pay attention to spirituality. This issue has a more complicated response than one might imagine. Business may benefit from allowing employees to engage in practicing their spirituality. Companies have been doing this with some degree of frequency. Many companies explicitly allow, even encourage, employees to find times and places to express and share their spirituality. Thierry Pauchant (2002) has documented dozens of major multinational companies that follow such spirituality-friendly policies. Beyond such explicit policies, however, there is an advantage for businesses to foster passionate commitments to excellence on the part of their employees. Such passions deal with the emotions and with aesthetics, and those sentiments are an expression of spirituality, sometimes with a religiously transcendent dimension, sometimes not.

What is vital to business is to provide an atmosphere where individuals find a sense of identity that they can passionately pursue at the workplace. There is a specific reason why this is important. Businesses are required to follow a myriad of demands to be ethical today, including complying with the laws of relevant government organizations. They also arise from public pressure to find ways to integrate doing well and doing good. Individuals do respond to external incentives in modifying behavior, but there are also important internally-driven motivations that, if left out, underutilize the motivations that could make doing good in business something that is valued.

I refer to these three kinds of practices as Hard Trust, Real Trust and Good Trust. They do not come from nowhere. Indeed, they can be traced to basic biological urges that exist within all humanity, and non-humans as well. William Frederick (1995) has detailed these three value clusters, calling them Economizing, Ecologizing and Power-Aggrandizing. Frederick's point is not whether these are good or bad; they simply are there and we do well not to ignore them. Instead, integrating them is a more effective strategy. In my lexicon, Power-Aggrandizing connects with Hard Trust and therefore with the law. Economizing connects with Real Trust and therefore most directly with profit-making business. Ecologizing connects with Good Trust and therefore connects with the affective dimension of human nature. Good Trust motivates individuals to care about being ethical from sources deep within them.

Spirituality directed toward religious beings is one form of Good Trust and it is one that many individuals will embrace. An existential affective spirituality, one that is shared by all faiths, is a commitment to peace. So, if businesses commit to practices that foster peace, they may also find that they are able to open the door to the better angels of spiritual natures. In other words, a powerful, affective spirituality could provide a positive common ground among various religious and spiritual traditions. Not only might this engage the affective enthusiasm of workers in their work, but it might also create a platform for people of differing spiritual traditions to come together to pursue peace through commerce. So, while being specifically open to spiritual practices may be a good thing, even an indirect openness through peace through commerce practices would provide a similar kind of opening.

The fourth issue is, whose religion or spirituality should one follow? There can be only one answer to this question: ours. That is, any effort to prioritize one belief over another is bound to run into contention and potential animosity. Instead, the religion and spirituality needs to be one that is shared. Seeking to find shared values does not mean unanimity of values; non-shared values can still be powerful. However, here again, an approach fostering peace through commerce provides an "ours" that can link individuals together even when they differ, while preserving the uniqueness that differentiates one spiritual tradition from that of another.

In other words, it may be powerful if in sharing our individual spiritualities, we are able to find common ground. But even if a Sikh cannot find common ground with a Christian evangelical, *all* religious traditions venerate peace as the ultimate goal. Peace is an ideal promised to believers. It is a kind of ideal that, if practiced, allows people to live together. It is also an ideal that allows most businesses to flourish. Most businesses do better in peaceful stability rather than in the midst of violence. So, if businesses actively pursue peaceful practices, they may plug into the peaceful elements of religious traditions that constructively reinforce both the business practices of peace and also the commitment to emphasize the peaceful dimensions of religious traditions themselves. This recursive process creates a spirituality of peace that is an "ours" and it is possible through a business commitment to peace itself.

The fifth issue is what kind of socio-political environment might be receptive to this integration of spirituality, business and politics. Here, I offer the notion of civic republicanism. This enjoyed a brief resurrection in the 1980s, and deserves further consideration today. The idea of civic republicanism is that members of society engage in full, honest debate about political issues that govern them. In such democratic dialogue, public policies are developed with a sense of ownership of all members of society. However, two critical kinds of institution are necessary for civic republicanism to flourish. Those are religious institutions and mediating institutions, both of which are frequently shunted to the side in analysis of civic republicanism.

In other words, the literature that develops republicanism as well as its cousin, communitarianism, tends to focus on the negative aspects of mediating institutions and religious institutions and so tends to remove them from public dialogue. But mediating institutions – those small communities of families, neighborhood, business and religion – are where we develop our moral character and learn our public responsibilities. They are critically important in teaching the kind of virtues necessary to create peace through commerce. The same holds true with religious institutions. So, our political processes would do well to include them in public debate provided that these institutions constructively aim toward the common good. The likelihood of that aiming being successful would increase with a commercial emphasis on peace for the reasons detailed in the previous paragraphs.

Finally, when will all of this occur? The answer is pretty much now and never. That is, the resources for a spirituality that fosters understanding have been with us for a very long time. Businesses are capable of quickly integrating them because the ideas are basic ones of business ethics, simply more mindfully practiced. At the same time, one must not become utopian. There will *never* be peace through commerce. But what can occur is that the quest for peace can create more peace than we thought we would be able to achieve. In pursuing peace through commerce, the ethical practices that are necessary to do so become more prominently engrained. More ethical business would itself be a welcome social contribution. Thus I prefer to look at the prospects for peace through commerce through metaphors of rocks.

The first rock is Sisyphus's. As Albert Camus argued, Sisyphus should accept his lot of pushing the rock up the side of the hill. At least he knows what it is he is to do. Abstracting Camus' recommendation from the philosophy of the absurd, we might take actual delight in pushing the rock of peace up the hill, even if we know that we may not be ultimately successful in getting it all the way there. It is a motivating quest and we may see more gain from our efforts than we initially expected.

The other rock is that of the Prophet Mohammed. When the Kaaba Stone, the ancient stone set in what is now Mecca by Abraham, fell into disrepair, a dispute broke out among the various tribes as to who should have the honor of returning the repaired stone to its sacred spot. Before the tribal leaders broke into fighting, the Prophet Mohammed proposed a solution: the Stone would be placed in the middle of a blanket and then the tribal leaders would take sides and corners of the blanket and together – and equally – carry the stone back to its resting spot. This suggestion, from the only leader of a religion founded by a merchant, might suggest a practical wisdom of commerce that we would find helpful today.

4.4 NEXT STEPS AND CONCLUSION

It may seem far-fetched to think of business pursuing peace through commerce. It may be farther-fetched to think of religion as a constructive force for peace as opposed to a force for sectarian violence. And it may be beyond the imagination of many academic scholars to think of religion and business joining together in a common search for peace. At the same time, is it realistic to think that we can avoid the possibility? As has been extensively documented by evolutionary biologists, religious belief seems to be an essential aspect of human nature. Indeed, they have argued that it is part of a competitive evolutionary advantage because religious institutions teach individuals to sublimate short-term self-interest for the greater good of the community. This teaching allows culture to develop and to thrive. Sometimes those teachings go awry, but religion is not likely to go away any time soon, so we might as well stop trying to marginalize it and instead deal directly with it.

Similarly, business is not going away any time soon either, and today's globalization, whether one likes it or not, provides the capability for interaction that forces us to deal with our diversity. Like open religious engagement, there is danger in that. But it is a reality that we must face. So the question isn't whether or not it is far-fetched to think of religion, business and peace together in a constructively imagined engagement; the fact is that they are in the mix with each other, for better or worse. What can we make of it? This chapter, itself following the six chapters of my Yale book, has suggested that there are ways that they can make the best of the possibilities and foster each others' better angels.

   If there is any truth to this argument, then there are huge issues that arise for scholarly inquiry. The argument I have made simply tries to insist that marginalization and compartmentalization are not a good idea. Those strategies contribute to religious illiteracy, which itself can be destructive and deadly. Yet if we are to have engagement, each argument and point I have made simply raises about a dozen additional questions as to how to foster the engagement optimally and how to deal with the inevitable difficulties that *will* arise when such powerful social sectors interact. Sifting through and analyzing all these issues will be hard work. But if we as academics desire to have our work make real contributions to the betterment of our world, it is hard to think of a richer place to begin than to deal with the intersection of religion, business and peace.

REFERENCES

Fort, T.L. (2007) *Business, Integrity, and Peace*. Cambridge: Cambridge University Press.

Fort, T.L. (2008, forthcoming) *Prophets, Profits, and Peace*. New Haven, CT: Yale University Press.

Fort, T.L. and Schipani, C. (2004) *The Role of Business in Fostering Peaceful Societies*. Cambridge: Cambridge University Press.

Frederick, W.C. (1995) *Values, Nature, and Culture in the American Corporation*. New York: Oxford University Press.

Hinduism Today (2003) *McDonald's Fries: Not Done Yet*, October/November/December, available at www.hinduismtoday.com/archives/2003/10-12/66-67% 20McDonald's.shtml, accessed 14 January 2008.

Lim Kooi Fong (2004) Global Buddhist Outrage over Firm's Swim Suit Product. *Buddhist News Network*, 22 April.

Nelson, J. (2000) *The Business of Peace: the Private Sector as a Partner in Conflict Prevention and Resolution*. London: International Alert.

Pauchant, T.C. (2002) "Introduction: Ethical and Spiritual Management Addresses the Need for Meaning in the Workplace", in T.C. Pauchant (ed.), *Ethics and Spirituality at work*. Westport, CT: Quorom Books, pp. 1–27.

Priyadarshi, R. (2004) *Harrods apology over Hindu bikinis*, 9 June, available at http://news.bbc.co.uk/1/hi/world/south_asia/3790315.stm, accessed 14 January 2008.

5. Expropriation of minority shareholders or social dividend? Beware of good corporate citizens

Wladimir M. Sachs and Marleen Dieleman

5.1 INTRODUCTION

Terrorists terrorize us, and they often say that they do this for our own good, to force us to correct ethical flaws in our societies and individual behavior. Some of the ethical flaws they point out are not seen as such by us (for example, we do not think that treating women as inferior living property of men is right), but we agree with other critiques on unfair distribution of wealth, poor performance of social welfare, government corruption or excessive consumerism in general. Therefore, one natural response to the threat is to advocate removal of undesirable characteristics and thus to remove, at least partially, the "reason for terrorism". Corporations, as the most influential and powerful actors of modern post-industrial societies, are asked to play their role, and thus become "good corporate citizens".

While the current terrorist threat is new in many ways, the argument presented above is not. It has a long tradition in Western political thought: communism was to be fought by developing capitalist societies faster and better. At times, when faced with a deficit of positive accomplishments to boast about, communist propaganda claimed that the development of the economies and of institutions (such as trade unions) in the West was entirely due to the Soviet threat, and therefore the altruistic and internationalist Soviet worker and concentration camp laborer ought to be proud that his sacrifices improved the lot of his counterparts in the West, who otherwise would have been living in sordid Dickensian conditions. Thus Soviet propaganda managed the daring feat of pointing to successes in the "enemy" camp as their own.

Similarly, in the words of two eminent French historians, anti-Americanism is the only consensual value in French politics; and has been since the times of Louis XIV (Revel, 2002; Roger, 2002). Those in modern France that attack McDonald restaurants are no different from those in the

19th Century who decried as barbarism elevators and taps with running water. The hamburger is not the cause of the trouble; for McDonald to serve *bisque de homard* and *rognons à la sauce normande* would be unlikely to calm the neurosis that led to the attacks.

The argument is flawed now as it has always been. Corporations are social constructs and to be successful they must operate within the current norms of society. Maybe in the case of foreign multinationals, they can be a bit ahead of the norm, and thus pull the society forward through positive example. But this is at best marginal.

The stark reality is that corporations in many places behave in ways that would be judged corrupt by external standards, and that they do this consciously and with the approval of significant parts of the population. In places that have weak institutions, the social capital of businesses or business owners is a pretty good substitute. We illustrate this by exploring theoretical reasons why under some conditions minority shareholders in a business may willingly accept expropriation of their wealth by controlling parties, and support this with material derived from a longitudinal study of the Salim Group of Indonesia.

We present a conjecture: in some cases minority shareholders willingly accept expropriation by majority shareholders, considering it to be a form of remuneration of social capital put at the disposal of the firm by the majority shareholders. Social capital, discussed more precisely in the next section, is understood here to be the goodwill resulting from privileged relationships of the majority shareholders and which can be used to procure tangible economic benefits for the firm. For instance, if the majority shareholder arranged through his or her personal influence for the firm to have an exclusive import license, then we consider this to be an investment of social capital, entitling the majority shareholder to economic benefits from the firm in excess of those stemming from ownership rights. We propose to dub such excess remuneration social dividend. We also introduce related concepts of social depreciation, social assets, social liabilities and social equity.

All around the world, business groups have minority investors in parts of their empires. Frequently the "majority owners" in fact have only a minority economic interest, either through dual-class shares with differing voting rights or when they invest in the company through a pyramid scheme in which at each stage to maintain control they only have to own a little more than 50 per cent of shares (Amit and Villalonga, 2006; Anderson and Reeb, 2003; Bebchuk, Kraakman and Triantis, 2000; Daily and Dalton, 1992; Demsetz and Lehn, 1985; Fama and Jensen, 1983; Shleifer and Vishny, 1986; Wolfenzon, 1999).

This chapter focuses on the case where the majority shareholder is an individual or a family, which is the case in many developed and developing countries (La Porta *et al.*, 1999). It is often argued that the classical agency problem of aligning owners and managers in a firm (Jensen and Meckling, 1976) does not apply to family firms, as their governance structures often combine ownership and management. Instead, scholars argue that family firms face a different type of agency problem, which is the possible conflict of interest between different groups of shareholders (Chrisman *et al.*, 2004; Morck and Yeung, 2003). In family companies, the non-family investor faces an important question: is the business managed to maximize the wealth of all investors or is some of its performance sacrificed to the benefit of the family? Because the family controls management, it has myriad opportunities to expropriate the company: overpaying purchases, underpricing sales, nepotism, and other practices known collectively as "tunneling" (see for example, Bae *et al.*, 2002; Barclay and Holderness, 1989; Bertrand, Mehta and Mullainathan, 2002; Friedman, Johnson and Mitton, 2003; Johnson *et al.*, 2000). Such private benefits are described by Coffee (2001) as "all of the ways in which those in control of a corporation can siphon off benefits to themselves that are not shared with the other shareholders". Modern auditing and oversight methods are designed to prevent such practices. But countries have imperfect institutional environments, and barriers to expropriation are fairly fragile. Such expropriation is common in transitional economies in general (see for example, Claessens, Djankov and Lang, 2000; Firth, Fund and Rui, 2006; La Porta *et al.*, 1999; Leuz, Nanda and Wysocki, 2003; Lemmon and Lins, 2003; Mitton, 2002), and in Asian economies in particular, such as Korea (Chang and Hong, 2000), India (Bertrand *et al.*, 2002) or Hong Kong (Cheung, Rau and Stouraitis, 2006; Dieleman, 2007). But European countries are also known to experience this phenomenon. In France, expropriations of minority shareholders by business tycoons Pinault (Roche, 2003) and Arnault (Routier, 2003) have been well documented. Yet family-controlled companies frequently are a popular choice of the investing public (Miller and Breton-Miller, 2005), which seems to mean that some degree of expropriation is accepted. This is puzzling, especially in an open global investment market with plentiful options to invest in companies without concentrated ownership.

The ideas presented here emerged from the sense-making phase of an extensive case study of the strategic evolution of the Salim Group, founded in the late 1930s by a proverbial "barefooted" immigrant from China, and some 60 years later representing in turnover 5 per cent of Indonesia's GDP, with over 200 000 employees and hundreds of companies (Carney, Dieleman and Sachs, 2006; Dieleman and Sachs, 2006; Sato, 1993; Soetriyono, 1989). The spectacular success of the Group is largely attributed to the very close relationship between the owning family and Suharto,

Indonesia's dictator for 32 years, but also to the family's extensive network of ethnic Chinese connections. The family had many partners, usually retaining controlling rights, and several of its companies were publicly listed on various Asian stock exchanges. Accounting and reporting practices were far below the standards of dominant international markets, and the Group was not known for being overly committed to transparency. It was widely assumed in Indonesia that the Group played all kinds of games with its minority shareholders, although pinning down irrefutable evidence is difficult. It appeared obvious to us that many minority shareholders accepted a priori that they would not be getting their fair share of the fruit from their investments.

We conjectured that this acquiescence resulted from the acceptance that the Salim family was entitled to be remunerated for "lending" their connections to their individual companies, and that they needed the economic means to maintain and further develop their network of relationships. Furthermore, it became clear to us that this modus operandi was necessary in the institutional environment of Indonesia. We thought that a somewhat formalized concept of social capital and the derivative one of social dividend were well suited to describe these conditions. Together with theories of conglomeration and of institutional development, they provide a theoretical framework to explain the phenomenon.

The next two sections offer a possible explanation using the concept of social capital, which is the set of privileged relationships that the family employs to the benefit of the company, expecting in return to be remunerated as it would be for a pecuniary investment. An adaptation of accounting concepts is then proposed to identify ways in which social capital can be remunerated.

5.2　THE CONCEPT OF SOCIAL CAPITAL

The concept of social capital arose as the response of sociologists to the economic concept of human capital. The latter was formulated as a way of broadening the classical model of an economic entity, in which (financial) capital and labor are used to transform inputs into outputs (see for example, Leontief, 1973). The idea is to recognize that education and skills are a source of wealth, frequently more important than money (Becker, 1964; Mincer, 1958).

Sociologists expanded on this concept by pointing out that human capital accounts only for intrinsic qualities of human beings – and by extension of social entities – such as education and skills. But social entities also have extrinsic qualities by deriving positional benefits from relationships.

Expropriation of minority shareholders   61

They can call on social networks for support and solidarity, or just to gain access to scarce resources, and they contribute in turn to other members of the network. Thus social capital is as "real" as human capital or just capital (Bourdieu, 1985; Coleman, 1988; Lin, 2001; Putnam, 2000; Uzzi, 1997; Woolcock, 1998).

Since its inception, the concept of social capital has proved to be very fertile, used in myriad fields of inquiry. It is generally viewed as a "good thing", as when development experts argue that it can help in rendering poor communities more resilient or when students of transitional dynamics in post-communist countries see it as a key element in fostering democracy and other modern institutions. Theories of the firm also use the concept to advance their understanding of the role of culture and group cohesion in producing desirable outcomes such as client orientation or innovation (Adler and Kwon, 2002; Nahapiet and Ghoshal, 1998; Uzzi, 1997). This chapter proposes a more instrumental perspective, arguing that the social capital of the firm or of the firm's owners – seen here as political and business relationships with powerful players – is a direct producer of significant strategic results, as when a firm benefits from a state-granted monopoly.

There is ample evidence that social capital is a key corporate success factor in countries with underdeveloped institutional environments (see for example, Blyler and Coff, 2003). During the years of import-substitution industrialization, the governments in developing economies promoted local companies, providing them with subsidized loans, exclusive rights and tax advantages, frequently with the blessing and participation of international institutions (see for example, Wu and Wu, 1980). For private entrepreneurs, it was critically important to be chosen as beneficiaries of government largesse, and that depended on their relationships and willingness to remunerate corrupt officials. Many countries saw the emergence of what was dubbed "crony capitalism" (Kang, 2002).

Some authors (for example, Adler and Kwon, 2002) distinguish between bonding and bridging forms of social capital. Bonding capital accrues to an individual by virtue of belonging to a close-knit group, such as an ethnic minority or an "old boy's network". Members of the group exhibit greater goodwill to each other than to outsiders, are bound by some kind of code of conduct, and are obliged to participate in some sort of trading of favors. Bridging capital accrues to an individual by virtue of his or her intermediation position, establishing useful relations across boundaries that are not easily crossed. Such capital is more ephemeral than the bonding form; it requires maintenance through a continuing transaction stream and does not transfer easily to others. Both forms of social capital need to be maintained by continued investments, implying that social capital comes at a cost to the firm or its owners. In some cases the costs of social capital may exceed the benefits, and it is therefore necessary to manage it carefully (Carney, Dieleman and Sachs, 2006).

5.3   THE ROLE OF SOCIAL CAPITAL

In environments with poorly developed market institutions, economic transactions are difficult: the legal framework may not be able to enforce contracts, business partners may be unreliable and dishonest, financial institutions may not be able to provide the necessary support instruments, infrastructure may be deficient, regulatory bodies may not be able to ensure a level playing field, government officials may be incompetent and/or corrupt, and the political system may be unstable (see for example, Peng, 2003). It is well established that in such environments, tightly knit social networks, such as army officers, school networks, families or minority groups, have a significant advantage (Bonacich, 1973; Cook, 1977; Davis, Trebilock and Heys, 2001; Granovetter, 1992; Keister, 1999; Portes and Sensenbrenner, 1993). Contracts can be enforced by internal group bodies, such as an honor court or a religious council, or more informally by the exercise of heavy social sanctions for deviant behavior. Reliability and honesty of partners is checked through the social "grapevine", credit can be extended among group members without much formality, and internal rules can substitute for government regulation. The bonding social capital of the group creates an environment that is more propitious for business than the context at large. In fact it becomes a necessary ingredient of business success.

Bridging social capital is also necessary. For example, when a government allocates scarce resources on other-than-market bases, it is necessary to establish bridges with the clique controlling such decisions (Frynas *et al.*, 2006) and to arrange for some form of payment for favorable outcomes. The natural response of a business operating in a corrupt environment is to corrupt, and this tends to create lasting relationships between members of a particular business community and members of the government circles.

Traditionally, minority groups played an important role in economic activity, as in the cases of the Jewish, the Chinese and the Indian diasporas. Their internal codes of conduct enforced through strong social pressure made up for the deficiencies of the institutional environment that rendered trust-based legally-enforceable economic transactions difficult. Some ethnic groups have elaborate systems to regulate and even account for favors traded within the group, such as the Jewish Talmud (Attali, 2002), or the Chinese *guanxi* system (Redding, 1990; Szeto and Wright, 2006; Xin and Pearce, 1996). Modern groups that are not defined on ethnic lines also use implicit systems regulating the trading of favors, as described by Michel Ferrary (2003) in his discussion of "gift exchange" in the Silicon Valley venture capital scene.

Persecuted minority groups frequently play an important role in transforming their social capital into successful business ventures. Authoritarian rulers tend to prefer doing business with such minorities, since they are more vulnerable, subject to arbitrary expropriation, less likely to transform their economic wealth into competing political power, and easily blamed to canalize popular resentment. Such groups tend to have a higher degree of social cohesiveness than the population at large, and their members can call on each other, including in trans-border networks, to trade favors and mutually advance their fortunes. In institutionally undeveloped environments, where trust and enforcement of contracts are lacking, this social cohesiveness can be a significant asset.

In the Indonesian case we have seen all of these phenomena at work. The Salim family relied on their Chinese networks, both domestically and throughout South East Asia. The caste of army officers, Suharto chief among them, that exercised authoritarian control over the country, favored a select group of Chinese businessmen, lavishing on them subsidized credits, exclusive import licenses, tailor-made protectionist barriers and regulations, and other favors that translated into billions of dollars. They did so in exchange for private economic benefits, but also to build up a modern economy. At the same time they maintained a climate of nationalistic hostility toward the Chinese minority, focusing on it the wrath of the population when the Asian crisis erupted in mob violence.

One puzzling element of the Salim case, and of many similar cases around the world, is why the government largesse focused so much on one group. Why did Suharto favor the Salims quite so much, and forego diversification of his "portfolio of corrupt advantages" among a wider spectrum of cronies? We think that there is a double answer to that question. First, it is well known that diversified conglomeration is an advantageous business strategy in weak institutional settings (Carney, 2005; Hoskisson *et al.*, 2000; Khanna and Palepu, 1997, 2000; Kock and Guillen, 2001). Controlling as much of the value chain as possible, including financial and media institutions, is a clever way of dealing with the deficiencies of the market, by substituting a tightly managed internal market for the vagaries of the economy at large. Second, contrary to the widespread misconception that corrupt companies are incompetent, Salim emerged to be one of the most respected companies in the country, not for its ethics, but for its efficacy. It was in the interest of Suharto to deal with competent cronies, because he derived his political legitimacy from the relative success of his development policy for the nation. Thus to be successful, the Salim Group had simultaneously to develop its social capital and to run a good business (Dieleman and Sachs, 2006).

In corrupt institutionally unstable environments, family groups tend to be widely dispersed (Carney, 2005; Khanna and Palepu, 1997, 2000; Kock and Guillen, 2001), but also opaque. Secrecy and opaqueness are good protection against expropriation or political upheaval. To maintain a better control over the complex web of relationships that constitutes the family's social capital, it is important to separate the various participants, and thus not to bring them together under a single corporate umbrella. Also, different cronies are entitled to different levels of remuneration, and therefore the business structure has to be "portioned out", resulting in fragmentation. Some partners, such as multinational corporations, provide key skills and prefer to be isolated from the ambient corruption. They tend to be associated in separate corporations, and little "funny business" takes place in such entities. Other partners are corrupt officials and the profitability of ventures must be assured regardless of business performance, leading to propping: the opposite of tunneling (Friedman, Johnson and Mitton, 2003). Some ventures are entered into as "repayment of past favors" or under some sort of duress, and they may not make much business sense. Only a portion of businesses have "traditional investors" that provide capital in exchange for profits.

Even in such companies, the social capital motivation may not be negligible, since the family may need for its own preservation the goodwill of the investors. Thus even in public companies owned through a pyramidal scheme – the ideal vehicle for minority shareholder expropriation in economies with weak law enforcement records for corporate governance – the family must limit its appetite to preserve public goodwill. This suggests a self-regulatory mechanism that may explain why minority investors may not worry too much about being excessively expropriated.

If the company enjoys a wealth-generating advantage due to the family's social capital, it is natural that minority investors will accept that this capital be remunerated. Thus, what may appear as "expropriation of minority investors" in classical economic theory may in fact be a "legitimate remuneration of non-monetized investment" in the eyes of the minority investors. Naturally, the term "legitimate" is used here in a narrow utilitarian sense, distanced from broader ethical considerations.

Consider a simple example. A well-connected person decides to start an arbitrage company whose business success will depend on privileged access to information gleaned from the network. The entrepreneur has no capital, which is needed to buy low and hold before reselling at a higher price. He approaches a potential investor, and agrees to sell 40 per cent of the newly created company in exchange for the capital. The transaction assigns an a priori weight of 60 per cent to the social capital brought in by the entrepreneur. Future gains will accrue 40 per cent to the investor and 60 per cent to the entrepreneur. If the entrepreneur delivers on his promises, the investor is likely to be satisfied and the transaction described here is perfectly legitimate in any jurisdiction.

It is reasonable to postulate that a similar logic governs decisions of minority investors in family businesses. The key difference is that the agreement is not explicit, and that the value placed on social capital is unclear. Advanced jurisdictions frown upon such non-explicit arrangements because of ethical standards, but also because they risk expropriating the taxman when remuneration takes place through inflated costs. Thus there is a considerable body of financial auditing practices aimed at detecting cases of confiscation and expropriation. The next section uses a simple accounting scheme to conceptualize ways in which social capital can be remunerated.

5.4   REMUNERATING SOCIAL CAPITAL

Regulatory, judicial and fiscal systems in advanced market economies are designed to force companies into maintaining transparent accounts, in particular to protect minority shareholders from asset expropriation and rent confiscation by majority owners (AICPA, 2001; Bushman and Smith, 2001; Bushman *et al.*, 2004; FASB, 1982; Gordon and Palia, 2004; Hirst and Hopkins, 1998; Sherman and Young, 2001). Figure 5.1 shows a simplified version of corporate accounts annotated with the kind of questions that may be asked by an auditor looking for signs of expropriation and confiscation.

The firm's profitability, and therefore all shareholders, including minority ones, can be hurt when products or services are sold at a cost lower than the fair market value. If such sales are made to an entity in which the controlling shareholder has an interest greater than in the focal firm, then the possibility of confiscation arises. For example, if a family owns 60 per cent of the seller and 80 per cent of the buyer, then by causing the seller to under-price, it transfers profits from an entity in which it would partake in only 60 per cent of the profits to an entity where it can claim 80 per cent. Hence the auditor's focus on sales to related parties. The same reasoning goes for purchases from related parties, where the danger is of overpaying for goods and services acquired from an entity in which the controlling shareholder has a stake greater than in the focal company. A particular

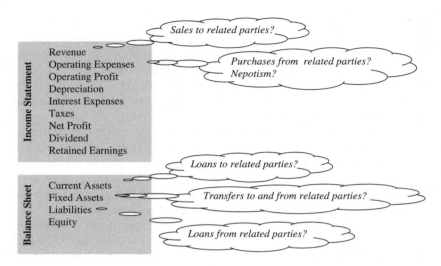

Figure 5.1   Expropriation audit

form of such transaction is nepotism, paying for employment of a kin of the controlling family with a salary above fair market value.

Loans to and from related parties both follow the same kind of logic. There is the possibility of loaning money cheaply (or extending payment terms) to entities in which the controlling shareholder has a greater stake, and in borrowing expensively (or shortening payment terms). Transfers of assets to and from related parties are also a potential instrument of expropriation. They can be bought too dearly or sold too cheaply to an entity with a greater stake by the controlling shareholder.

The central thesis of this chapter is that in some situations, what would otherwise appear as an illicit transaction aimed at confiscating rents or expropriating assets from minority shareholders, may in fact be viewed by those as "legitimate" remuneration of the controlling family's social capital vested in the firm. Conceptually, this may be captured by amending Figure 5.1 as shown in Figure 5.2. Several conceptual categories, printed in bold, have been added to the company's income statement and balance sheet. They call for brief definitions.

Social assets are advantages stemming from the controlling family connections that produce benefits to the firm. An exclusive license or import barriers obtained from the government are examples of such assets. In corrupt economies such assets are generally associated with a corresponding liability, such as remunerating the official that granted the favor. Such a liability can be assumed directly by the family, for example by setting up an

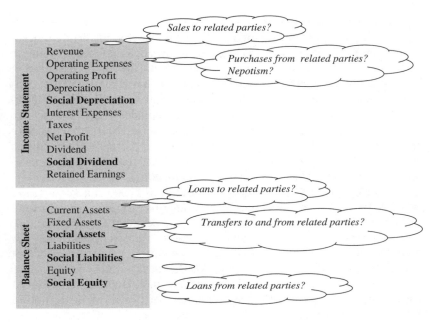

Figure 5.2   Social capital audit

unrelated business with an official's kin. In some cases, however, the liability may be assumed by the focal firm, thus giving rise to a social liability. The difference between social assets and social liabilities forms social equity: the net social capital invested by the family. Social equity entitles one to a social dividend: economic benefits derived by the family above and beyond the amount based on its shareholding.

While many modern businesses treat depreciation as simply a fiscal advantage that shelters part of the income stream from taxes, originally the concept was used as a way of accounting for the costs of wear and tear of fixed assets, such as machines, creating a reserve to replace them eventually. Social assets may also have this kind of cost associated with them. In the complex web of mutual obligations that characterize social networks, some social capital flows from IOUs: favors owed in exchange for past services. Such a form of social capital decreases in value when used and/or with time, and therefore it is appropriate to think of a "replenishment reserve" or social depreciation.

This completes the conceptual scheme to incorporate the notion of social capital into an accounting view of the firm. The auditor's annotations in Figure 5.2 and those in Figure 5.1 are identical, looking for dealings with related parties. This is because from a purely formal point of view it is impossible to distinguish between vulgar "cheating of minority shareholders out of their due" and "paying for social capital vested in the firm". Indeed, the distinction between the two is based on knowledge that firm advantages are due to the controlling shareholder's social capital and on the assumption that the minority shareholder agrees to pay for that capital. Indeed, confiscation and expropriation on the one hand, and remuneration of social capital on the other, can coexist. Controlling shareholders may cause the firm to pay them a "legitimate" remuneration for their social capital, but also take advantage of their control simply to steal from their partners. This confirms the widely accepted notion that it is difficult to construct operational measures of social capital (see for example, Schmid, 2002).

The concept of "related party" (La Porta *et al.*, 2000; La Porta *et al.*, 2002; La Porta, Lopez-de-Silanes and Zamarripa, 2003) is crucial to the auditor's task of detecting the various forms of payment for social capital. In legal terms it is a fairly simple concept to render operational. For example, one may define a related party as an entity or a person owned in part, directly or indirectly, by an owner of the focal business or his kin, or as a person related to an owner of the focal business. But even in advanced modern economies such as France, a definition of this sort fails to capture favors traded among members of a group such as alumni of an elite school or members of a particular professional corporation. These problems are worse in corrupt emerging market environments populated by opaque family firms.

5.5 CONCLUDING REMARKS

In the era when corporate social responsibility has become fashionable, it is well worth remembering that corrupt societies lead to corrupt business practices. Many of those practices – indeed those that are most profitable – consist in cronies of power holders arranging for advantages that give their businesses a competitive edge. This is transforming a social capital vested in personal relationships into a business asset. Therefore, the concepts of social capital, social dividend and other related concepts, even if difficult to measure, provide a valid way in which to think about businesses in many transitional economies and beyond.

REFERENCES

Adler, P.S. and S. Kwon (2002), Social Capital: Prospects for a New Concept, *Academy of Management Review*, **27**, 17–40.

AICPA (2001), *Staff of the American Institute of Certified Public Accountants: Accounting and auditing for related parties and related party transactions*, American Institute of Certified Public Accountants, Ewing, NJ.

Amit, R. and B. Villalonga (2006), How do Family Ownership, Control, and Management Affect Firm Value? *Journal of Financial Economics*, **80**, 385–417.

Anderson, R.C. and D.M. Reeb (2003), Founding Family Ownership and Firm Performance: Evidence from the S&P 500, *Journal of Finance*, **58**, 1301–1328.

Attali, J. (2002), *Les Juifs, le monde et l'argent*, Fayard, Paris.

Bae, Kee-Hong, Jun-Koo Kang and Kim Jin-Mo (2002), Tunneling or Value-added: Evidence from Mergers by Korean Business Groups, *Journal of Finance*, **57**, 2695–2740.

Barclay, M.J. and C. Holderness (1989), Private Benefits from Control of Public Corporations, *Journal of Financial Economics*, **25**, 371–395.

Bebchuk, L., R. Kraakman and G. Triantis (2000), Stock Pyramids, Cross-ownership, and Dual Class Equity: the Mechanisms and Agency Costs of Separating Control from Cash Flow Rights, in: R. Morck, (ed.), *Concentrated Corporate Ownership*, A National Bureau of Economic Research Conference Report, University of Chicago Press, Chicago, IL: pp. 445–460.

Becker, G.S. (1964), *Human Capital: A Theoretical and Empirical Analysis, with Special Reference to Education*, Columbia University Press, New York.

Bertrand, M., P. Mehta and S. Mullainathan (2002), Ferreting out Tunneling: An Application to Indian Business Groups, *The Quarterly Journal of Economics*, **117**, 121–148.

Blyler, M. and R.W. Coff (2003), Dynamic Capabilities, Social Capital, and Rent Appropriation: Ties that Split Pies, *Strategic Management Journal*, **24**, 677–686.

Bonacich, E. (1973), A Theory of Middleman Minorities, *American Sociological Review*, **38**, 583–594.

Bourdieu, P. (1985), The Forms of Capital, in: J.G. Richardson (ed.), *Handbook of Theory and Research for the Sociology of Education*, Greenwood, New York: pp. 241–258.

Bushman, R.M. and A.J. Smith (2001), Financial Accounting Information and Corporate Governance, *Journal of Accounting and Economics*, **32**, 237–333.

Bushman, R.M., Q. Chen, E. Engel and A.J. Smith (2004), Financial Accounting Information, Organizational Complexity and Corporate Governance Systems, *Journal of Accounting and Economics*, **37**, 167–201.

Carney, M. (2005), Corporate Governance and Competitive Advantage in Family-controlled Firms, *Entrepreneurship: Theory and Practice*, **29**, 249–265.

Carney, M., M. Dieleman and W.M. Sachs (2006), Years of Living Dangerously: Family Firm Advantage in Hostile Environments, *Journal of Business Venturing*, Special Issue, Conference on Entrepreneurs in Emerging Regions, Hyderabad, India, 13–15 December 2006.

Chang, S.J. and J. Hong (2000), Economic Performance of Group-affiliated Companies in Korea: Intragroup Resources Sharing and Internal Business Transaction, *Academy of Management Journal*, **43**, 429–448.

Cheung, Y., P.R. Rau and A. Stouraitis (2006), Tunneling, Propping and Expropriation: Evidence from Connected Party Transactions in Hong Kong, *Journal of Financial Economics*, **82**, 343–386.

Chrisman, J.J., J.H. Chua and R.A. Litz (2004), Comparing the Agency Costs of Family and Non-Family Firms: Conceptual Issues and Exploratory Evidence, *Entrepreneurship: Theory and Practice*, **28**(4), 335–354.

Claessens, S., S. Djankov and L. Lang (2000), The Separation of Ownership and Control of East Asia Corporations, *Journal of Financial Economics*, **58**, 81–112.

Coffee, J.C. Jr (2001), *Do Norms Matter? A Cross-country Examination of the Private Benefits of Control*, The Center for Law and Economic Studies Working Paper No. 183, Columbia Law School, New York.

Coleman, J.S. (1988), Social Capital in the Creation of Human Capital, *American Journal of Sociology*, **94**, S95–S120.

Cook, K.S. (1977), Exchange and Power in Networks of Interorganizational Relations, *Sociological Quarterly*, **18**, 62–82.

Daily, C.M. and D.R. Dalton (1992), The Relationship Between Governance Structure and Corporate Performance in Entrepreneurial Firms, *Journal of Business Venturing*, **7**, 375–386.

Davis, K., M.J. Trebilcock and B. Heys (2001), Ethnically Homogeneous Commercial Elites in Developing Countries, *Law and Politics in International Business*, **32**, 331–361.

Demsetz, H. and K. Lehn (1985), The Structure of Corporate Ownership: Causes and Consequences, *The Journal of Political Economy*, **93**, 1155–1177.

Dieleman, M. (2007), *The Rhythm of Strategy: A Corporate Biography of the Salim Group of Indonesia*, Amsterdam University Press, Amsterdam.

Dieleman, M. and W.M. Sachs (2006), Oscillating Between a Relationship-based and a Market-based Model: The Salim Group, *Asia Pacific Journal of Management*, **23**(4), 521–536.

Fama, E.F. and M.C. Jensen (1983), Separation of Ownership and Control, *Journal of Law and Economics*, **6**, 301–325.

FASB (1982), *Statement of Financial Accounting Standard No. 57: Related Party Disclosures*, Financial Accounting Standards Board, Norwalk, CT.

Ferrary, M. (2003), The Gift Exchange in the Social Networks of Silicon Valley, *California Management Review*, **44**(4), 120–138.

Firth, M., P.M.Y. Fung and O.M. Rui (2006), Firm Performance, Governance Structure, and Top Management Turnover in a Transitional Economy, *Journal of Management Studies*, **43**, 1289–1330.

Friedman, E., S. Johnson and T. Mitton (2003), Propping and Tunneling, *Journal of Comparative Economics*, **31**, 732–751.

Frynas, J., K. Mellahi and G.A. Pigman (2006), First Mover Advantages in International Business and Firm-specific Political Resources, *Strategic Management Journal*, **27**(4), 321–345.

Gordon, E., E. Henry and D. Palia (2004), Related Party Transactions and Corporate Governance, *Advances in Financial Economics*, **9**, 1–28.

Granovetter, M. (1992), Economic Institutions as Social Constructions: A Framework for Analysis, *Acta Sociologica*, **35**(1), 3–11.

Hirst, D.E. and P.E. Hopkins (1998), Comprehensive Income Reporting and Analysts' Valuation Judgments, *Journal of Accounting Research*, **36**(Supplement), 47–75.

Hoskisson, R.E., L. Eden, C.M. Lau and M. Wright (2000), Strategy in Emerging Economies, *Academy of Management Journal*, **43**(3), 249–267.

Jensen, M. and W. Meckling (1976), Theory of the Firm: Managerial Behavior, Agency Costs and Ownership Structure, *Journal of Financial Economics*, **3**, 305–360.

Johnson, S., R. La Porta, F. Lopez-de-Silanes and A. Shleifer (2000), Tunneling, *The American Economic Review*, **90**, 22–27.

Kang, D.C. (2002), *Crony Capitalism: Corruption and Development in South Korea and the Philippines*, Cambridge University Press, Cambridge.

Keister, L.A. (1999), Where Do Strong Ties Come From? A Dyad Analysis of the Strength of Interfirm Exchange Relations During China's Economic Transition, *International Journal of Organizational Analysis*, **7**(1), 5–25.

Khanna, T. and K. Palepu (1997), Why Focused Strategy May be Wrong in Emerging Markets, *Harvard Business Review*, **75**, 41–51.

Khanna, T. and K. Palepu (2000), Is Group Affiliation Profitable in Emerging Markets? An Analysis of Diversified Indian Business Groups, *The Journal of Finance*, **55**, 867–892.

Kock, C. and M. Guillen (2001), Strategy and Structure in Developing Countries: Business Groups as an Evolutionary Response to Opportunities for Unrelated Diversification, *Industrial and Corporate Change*, **10**, 77–113.

La Porta, R., F. Lopez-de-Silanes, A. Schleifer and R. Vishny (1999), Corporate Ownership Around the World, *Journal of Finance*, **54**, 471–517.

La Porta, R., F. Lopez-de-Silanes, A. Schleifer and R. Vishny (2000), Investor Protection and Corporate Governance, *Journal of Financial Economics*, **58**, 3–27.

La Porta, R., F. Lopez-de-Silanes, A. Shleifer and R. Vishny (2002), Investor Protection and Corporate Valuation, *Journal of Finance*, **57**, 1147–1170.

La Porta, R., F. Lopez-de-Silanes and G. Zamarripa (2003), Related Lending, *The Quarterly Journal of Economics*, **118**(February), 231–267.

Lemmon, M.L. and K.V. Lins (2003), Ownership Structure, Corporate Governance, and Firm Value: Evidence from the East Asian Financial Crisis, *The Journal of Finance*, **58**, 1445–1468.

Leontief, W. (1973), *Input-Output Economics*, Oxford University Press, New York.

Leuz, C., D. Nanda and P.D. Wysocki (2003), Earnings Management and Investor Protection: An International Comparison, *Journal of Financial Economics*, **69**, 505–727.

Lin, N. (2001), *Social Capital*, Cambridge University Press, London.

Miller, D. and I.L. Breton-Miller (2005), *Managing for the Long Run: Lessons in Competitive Advantage from Great Family Businesses*, Harvard Business School Press, Boston, MA.

Mincer, J. (1958), Investment in Human Capital and Personal Income Distribution, *The Journal of Political Economy*, **66**, 281–302.

Mitton, T. (2002), A Cross-firm Analysis of the Impact of Corporate Governance on the East Asian Financial Crisis, *Journal of Financial Economics*, **64**, 215–241.

Morck, R. and B. Yeung (2003), Agency Problems in Large Family Business Groups, *Entrepreneurship: Theory and Practice*, **27**(4), 367–382.

Nahapiet, J. and S. Ghoshal (1998), Social Capital, Intellectual Capital, and the Organizational Advantage, *Academy of Management Review*, **23**, 242–266.

Peng, M.W. (2003), Institutional Transitions and Strategic Choices, *Academy of Management Review*, **28**, 275–285.

Portes, A. and J. Sensenbrenner (1993), Embeddedness and Immigration: Notes on the Social Determinants of Economic Action, *American Journal of Sociology*, **98**, 1320–1351.

Putnam, Robert (2000), *Bowling Alone: The Collapse and Revival of American Community*, Simon and Schuster, New York.

Redding, G. (1990), *The Spirit of Chinese Capitalism*, De Gruyter, New York.

Revel, J.-F. (2002), *L'obsession anti-américaine: Son fonctionnement, ses causes, ses inconséquences*, Plon, Paris.

Roche, F. (2003), *François Pinault: l'empire menacé*, Editions du Carquois, Paris.
Roger, P. (2002), *L'Enemi américain: Généalogie de l'antiaméricanisme français*, Seuil, Paris.
Routier, A. (2003) *L'Ange exterminateur: La vraie vie de Bernard Arnault*, Albin Michel, Paris.
Sato, Y. (1993), The Salim Group in Indonesia: The Development and Behavior of the Largest Conglomerate in Southeast Asia, *The Developing Economies*, **31**, 408–441.
Schmid, A.A. (2002), Using Motive to Distinguish Social Capital from its Outputs, *Journal of Economic Issues*, **36**, 747–768.
Sherman, H.D. and S.D. Young (2001), Tread Lightly through these Accounting Minefields, *Harvard Business Review*, **79**(7), 129–135.
Shleifer, A. and R.W. Vishny (1986), Large Shareholders and Corporate Control, *The Journal of Political Economy*, **94**, 461–488.
Soetriyono, E. (1989), *Kisah Sukses Liem Sioe Liong*, Indomedia, Jakarta.
Szeto, R. and P.C. Wright (2006), Business Networking in the Chinese Context: Its Role in the Formation of *Guanxi*, Social Capital and Ethical Foundations, *Management Research News*, **29**, 425–438.
Uzzi, B. (1997), Social Structure and Competition in Interfirm Networks: The Paradox of Embeddedness, *Administrative Science Quarterly*, **42**, 35–67.
Wolfenzon, D. (1999), *A Theory of Pyramidal Ownership*, Working paper, New York University, New York.
Woolcock, M. (1998), Social Capital and Economic Development: Toward a Theoretical Synthesis and Policy Framework, *Theory and Society*, **27**, 151–208.
Wu, Y.-I. and C.H. Wu (1980), *Economic Development in Southeast Asia*, Hoover Institute Press, Stanford, CA.
Xin, K. and J. Pearce (1996), Guanxi: Good Connections as Substitutes for Institutional Support, *Academy of Management Journal*, **39**, 1641–1658.

6. Information management and communication technology for conflict prevention and peace

Jeffrey Soar

6.1 INTRODUCTION

Information management and communication technology has much to offer to support public safety and policing in conflict prevention and peace. Police and public safety agencies have been using information and communication technologies (ICTs) for several decades for managing the processes of investigation and preparation of documents for prosecution. The processes of receiving calls for assistance and dispatching response vehicles are increasingly managed through intelligent systems linked to radio communications. These have been enhanced with the availability of GIS (Geospatial Information Systems) for interactive mapping of locations of events and GPS (Global Positioning Systems) for tracking of vehicles. Bio-identity, such as fingerprints and DNA, has been used for some time by public safety jurisdictions. Fingerprints are increasingly used for buildings access, border control and access to computer systems. Community use of ICTs for enhanced public safety include CC-TV (Closed-Circuit Television), and anti-theft devices in retail.

The current environment of international uncertainty requires both public safety agencies as well as international businesses to explore the adoption of new and emerging ICTs as well as to ensure that their security practices are current and appropriate to the changes. Much of the world's business crosses continents and jurisdictions; many with increased risks of conflict, crises and terrorism. There is a corporate responsibility to contribute to world peace as well as to close gaps for or exposures to conflict or terrorism that might not only harm the individual enterprise but whole industries or countries. There is a need to identify and adopt ICTs that minimise or eliminate risks as well as to ensure that appropriate policies are in place and actively managed. Policies should promote a culture of awareness and risk minimisation.

This chapter will review some of the ICTs used by police and public safety agencies as well as approaches that might be used by international business. Of particular interest is the adoption of e-commerce, and e-procurement in particular, in international business for its potential in reducing opportunities for corruption and other inappropriate activities and providing audit trails for investigation. The chapter ends with a discussion of security systems for the new world of internet interconnectivity where business is conducted in the largely unsecured world of the web.

6.2   ROLE OF PUBLIC SAFETY AND POLICING AS A CONDITION FOR INTERNATIONAL BUSINESS

Public safety is a critical infrastructure for the conduct of international business. While illegal or semi-legal businesses might arise from, take advantage of and even promote disorder, most businesses operate more successfully in environments of certainty. Aspects of certainty include peace and order, legal protections of contracts and property, security of staff, open and contestable hiring and purchasing practices, open markets, the absence of trade barriers and the absence of corruption.

One indication that business operates more successfully in environments of certainty is that the majority of the world's business is conducted between developed countries which tend to be more ordered environments. Similarly, economic development is associated with peace. Most democratic countries are those with strong economies, while despotic nations experience difficulties in retaining skilled human resources, building infrastructure, attracting investment and sustaining business activity.

Difficulties of operating in unsafe environments include restrictive hiring practices where staff are hired on the basis of patronage or other means rather than open recruitment and replacement practices based on merit. This leads to performance and management issues. Purchasing practices similarly need to be open and contestable. Government regulation can be an aid or a barrier to business. It can obstruct or facilitate. Corrupt practices of officials cause delay, confusion on the part of the agents of international companies wishing to invest due to the difficulties of the unofficial "rules" of bribery and corruption, and other associated uncertainties.

With the world's leading economies currently in a cycle of boom, it can be difficult to attract qualified staff. This is even more the case for companies wishing to operate in environments where staff may not feel safe. Companies have withdrawn even from areas rich in resources where it has become difficult to operate due to instability, leading to adverse economic impacts for the host nation.

ICT has potential to assist international business to operate under adversity, to strengthen corporate responsibility, reduce conflict and promote peace. ICTs already support conflict reduction and peace promotion in the form of security cameras, anti-theft devices on products for retailing, and digital security access controls to information and property. ICTs offer increased speed of transactions, reduced processing steps and cost, standardised business processes and decision making, and the capacity to conduct business 24/7. In addition business has a responsibility to adopt ICT systems for enhanced safety, reduced opportunities for theft and corruption, and robust audit trails.

The role of ICT in supporting international business under adversity, corporate responsibility, conflict prevention and peace includes better equipping police and other public safety agencies, securing business transactions, securing and managing knowledge assets, providing secure audit trails, reducing opportunities for bribery and corruption, and overall reducing risks.

6.3 ICTs IN POLICE AND OTHER PUBLIC SAFETY AGENCIES

There is a range of ICTs that are used around the world by public safety agencies such as police, ambulance and other emergency response services. Many jurisdictions already make use of ICTs for emergency call taking and response to and analysis of intelligence data. Information systems and technology such as automated systems for detection of traffic law infringements have further potential to assist greatly in improving public safety and even to eliminate the need for certain types of policing (Soar, 1998a). Quality information can assist in decisions about where best to deploy our limited police resources, can inform policy and ensure that our operational decisions are supported by research. When officers provide a service to the public, timeliness and access to appropriate information can enhance the effectiveness and safety of those interactions.

Technology already reduces public trauma through traffic controls, speed and alcohol detection devices, tools for safer road design, controlling commercial vehicle loading and safety features in vehicles (Soar, 1998b).

Future and emerging technologies might disable a vehicle when alcohol is detected, automatically fasten seat belts, limit a vehicle's speed to the maximum allowed in each speed zone, allow patrol cars to disable an offender's vehicle remotely, make vehicles more collision-proof, provide alerts to drivers or assist vehicles to avoid collision, track and monitor the movement of vehicles, monitor the roadworthiness of a vehicle's systems and even make an emergency call in the event of a collision. Mobile data terminals will provide information about vehicles, drivers, alerts, maps and safety information for officers. Automatic vehicle location can improve the effectiveness of computer-aided dispatch systems as well as improve coordination of operations and staff safety.

Over the last decade, governments have undertaken sweeping reforms of social and economic policies, including those of the public safety sector. This has seen a greater focus on measuring outputs and outcomes and away from measuring inputs. The police are increasingly funded on the basis of output classes, which include deliverables relating to crime reduction and improvements in traffic safety. Improving outcomes requires effective inter-agency collaboration across the justice and public safety agencies. Key agencies concerned with traffic and public safety also share a joint information approach – there is a need for an integrated justice sector information strategy. The goal needs to be to ensure that relevant, timely and accurate information is available and accessible to authorised users to support the business needs of all agencies in the justice sector and their customers and to monitor the justice environment.

Integration of public safety will be difficult without policy and planning, integrated information networks, a communications infrastructure with technical standards, common definitions, technology for interactive sharing of information across providers, and protocols for access to information for event management purposes as well as for monitoring. There is interest in providing knowledge-driven services as well as reinforcing individual responsibility. Both of these are dependent upon the provision of information to planners, professionals and front-line officers.

Policing has traditionally been dependent on the processing of paper-based forms for preparation of documents for prosecution and presentation of evidence in courts. That is rapidly changing. Automation of processes has benefits other than elimination of manual processing and form-filling. It provides data for immediate access for officers at the point of service and provides electronic exchanges of information between agencies, thus reducing errors and lost paperwork.

When officers deliver a service to a member of the public, they will be supported in the availability of information to aid their effectiveness. Police systems include an on-line electronic library to provide access to legal reference and other material. The communications facility provides links to mobile data terminals in patrol cars. Mobile computers enable officers to interrogate central databases as well as issue computer-generated infringement notices with reduced errors and more complete information. These can reduce much of the radio voice traffic. The police maintain detailed maps. Both emergency dispatch operators and mobile patrols use ICTs to improve response times and better coordinate events. GPS (Global Positioning Systems) linked to GIS (Geospatial Information Systems) assist dispatch operators to locate vehicles in relation to a need for police attendance. This ensures that the closest available unit can attend as well as providing better protection for mobile staff. Intelligence analysts use the mapping facility to log and track events, and to identify patterns of incidents and associated factors.

A major development in geospatial technology has been through the European Galileo project, which is making geo-localisation more precise than GPS. It has a much better precision factor, of about 1 meter, is already functioning over Europe and is intended for worldwide coverage. Emergency services staff in the field will be able to use mobile telephones and other handheld devices for geospatial location of objects and incidents.

Technology and information management are key components of a strategy to strengthen the police as a knowledge-based service. With this knowledge base, the police can be confident that their IT-supported public safety interventions are targeted, grounded in research, evaluated and stand a high chance of returning an improvement in public safety.

6.3.1   CC-TV

Closed Circuit Television or CC-TV has been deployed extensively in many countries, in airports, banks, retail outlets, shopping centres and malls, sporting stadiums, beaches, within public transport systems including inside vehicles such as buses and taxis, and in other areas where it can be used to monitor risks, direct responses and later provide evidence for investigation and prosecution. CC-TV is deployed extensively across many road systems, allowing controllers to manage traffic flows better, identify problems and similarly deploy response services. CC-TV is also used by many police services in interviews. This provides a record of the interview to be provided as evidence in court proceedings and reduces the opportunity for either police or suspects to claim that a transcript of the interview was tampered with.

CC-TV recordings from retail outlets have assisted police in cases such as the Jamie Bulger murder in the UK and the Peter Falconio murder in Australia. A feature of CC-TV is the high level of public acceptance. It is ubiquitous in many countries and there has been surprisingly little public dissent.

Further advances in technology will provide cameras with their own IP addresses, allowing them to be directly connected to the internet and easily accessed. Ethernet over power allows the power supply cable to be used for internet connectivity. Even where an electricity connection is not readily available, new battery technology is ever extending battery life. Satellite connection powered by solar power is well developed and deployed in some jurisdictions such as Australia and Canada, where services are required in remote locations.

It is an example of a relatively low-cost and successful technology with a high level of public acceptance. The further deployment of CC-TV is to be encouraged in all areas where monitoring, capture of images and even the presence of CC-TV cameras might discourage anti-social behaviour.

6.3.2   Facial Recognition

An enhancement to television and CC-TV is facial recognition. This works in a similar way to other bio-identity systems in that the relative distances between points on the face are measured and converted to an algorithm. Facial recognition is still in the early stages of refinement, and adoption has not yet been widespread. It can supplement other approaches to identification and select subjects requiring further investigation.

6.3.3   Automatic Number Plate Registration

Automatic number plate readers are a further enhancement of video or visual recording technologies. In some jurisdictions these are used to identify stolen vehicles or other vehicles of interest, and may be handheld or vehicle-mounted. The technology can track vehicles from fixed readers and even detect speed infringements or otherwise provide alerts on vehicles of interest.

6.3.4   Emergency Call Taking and Response

A core technology for police and other emergency services is call taking and despatch systems. These support call centres for taking calls and radio links to patrol cars and other units. Call centre operators can usually see the details of the caller's number, including the name of the person and the address if a fixed rather than mobile phone; they may have available to them any history of calls from the same number and a link to a GIS system showing the location of the telephone. On the same GIS screen they can see the available response units and their status in terms of availability to respond.

6.3.5   Mobile Telecommunications and Data Services

Mobile units can increasingly use pre-programmed keys to communicate to the call centre, supplemented by data screens that enable them to link directly to police or other service databases. These too can be supplemented by GPS and GIS systems to improve speed of response.

6.3.6 Investigation Processing System and Database

A core police and public safety system manages the data related to preparing a case for court and keeps a history of investigations. The police maintain information about key items such as persons (victims, suspects, witnesses, reporters of crimes, associates), vehicles, weapons and places.

6.3.7 Intelligence Analysis

The police are trained to take notes of every event and of their observations even when no prosecution results. All of this data is entered into intelligence systems that allow analysts to identify patterns and alert investigators or to guide patrols, or for investigators to search for data that might be related to an event. Systems can link data including the connections between individuals. GIS can assist in mapping incidents or observations by time, place or any other factor to identify patterns.

6.3.8 Bio-identity Databases

Fingerprints and DNA are well-established tools for investigators and provide evidence that is effectively absolute. Fingerprint identification is a very well-established technology. New technology uses an algorithm that converts analogue fingerprints into a digital format that can be easily stored or transmitted.

In some jurisdictions, electronic bio-identification can be used, for example in circumstances where offenders are required to report regularly to a police station. A fingerprint reader can record attendance, reducing staff time and queues and providing certainty of identification.

6.4 RFID TAGS

A new technology with significant potential for positive impacts on business is RFID (Radio-Frequency Identification). RFID is likely to replace or supplement barcodes. An advantage of RFID is that the RFID tag can be read from a distance. Active tags have a power source and can be read from a significant distance. These are already deployed in vehicles for motorway toll payment. Passive tags do not have power and a scanner needs to be much closer. The scanner can provide enough power for the tag to respond, for example with its unique number for registration. Passive tags are currently used for airport baggage tracking.

RFID tags are expected to become as ubiquitous as barcodes and have the potential to combine the function of item identification that barcodes provide as well as anti-theft functionality. Entrances can be equipped with scanners that can detect and provide alerts on the passage of goods with RFID tags. A small number of airports such as Hong Kong International Airport are using RFID tags to track checked luggage and reduce the time required to read barcodes.

6.5   ICT FOR KNOWLEDGE MANAGEMENT IN PUBLIC SAFETY AGENCIES

Knowledge management is an approach to recognising and managing corporate knowledge as an asset. Corporate knowledge can be embedded in business processes, structured and standardised. The goal is to ensure that relevant, timely and accurate information is available and accessible to authorised users to support the business needs of all agencies in the justice sector and their customers and to monitor the justice environment. Integration of public safety will be difficult without policy and planning, integrated information networks, a communications infrastructure with technical standards, common definitions, technology for interactive sharing of information across providers, and protocols for access to information for event management purposes as well as for monitoring. There is interest in providing knowledge-driven services as well as reinforcing individual responsibility. Both of these are dependent upon the provision of information to planners, professionals and to relevant staff when mobile.

First among these is targeting attention toward prevention. Then there is the issue of targeting services toward areas of need and developing a research-based knowledge of the demographic and physical needs of customers. The knowledge database would help in answering questions such as:

● Where are the unsafe communities, both in terms of social strata and behaviours defined by locality, age or social strata?
● Who is most likely to drive too fast or adopt anti-social behaviours so that we can target our services appropriately?
● Are front-line staff equipped with the knowledge to optimise the effectiveness of their interventions?

A knowledge base should drive needs assessment, service planning, information delivery at the point of service, and evaluation, which should feed back into the knowledge base. Users of the system can find out about their communities and their needs so they can select, plan and direct services appropriately. The knowledge base should provide information on the research base for the selection of interventions in response to events or patterns of events. For example, what might be the most effective response in areas that are impacted by graffiti or groups of youth who may make others feel less safe? Increased police presence may not be appropriate.

The knowledge base should also equip the response unit with the information it needs at the point of delivery of service. The tie-up in that loop is evaluation. The knowledge base needs to know about the intervention selected and what impact it had on the part of the community being targeted. Did it impact the incidence of the behaviours that were targeted, or did it just result in the perpetrators moving elsewhere?

Knowledge management supports a model for policing under which the focus can broaden from response resolution and include specific and general prevention. One issue driving the police quest for a suitable knowledge-based system is recognition that some traditional interventions do not always produce the best results. This refocus cannot occur without the appropriate knowledge-based ICT infrastructure.

6.5.1 Eliminating Paper

Paper is inherently inefficient in any organisation or sector. Only one person can view a paper file at any one time, making it difficult to share information. Audits are more difficult, it is difficult to record occasions of access to paper records and paper records can be tampered with. Electronic records can similarly be altered unless the available software security systems are installed that record all occasions of access and modification. Eliminating paper and the adoption of electronic records, as well as a good audit trail, are essential first steps for knowledge management.

6.6 ICTs FOR BUSINESS IN ADVERSITY

Some of the ICTs used by public safety agencies are also available for deployment by business. Retail outlets have been using CC-TV for well over a decade, and anti-theft tags are also widely used. RFID combined with GPS allows people and assets to be tracked against digital maps. A general move by business to adopt automated systems and e-commerce generally provides better control, security and audit trails than when they use manual systems. Business needs to move to eliminate paper as much as possible. E-commerce and e-procurement offer potential for reducing opportunities for corruption and other inappropriate activities and provide audit trails for investigation. All organisations need to actively manage security policies that address and manage risks in a world where much of the world's commerce is conducted in the unsecured environment of the Internet.

6.6.1   e-Commerce and e-Procurement

One of the ways that businesses can better protect themselves, their customers and suppliers, is through taking advantage of the security that electronic transactions can have. E-commerce is usually adopted for reasons of the efficiencies offered but can also provide benefits of more transparent transactions and reduced opportunities for theft, bribery or other illegal or inappropriate activities. E-commerce offers an audit trail, the capacity to reverse incorrect transactions, the capacity for immediate response and an easily searchable database of transaction histories. Electronic systems can have their own associated problems, including identity fraud, and implementations need to be accompanied by the adoption and active maintenance of rigorous security software supported by security policies.

Purchasing is the act of buying goods and services, whereas procurement encompasses all activities, including purchasing, involved in obtaining goods and services for the end users (Gebauer and Segev, 1998a). Electronic procurement (e-procurement) is defined as the use of electronic commerce (e-commerce) for procurement. It involves the use of electronic technologies such as the Internet to automate and streamline an organisation's processes – from requisition through to payment (DPWS, 2002; Thomson and Singh, 2001). Kalakota and Robinson (2000) define supply chain management as the coordination of material, information and financial flows among all the participating parties. Undoubtedly, e-procurement is one of the most important enablers of supply chain management.

The term "e-procurement" refers to individual components of a full e-procurement system such as online supplier catalogues, e-tendering and so on; the full e-procurement system encompasses procurement/purchasing, audit, finance and information technology (IT). It includes the electronic means for the following actions (Vaidya *et al.*, 2004):

- selecting goods and services (e-catalogues, on-line e-auctions);
- raising and approving purchase orders;
- forwarding purchase orders to suppliers;
- receiving invoices;
- tracking purchase orders through the system;
- linking purchase orders with invoices received;

- linking the e-procurement system and the accounting system; and
- payment of invoices.

There are various approaches to classifying e-procurement models and applications in the literature. Thomson and Singh (2001) propose an e-procurement model consisting of four quadrants namely, Buyer Model (few buyers, many sellers), Marketplace Model (many buyers, many sellers), Longer Term Relationship Model (few buyers, few sellers) and Seller Model (few sellers, many buyers). Similarly, Knudsen (2002) proposes various e-procurement activities such as e-sourcing, e-tendering, e-reverse auctions, that can be utilised in many ways to support the seven phases of the procurement life cycle, namely 1) information gathering; 2) supplier contact; 3) background review; 4) negotiation; 5) fulfilment; 6) consumption, maintenance and disposal; and 7) renewal (Archer and Yuan, 2000).

Procurement is an area where organisations can often make significant improvements and savings. This can include savings through improved rapidity of delivery of goods in time for processing, reducing the cost of holding stocks of raw materials, and reduction of warehousing, insurance, labour and other stock handling costs. There is also a reduction of waste and spoilage, reduction of opportunities for theft, and minimisation of corrupt purchasing practices and associated costs. Electronic management of purchasing and warehousing also reduces the opportunity for departments or units within an organisation to hoard their own supplies, with associated risks of misuse, spoilage and waste.

The elimination of manual processing frees up the time of procurement personnel, allowing them to accomplish more strategic aspects of procurement, such as better management of relationships with suppliers. Although each organisation has a specific business case for e-procurement, Birks et al., (2001) have identified the most common drivers as increase in contract compliance, collaboration, process improvement, order accuracy, improved value for money and better management information. They further state that benefits for e-procurement depend on the ability of the organisation to achieve purchase price reduction and process cost savings, which need to be identified and measured against the cost of the initiative.

There are two major categories of traditional procurement: indirect and direct. Indirect procurement can be further divided into two groups: ORM (Operating Resource Management, for example, office products and travel services) and MRO (Maintenance, Repair and Operations, for example, replacement parts). Neef (2001) says that e-procurement has changed the boundary between indirect and direct procurement. Table 6.1 outlines the performance of procurement activities in the traditional versus e-environment.

Table 6.1   Performance of procurement activities

Procurement Activity	Traditional Procurement	e-Procurement
Product Research	Slow and laborious. Process involves catalogue and phone calls.	All product information in one place, real time and accurate.
Approval	Time-consuming process to document quotes, long lead time for bids.	Audit trail, approval history, automated approvals.
Purchase	Time-intensive, redundant data entry, high processing cost.	Bids, quotes, purchase orders automated, stop "reinventing the wheel".
Technology	Installation, training and updates can be expensive or time-consuming.	Software updates should be automatic.

Source: Rohleder (2001).

The characteristics of the Internet, such as "ubiquity and connectivity, immediacy and interactivity, multimedia and universal interface and ease of use" (Ware *et al.*, 1998), have the potential to trigger significant changes in traditional procurement (Gebauer *et al.*, 1998b). More specifically, as Subramaniam and Shaw (2002) state, "use of e-procurement impacts four major B2B [business to business] procurement activities – search, negotiation and contracting, coordination, and monitoring and control". Although some of the issues in traditional procurement are relevant for e-procurement, other issues and critical "e"-variables are of increased importance. Therefore, performance measurement established for traditional procurement is not applicable to procurement in the electronic environment. It is inevitable that obsolete metrics will be deleted and that a dynamic measurement system will be established that focuses on e-Procurement.

While management and IT companies such as BuyIT, Gartner, Aberdeen and Oracle have carried out market research into e-procurement measurement, most of this work is limited to measure the financial savings (return on investment) only. Most organisations are trying to compute the value of and justify their e-procurement investment by estimating average savings for a procurement transaction and the transaction volume (Subramaniam and Shaw, 2002). Talero (2001) suggests that effective transparency in public procurement depends on the timeliness, quality and accessibility of procurement information. The objective is to improve the transparency of procurement expenditures while maintaining competition.

Other systems that can improve an organisation's security include Decision Support Systems (DSS). These can either make a decision or guide an operator to a decision based on pre-set parameters. DSS can consequently reduce operator error, opportunity for fraud or other inappropriate decision making. Engineered or "built-in" decision making has long been used to improve safety in vehicles and aircraft. Examples include the need in most automatic vehicles to place your foot on the brake in order to move the gear selector into reverse. Aircraft are rich in engineered safety features, including collision-avoidance technology. Companies similarly need to engineer decision-support systems into their business processes so as to reduce costly operator error, other risks and inappropriate behaviours.

6.6.2   Data Security Mechanisms and Policies

Computers continue to be connected to the Internet at a rapid pace and at higher interconnection speeds, driven primarily by the need for information exchange that is efficient and cost-effective. In some industry sectors, critical information systems are still largely paper-based. One of the major challenges society faces is the transfer of such sensitive information into a readily accessible electronic format. It is vital that customers and/or the community trust the computing systems put to use. However, exposing databases holding such data sets over the global and unregulated Internet greatly increases the risk of information compromise. Consequently, there is a need for businesses to adopt and maintain appropriate policies and security systems to minimise or eliminate inappropriate activity.

6.6.3   Security Mechanisms for Access to Sensitive Data

Advances in storage and communication technologies have made large repositories of data available even when they are maintained on separate systems and geographically distributed. The access to such data sets is often subject to varying degrees of legal, social and ethical constraints. Further, the data sets may not be available for open interrogation due to the sensitive and private nature of the information they contain. For example, in healthcare, the causes for this state include the need to abide by national privacy legislation, the reluctance to change to an electronic record format due to security fears, and the requirement to maintain end-users' trust in the overall healthcare information system (Croll and Croll, 2004).

Information security mechanisms of increasing sophistication are available to ensure that sensitive information is protected and only accessible on a "need-to-know" and approval basis. It is imperative that adversaries such as external system "hackers" and technical personnel with in-house knowledge be denied inappropriate access. The security mechanism known as Mandatory Access Control (MAC) can be used to enforce the necessary security and privacy processes required for handling sensitive data. Such mechanisms have been studied and understood for over 30 years, mainly in defence-related systems. However, they have not been evident in contemporary commodity-level operating systems or allied environments. The same holds true for contemporary computer grid technologies, for example, the Globus (Foster and Kesselman, 1998). In other words, trying to secure adequately the shared virtual machine environments that grid technologies currently exploit is next to impossible (that is, far too challenging for the foreseeable future). Through trusted computing nodes, the need to secure contemporary commodity operating systems can be alleviated. These systems can be built using technology that can provide dependable access control mechanisms and yet still be able to interface with existing technologies.

6.6.4   Mandatory Access Control

There is a strong vested business interest by the mainstream suppliers of computer operating systems in perpetuating the belief that computer applications can be "made secure from within", irrespective of other software or even hardware components. In other words, the correct use of their technology will ensure a sufficiently secure operating environment upon which application programs can run safely. Unfortunately, any such assumption is flawed since in reality they represent a "fortress built upon sand" (Loscocco, *et al.*, 1998). The applications will not be secure unless the underlying operating system and hardware have been specifically developed with security in mind. A system that is built to utilise a Mandatory Access Control (MAC) mechanism will provide levels of security relating to all aspects of the computing system, that is, it will, "enforce an administrative set policy over all subjects and objects in a system, basing decisions on labels containing a variety of security-relevant information" (Loscocco and Smalley, 2001).

A major problem with the classic Mandatory Access Control approach is the cost and complexity involved in administering such systems. To reduce this overhead, Role-Based Access Control (RBAC) has been increasingly adopted. In RBAC systems, rather than directly associating users with the right to access resources, users manifest into one or more roles, and roles become associated with access to resources (Ferraiolo and Kuhn, 1992).

6.6.5 Controlling Access

The advent of computers has enabled rapid and purposeful access to vast amounts of previously almost inaccessible information. Controlling access to confidential and valuable information is therefore essential. Of particular importance is maintaining the confidentiality of individual records and providing acceptable levels of privacy and trust. Butler *et al.* (2000) describe access issues facing grid-based virtual organisations as follows: "The dynamic nature of sharing relationships means that we require mechanisms for discovering and characterizing the nature of the relationships that exist at a particular point in time".

The enhanced security of this system comes from the fact that the systems managers or maintenance staff cannot change the access rights on-the-fly (and cover their tracks). Note that this is relatively straightforward with current systems for both staff and adversaries who have good technical knowledge.

6.6.6 Security Policy

All businesses need to have a documented and tested policy relating to the security and privacy of information and intellectual assets. This needs to analyse where information is held and the transaction processes involved, and specify policies for access, release, retention and destruction. The security policy needs to address both physical security as well as systems security. For physical security there is increased usage of bio-identification. Staff should be required to wear identity badges and these need to be checked on entry.

The security policy needs to identify the resourcing of security staff. While many organisations may have a security officer at the front entrance to their building, not all organisations will recognise the need to manage systems access privileges actively. This is particularly relevant in the current environment of e-commerce, where the people accessing a company's computer system include customers, sales channels, contractors and consultants, suppliers as well as internal staff.

An allied document should be the disaster recovery plan. The DRP is a vehicle for monitoring and assessing risk, severity, probability, contingency and priority for recovery and restitution of services.

6.7 CHAPTER SUMMARY

This chapter explored the potential for ICT in the context of the international business environment of heightened risk and apprehension. Police and other public safety organisations have long been users of ICTs and new systems are increasingly available. Whilst organisations across the world have responded to the heightened sense of risk by increasing monitoring and controls, there is still much to be done to enable companies to identify risk, develop mitigation plans and particularly to implement automated systems that in most cases will reduce opportunities for inappropriate behaviour and improve business data retention and recovery.

REFERENCES

Archer, N. and Yuan, Y. (2000) Managing Business-to-Business Relationships throughout the E-Commerce Procurement Life cycle, *Internet Research*, **10**(5): 385–395.

Birks, C., Bond, S., and Radford, M. (2001) *Guide to eProcurement in the Public Sector: Cutting through the Hype*, Winter, OGC (Office of Government Commerce), UK.

Butler, R., Engert, D., Foster, I., Kesselman, C., Tuecke, S., Volmer, J. and Welch, V. (2000) Design and Deployment of a National-Scale Authentication Infrastructure. *IEEE Computer*, **33**(12): 60–66.

Croll, P.R. and Croll, J. (2004) Q.U.i.P.S.: a Quality Model for Investigating Risk Exposure in e-Health Systems, paper presented at the *International Conference on Health Informatics, MedInfo2004*, San Francisco, September.

DPWS (2002) *Electronic Procurement Implementation Strategy: Guidelines*, March, NSW Department of Public Works and Services, Australia.

Ferraiolo, D. and Kuhn, D. (1992) Role Based Access Control, paper presented at the *NIST-NSA National (USA) Computer Security Conference*, October.

Foster, I. and Kesselman, C. (1998) The Globus Project: A Status Report, *Proceedings of the Seventh Heterogeneous Computing Workshop*, IEEE Computer Society Press, Los Alamitos, pp. 4–19.

Gebauer, J., Beam, C. and Segev, A. (1998b) *Impact of the Internet on Procurement*, February, Hass School of Business, University of California, Berkeley, USA.

Gebauer, J. and Segev, A. (1998a) *Assessing Internet-based Procurement to Support the Virtual Enterprise*, Hass School of Business, University of California, Berkeley, USA.

HHS (2003) *Standards for Privacy of Individually Identifiable Health Information*; Final Rule, 45 CFR Parts 160, 162, and 164 Department of Health and Human Services, Office of the Secretary, Washington, DC.

Kalakota, R. and Robinson, M. (2000) *e-Business: Roadmap for Success*, Addison-Wesley, Canada.

Knudsen, D. (2002) Uncovering the Strategic Domain of e-Procurement, paper presented at the *11th International IPSERA Conference*, Enschede, 21 March.

Loscocco, P.A. and Smalley, S.D. (2001) Meeting Critical Security Objectives with Security-Enhanced Linux, paper presented at the *2001 Ottawa Linux Symposium*, Ottawa, 25–28 July.

Loscocco, P.A., S.D. Smalley, P. Muckelbauer, R. Taylor, S.J. Turner, and J. Farrell (1998) The Inevitability of Failure: The Flawed Assumption of Security in

Modern Computing Environments. Paper presented at the *21st National Information Systems Security Conference*, Crystal City, VA, October.

Neef, D. (2001) *e-Procurement: From Strategy to Implementation*, Prentice Hall, NJ, USA.

Rohleder, R. (2001) Government Boundaries in e-Procurement, paper presented at the *E-Gov: Electronic Procurement Conference*, US Government/Accenture, Vienna, VA, January.

Soar, J. (1998a) Improving Road Safety Through Technology, paper presented at the *Road Safety Conference 1998: Research, Policing, Education*, Land Transport Safety Authority and New Zealand Police, Wellington, New Zealand, 16–17 November.

Soar, J. (1998b) The year of excitement for NZ Police, paper presented at the *Technology in Justice Conference*, Melbourne, February.

Subramaniam, C. and Shaw, M. (2002) A Study on the Value of B2B E-Commerce: The Case of Web-based Procurement, *International Journal of Electronic Commerce*, **6**(4).

Talero, E. (2001) *Electronic Government Procurement: Concepts and Country Experiences*, The World Bank, Washington D.C.

Thomson, T. and Singh, M. (2001) An e-Procurement Model for B2B Exchanges and Role of e-Markets, paper presented at the *6th Annual CollECTeR Conference on Electronic Conference*, Coffs Harbour, Australia, 3–4 December.

Vaidya, K., Riquelme, H., Gao, J.B. and Soar, J. (2004) Implementing e-Procurement Initiatives: Impact of Organisational Learning across the Public Sector, paper presented at the *5th International Conference of the Continuous Innovation Network (CInet)*, 22–25 September, Sydney, InCITe.

Ware, J.P., Gebauer, J., Hartman, A. and Roldan, M. (1998) *The Search for Digital Excellence*, McGraw Hill, NJ, USA.

PART III

Dealing with best and worst practice

7. Adversarial allies: the evolving China–India nexus

Nikhilesh Dholakia

7.1 THE ASIAN GIANTS: WARY NEIGHBOURS, OBLIQUE COMPETITORS, RETICENT PARTNERS

In global economic overviews, China and India get increasingly mentioned in the same breath. They are seen as rising economic powers as well as rivals. Spurred by rapid economic growth, these two most populous nations in the world are becoming two of the most prominent economic players on the global scene. On a Purchasing Power Parity (PPP) basis, China is already the second largest and India the fourth largest economy in the world. Even in nominal dollars, by mid-century China and India are projected to surpass all others and become two of the largest economies in the world.

Similarities of techno-economic strategies and trajectories of rival nations often mask subsurface simmering tensions that could flare into open conflict or transform into protracted, hostile Cold War stances. Drawing on earlier historical conflicts and tensions of the 20th century, Lal (2006) makes the following observations about China and India in the 21st century (p. 1):

> Countries often follow similar policies to attain competitive economic or military capabilities. In the period leading up to the First World War, Britain and Germany each constructed dreadnoughts. During the Cold War, the Soviet Union and the United States each built massive arsenals of nuclear tipped ballistic missiles . . . China and India have defined economic reform and defence modernization as policies for planning their national interests . . . Despite [facing] . . . similar threats . . . and the similarities of capabilities sought . . . these large, rapidly developing countries [have] arrived at different national interests.

From her analysis, Lal (2006) discerns the overwhelming weight of the Taiwan issue in China's national interests while India has a more diverse set. The provocative undercurrent in Lal's analysis is to make one think about the undeclared, tacitly hostile goals or possibly inexorable conflict trajectories of large rival nations, nations that seem to follow similar techno-economic-military development strategies. One wonders if these rival nations – China and India – are evolving the way they are merely to protect their fast-growing economies, or are they heading into open or cold conflict – intentionally or accidentally?

There is no definitive way to answer the question just raised, but examining the economic and business relations of China and India could throw some light on whether the future holds prospects of more-or-less peaceful prosperity for these two largest demographic entities or prospects of conflict.

All the economic successes and the resultant global visibility notwithstanding, China and India exhibit a complex pattern of mutual relations. They remain wary neighbours, are oblique rather than direct competitors in most global markets, and have a rapidly growing mutual trade and business partnership that retains a low, reticent profile.

7.1.1 Wary Neighbours

In the late 1940s, China rejoiced in India's independence from British colonial rule and India welcomed the communist people's revolution in China. There were celebrated exchange visits by political leaders and statements of mutually shared values and interests. Leaders of both nations employed slogans of fraternal relations. By 1960, however, the Sino-Indian relations had become extremely strained over border disputes. In late 1962, triggered by a Chinese attack on an Indian military patrol, the brief but high-altitude and high-intensity border war resulted in China controlling the Aksai Chin region of Indian Kashmir. Having shown decisive military superiority, the Chinese army ended the war with a unilateral ceasefire. Forty-five years after the border war, by 2007, some of the border issues had been resolved but India still claimed Aksai Chin and China refused to recognize Arunachal Pradesh, now a state within the Indian Union, as a part of India. The main issues of Sino-Indian border conflicts and relationships over the 1950–2007 period thus ranged from professed fraternity to open warfare to gradual reduction of tension and even some limited forms of military cooperation (Sisci 2005).

7.1.2 Oblique Competitors

In the global markets, China has become the dominant provider of manufactured products while India has emerged as a leader in providing software and other technology-enabled services. The orders of magnitude, however, are very different – with Chinese exports and China-directed foreign direct investments exceeding comparable figures for India by big multiples (Sarin and Sarin 2006). In most geographic markets and industry sectors, therefore, Chinese and Indian firms do not compete directly. When they do compete, the respective advantages of each side seem to prevail – Indian firms find it very difficult to claw market share from the Chinese in manufactures, and Chinese firms in 2007 were not able to threaten India's dominant position in software and related services (Ferguson 2007).

While each country seems to have carved out respective spheres of country-specific advantages, this does imply that China and India do not compete. The two countries compete obliquely rather than directly. In multiple political and economic spheres, the two countries are in a race to grab shares of attention and resources. In attracting foreign direct investment (FDI) or gaining attention of G8 leaders or projecting influence in Asia and Africa, China and India are in competition with each other – with China usually substantially ahead of India in most races. Through its political hierarchy of command, China is able to implement massive infrastructure projects expeditiously. In India, most such projects become contested political terrains, with interest groups blocking or slowing project implementation (Business Week 2007). The same (messy) political openness, however, sometimes gives India political advantages in dealing with democratic western nations that face similar issues in their own domestic political settings. India is thus able to exert what is termed "soft power" on selected occasions, without being perceived as an aspiring hegemonic nation (Nye 2005).

While the competition between China and India is oblique in most ways, the trend is for such competition gradually to become less oblique and more direct. China is rapidly developing its English language and software skills for IT services so as to become the recipient of outsourced work in these fields. India launched a massive program of Special Economic Zones (SEZs), similar to such zones in China, to develop manufacturing capabilities that could take on Chinese firms in selected sectors. After 2010, it would be reasonable to expect that Chinese and Indian firms would occasionally encounter each other as direct competitors in some global settings. On the broader political and economic fronts, however, the oblique forms of China–India competition seen today can be expected to continue.

7.1.3 Reticent Partners

Even in the face of continuing wariness across borders and oblique (but sometimes head-on) economic confrontations in global markets, the business and trade relationship between India and China is growing at a very rapid clip. The 2007 level of China–India trade was US$2 billion per month, making this a major trade relationship in Asia and the world. In relation to other bilateral trade relations among large neighbours – such as USA–Mexico, Brazil–Argentina or Germany–France–the China–India bilateral trade, however, was very low compared to the sizes of these economies (Khanna 2006). Moreover, raw material supplies from India to China, such as iron ore, account for a very substantial part of the trade (Khanna 2006).

While the trade linkages between China and India were relatively modest in 2007, the trajectory was set for such linkages to grow, albeit at a gradual pace. The following sections illustrate the roles of businesses in cementing India–China business relations, even as differences remained in political terms and in the economic systems of the two nations.

7.2   CHINESE BUSINESS INTERESTS IN INDIA

Chinese firms see India as a resource provider as well as a market. In terms of natural and especially mineral resources, China is tapping all corners of the world – and India is part of China's global resource quest. India has been a supplier of materials such as iron ore and refractory materials for steel plants in China for almost two decades. In recent years, China has tried to source knowledge-based products and services from India to some extent. Lenovo, the Chinese computer company that shot into prominence with the acquisition of the IBM notebook computer business, has decided to make India a hub for developing some of its global advertising. With long experience of developing advertising in English, Mumbai offers a much more economical base for developing advertising content than New York or London. For Chinese firms, the pace of making India a manufacturing base is much slower than for example the pace at which Japanese and Korean firms are making India a manufacturing base. Automobile makers from Japan and Korea, for example, have already made India a global supply base for some of their smaller car models. Chinese appliance maker Haier has announced plans to make India a manufacturing and export base for Southeast Asia, the Middle East and Africa. Overall, though, Chinese firms shy away from making India a manufacturing base for some obvious reasons. Chinese firms are generally low-cost producers in most manufacturing categories and they are loath to transfer manufacturing know-how to India because that would create new global competitors for Chinese manufacturers. This state of affairs could change, however, as third countries start making India a manufacturing and export hub. For example, APC – an American IT hardware firm that is now French owned – manufactures in both China and

India. Over time, however, for its low-end power supply units, India has turned out to be a higher quality and lower price global manufacturing base than China for APC. This is despite the atrocious state of road infrastructure linking the APC plant in Bangalore, India to the port city of Chennai located over 400 kilometres away.

India as a market is clearly quite attractive to Chinese firms, large and small. Not just Chinese giants like Haier and Lenovo, but also hundreds of small Chinese firms have started supplying merchandise to India's rapidly growing consumer markets. Unlike China, where the major driver of economic growth is exports, the Indian economy is booming primarily due to a rapid rise in domestic demand. This makes India an attractive destination for Chinese exports ranging from big-ticket items such as flat-screen TVs and large appliances all the way to minor items such as plastic household goods and firecrackers. The highly adaptive Chinese manufacturers have even emerged as significant suppliers of very traditional items such as resin-made statues of Hindu gods and garments with Indian folk art designs.

The Indian market, reflecting the vast income and wealth disparities of the country, is one of the most skewed in the world. This requires strategically savvy marketers to target all parts of the income pyramid in India: top, middle, and the very large bottom (Prahalad and Hammond 2002; Prahalad 2006). Having entered the Indian market at the high end of appliances, by 2006 Haier had launched a strategy to appeal to the bottom of the pyramid also. An India-specific range of low-end refrigerators, washing machines and TVs was under development (Economic Times 2006).

One impact of the Chinese "manufacturing invasion" of India, especially for low-end goods, has been to wake up Indian firms from their complacency about costs and quality (Khanna 2006). In part, the rising competitiveness of selected Indian manufactures after 2000 can be attributed to the pressure from Chinese imports in India. Writing from a business strategy perspective, Khanna (2006) opines that India should fling its doors wide open to manufactured goods from China. The resulting competitive pressure, he believes, would have the salubrious effect of India's mostly private sector manufacturing firms shaping up in terms of quality enhancements and cost reductions.

Apart from competitive business reasons, in some instances strategic political and military considerations come into play in China–India business relations. A project to build a major deep-water port on the southwestern coast of India went into limbo after it turned out that the most competitive bidder for the project was a Chinese firm. Indian political and military leaders did not want the Chinese to be the builders of an economically as well as militarily strategic port in India.

7.3　INDIAN BUSINESS INTERESTS IN CHINA

While the manufacturing competitiveness of Indian firms was increasing in selected categories, until 2007 Indian firms were not in a position to match Chinese firms in terms of production costs and sale prices of manufactures. For this reason, Indian firms viewed China somewhat differently from the way Chinese firms viewed India. By 2000, India had emerged as the world's pre-eminent provider of outsourced services such as software development and remote technology support. For India, China represents both a source of service-providing workers and a market for selected services where India has competitive strengths.

Illustrative of the Indian approach to the Chinese services market are the cases of two information technology (IT) training firms from India: NIIT and Aptech. NIIT was founded in 1981 and Aptech in 1986. By 2005, these firms – with their national (and now international) network of IT training centres – had become major pillars supporting India's competitive advantages in software and information technology-enabled services (ITES). China became attractive to both these Indian firms as a market when they realized that IT training needs in China were exploding, and these firms had operating models in place to provide such training at high quality and reasonable costs. Aptech estimated that its share of China's IT training market jumped from 27.3 per cent in 2005 to 32.1 per cent (Guliani 2007). Aptech entered China in 2000, much later than NIIT. It established a joint venture – Aptech Beida Jadebird IT Co. – an affiliate of Beijing University. By 2007, Aptech Beida Jadebird had over 250 IT training centres in 57 cities in China and trained nearly 400 000 students a year. NIIT had 165 training sectors in China, and estimated its 2007 market share of the Chinese IT training market at 7.6 per cent (Guliani 2007). The number of NIIT centres in China was projected to rise to 250 by 2010.

The source of the competitive advantage of these two Indian firms in China resided not so much in the technology elements but in the operational and managerial aspects of large software development projects. According to the CEO of NIIT, Vijay Thadani (quoted in Guliani 2007):

We [NIIT] found that Chinese programmers were very talented, very hard-working and highly disciplined, and that the cost of doing software projects in China would be lower than in India . . . however, many Chinese IT professionals, though possessing excellent mathematics, engineering and science background and blessed with impressive logic orientation, often lack proper training in software development. Most of them also lack experience of working in large software projects and hardly have any knowledge about project management. Therefore, we had come up with the idea that we should first take our education programs to China to train people before starting our software projects there.

In the global context, NIIT is not just a software and IT training firm but also a major provider of software development services to global clients. Thus, the above viewpoint of the NIIT CEO is indicative of the strategic stepping stones that some of the Indian IT services firms may follow in China: enter by providing training and education opportunities to a ready and waiting target population, develop a substantial trained workforce, and then use Chinese facilities (along with India and other locations) as production centres for global software and ITES projects and operations.

Another insight from Aptech and NIIT is about the structuring of the mode of entry into China. NIIT entered China before Aptech, but Aptech raced ahead to claim a market share almost five times larger than that of NIIT. This can most likely be attributed to the strategic partnership of Aptech with a Beijing University affiliated firm, and the creation of the Aptech Beida Jadebird joint venture. Indian firms may have to make trade-offs between the desire to maintain control of their China ventures and getting wide access to China's fast-growing markets by sharing control with Chinese partners.

In a few special cases, Indian firms have been able to make successful entries in the manufacturing sectors in China. Orind expanded its capacity for making refractory (bricks used to line steel smelters) four times in a 10-year period after the early 1990 entry. By 2007, Tata Refractory had also entered the Chinese market. Orind, however, moved its corporate head-quarters to Singapore, indicating the bureaucratic hurdles in running major China operations from a base in India.

7.4 THIRD-COUNTRY BUSINESS INTERESTS IN CHINA AND INDIA

Observing the interests of firms from third countries in 2007 – especially U.S. firms – it appears that the third-company businesses are making strategic moves that mesh their private corporate goals with the emergent capabilities of China and India. Such moves have already made China into the world's largest manufactory and India into the world's largest provider of offshore IT-enabled services. The biggest companies are beginning to approach both countries to meet multiple strategic goals – to hedge their bets, access markets, and tap talent pools. IBM's role in China and India is a case in point. The company has escalated its investments and commitments in both these areas (Yeo 2006):

- IBM moved its global procurement headquarters from New York to Shenzhen, China.

- IBM operates 25 facilities and employs over 43 000 people in India.
- In 2006, IBM announced a US$6 billion investment in India for developing hardware and software, creating services and conducting R&D work.
- China and India are important IBM hubs for business transformation outsourcing and business process outsourcing services.

As major firms such as IBM begin to distribute their investments, assets and technology bases across China and India, such firms develop a vested interest in ensuring that the two countries engage in competition that is healthy and cooperative – or co-opetition (Brandenburger and Nalebuff 1997). As Thomas Friedman (2006), who created the Flat World metaphor to describe the global levelling of assets and skills, is reported to have said, "No two countries that have a McDonald's have ever had a war". This logic extends even more strongly to rival countries that have major commitments from firms such as IBM, Intel and Microsoft. As major firms from third countries begin to invest and commit resources in China and India to achieve distributed strategic synergies, there will be rising global interest in ensuring that China and India remain political allies even as they compete economically.

7.5   THE TANGLED WEB: BUSINESS, TRADE, POLITICS AND SECURITY

As the world rolls further into the 21st century, China and India are increasingly moving to the centre stage – in economic, political and cultural terms. As these two countries begin to compete more directly (and less obliquely), they are also likely to increase mutual ties in terms of trade, investment and other linkages. This interdependence, however, would not reach the levels of interdependence observable in the USA–EU and USA–Japan linkages in the 20th century. This is because even by 2025, China, and especially India, will retain many characteristics of developing economies – and will continue to compete for global market access and global resource access. Also, unless a dramatic political transformation occurs – especially in China – these two nations will maintain some level of mutual distrust, and the rest of the world will continue to see the two nations as very distinct politico-economic systems.

The business institutions of China and India, however, can be expected to reach greater levels of interdependence than the governments or military forces of the two nations. In 2007, for example, a joint exercise by naval forces of the United States, Japan, Australia and India in the Indian Ocean was perceived negatively by China as a strategy of containment of China's rising military power by the navies of four democracies. Such rattling incidents and perceptual rifts are likely to keep on happening, although there are also some instances of China and India cooperating in military terms, especially when it comes to common threats such as terrorism (Sisci 2005). Overall, though, the military and political cooperation or rifts between China and India will remain sideshows to the growing business linkages of the two nations. Already by the 2000s in China, most national strategic decisions were made with business interests in view. By 2007, while political concerns still drove national and sub-national strategies in India, the tide was turning – business interests were gaining greater voices in government policy processes.

7.6 CONCLUDING OBSERVATIONS

Political, military and economic rivalry between China and India cannot be expected to disappear in the foreseeable future. At the same time, politicians and business leaders in both countries are well aware of the growing business and economic interdependence of the two nations. In September 2007, India's foreign minister made these comments in response to a question about India–China relations at a meeting in Seoul (Suryanarayana 2007):

> The leaders of both countries [India and China] recognise that co-existence and cooperation is the wise course of action; and sensitivity to mutual aspirations is the underpinning for building confidence and trust. There is enough space and opportunity for both of us to grow and develop and to bring benefit not only to us but also for other partners in Asia.

A key factor driving China–India business relations, according to political analysts, is the growing refinement of diplomatic skills of China as a regional superpower (Shambaugh 2004/05):

> Bilaterally and multilaterally, Beijing's diplomacy has been remarkably adept and nuanced . . . As a result, most nations in the region now see China as a good neighbor, a constructive partner, a careful listener, and a nonthreatening regional power. This regional perspective is striking, given that just a few years ago, many of China's neighbours voiced growing concerns about the possibility of China becoming a domineering regional hegemon and powerful military threat. Today these views are muted.

The China–India rivalries take a distant back seat in comparison to what has been called the "global labour arbitrage" – the availability of cheap labour to do almost any job, from unskilled to highly skilled, in countries

like China and India. This has resulted in a steady rise in outsourcing –
from manufacturing to services to knowledge work (Sarin and Sarin
2006), and from peripheral to increasingly central and core business
processes (Freeman 2005). At the core, then, there is a commonweal of
political-economic interest that puts China and India on the same side of
the global equation vis-à-vis the advanced Euro-American-Asian nations.
For the next few decades, China and India stand to gain more from a
growing web of tacit cooperation than from ruinous military rivalry or
open conflict.

REFERENCES

Brandenburger, A.M. and B.J. Nalebuff (1997) *Co-Opetition: A Revolution Mindset
That Combines Competition and Cooperation: The Game Theory Strategy That's
Changing the Game of Business*, New York: Currency.
Business Week (2007) "The Trouble with India", *Business Week*, 19 March, Cover
Story, available at: www.businessweek.com/magazine/content/07_12/b4026001.
htm?chan=search, accessed on: 3 October 2007.
Economic Times (2006) "Haier Sees Growth at Bottom of Pyramid", *The Economic
Times*, 3 July, available at: www.ibef.org/artdisplay.aspx?cat_id=591&art_id=
12802, accessed on: 18 September 2007.
Ferguson, T. (2007) "China no Tech Rival Yet, Says India", *ZD Net Asia*, 27 August,
available at: www.zdnetasia.com/news/business/0,39044229,62031385,00.htm,
accessed on: 30 September 2007.
Freeman, R. (2005) "China, India and the Doubling of the Global Labor Force:
Who Pays the Price of Globalization?" *The Globalist*, 3 June, available at:
http://hussonet.free.fr/freeman5.pdf, accessed on: 18 September 2007.
Friedman, T. (2006) *The World is Flat: A Brief History of the 21st Century*, updated
and expanded edition, New York: Farrar, Straus and Giroux.
Guliani, S. (2007) "Aptech, NIIT Encashing Upon IT Education & Training
Market in China", 21 September, available at: www.2point6billion.com/
2007/09/21/aptech-niit-enchasing-upon-it-education-training-market-in-china/,
accessed on: 30 September 2007.
Khanna, T. (2006) "India Needs to Encourage Trade With China", Harvard
Business School Working Knowledge, December 6, available at: http://hbswk.
hbs.edu/item/5573.html, accessed on: 30 September 2007.
Lal, R. (2006) *Understanding China and India: Security Implications for the United
States and the World*, New York: Praeger.
Nye, J.S. Jr (2005) *Soft Power: The Means to Success in World Politics*, New York:
PublicAffairs Books.
Prahalad, C.K. (2006) *The Fortune at the Bottom of the Pyramid: Eradicating
Poverty Through Profits*, Philadelphia: Wharton School Publishing.
Prahalad, C.K. and A. Hammond (2002) "Saving the World's Poor, Profitably",
Harvard Business Review, September, **80**(9), 48–57, 124.
Sarin, S. and A. Sarin (2006) *Why India can Never be China but can Become a Lot
More!*, paper presented at the *Fifth International Conference on Global Arena
Challenges of the Morrow*, Delhi, 28–29 December.

Shambaugh, D. (2004/05) "China Engages Asia: Reshaping the Regional Order", *International Security*, **29**(3), Winter, 64–99.

Sisci, F. (2005) "China and India Fall into Step", 2 June, available at: www.atimes.com/atimes/South_Asia/GF02Df03.html, accessed on: 30 September 2007.

Suryanarayana, P.S. (2007) "Strategic Partnership with China will Mature: Pranab Mukherjee", *The Hindu*, online edition, 18 September, available at: www.hindu.com/2007/09/18/stories/2007091861101200.htm, accessed on: 18 September 2007.

Yeo, V. (2006) "IBM: China, India Pivotal for Growth", *ZDNet Asia*, available at: www.zdnetasia.com/news/business/0,39044229,61972709,00.htm, accessed on: 5 October 2007.

8. Corporate social performance in a post-transition context: the case of Polish firms

Renata Kaminska-Labbé and Beata Buchelt

8.1 INTRODUCTION

The debate on the importance of ethics in businesses has recently gained momentum (Maignan and Raltson, 2002). In the developed world, especially North America, more and more corporations define themselves as "socially responsible". They emphasize that beyond serving the interests of their owners, they are equally committed to acting in the interests of society in general. They cite their role in creating employment, funding educational and research institutions, providing high-quality products or training their employees.

Sustainability of strategic success depends on the quality of corporate relationships with inside and outside stakeholders. Indeed, consumers, employees, business partners and citizens are increasingly well-informed and active in protecting their rights. Growing concerns about the effects of economic development on health and the environment, for example, modify the way many corporations produce and distribute. Employees expect good working conditions, decent salaries and equal chances for promotion. Suppliers want to be paid on time and to be treated fairly. Members of communities in which firms operate expect the latter to behave like "good citizens". Information travels quickly and almost at no cost. Corporate leaders are well aware of the fact that they have to apply societal ethical standards to business practices or otherwise one of the most valuable resources, reputation, may instantaneously be destroyed, exposing their companies to a serious risk.

In the countries with longstanding market economies, a growing focus on corporate social responsibility (CRS) appears to correspond to the evolution of society in general: on the one hand it is no longer enough to fulfil economic needs as people become affluent, and on the other hand, there is a growing awareness of high interdependency among the political, economic and social systems.

In Poland, the abolition of the centralized economic system created an unprecedented situation where firms, markets, and social and institutional systems underwent the process of complete reconstruction. During the first decade that followed the introduction of the market economy, local firms that were previously state-owned oriented all their efforts towards rebuilding their competence base, as a necessity for survival in the new increasingly competitive environment. They focused on modernizing production systems, protecting their existing market share and developing new markets, as well as differentiating their products. Beyond having to negotiate privatization programmes with trade union representatives and modernize production to lessen pollution, business ethics and CSR issues in a large sense were not at the top of managerial agendas. In the same way, new entrepreneurs conducting business in an unstable post-rupture context focused on generating rapid profits. Political instability, frequent corruption scandals, slow privatization processes and the lack of managerial competences resulted in opportunistic behaviours, low-quality goods and services and frequent strikes.

The complexity of this post-rupture context requires that local firms pay particular attention to their image. Indeed, the future international expansion of Polish firms will depend on the degree of trust foreign governments and firms have in them. Winning supply contracts from multinationals, for example, will require of them a high degree of adherence to international ethical standards. In this chapter we examine the nature and scope of social responsibility awareness in Polish firms over more than fifteen years of economic transition. Our analysis is partly based on the results of the "Best Practices in Human Resources Management" competition organized annually since the year 2000 by The Polish Institute of Labour and Social Studies. Interestingly, issues related to corporate social performance were included in the competition only in the year 2005.

8.2 WHAT DOES CORPORATE SOCIAL RESPONSIBILITY REALLY MEAN?

From the theoretical perspective, the major difficulty resides in the fact that there is no clear consensus on the definition of corporate social performance nor on the role that business organizations should play in exerting positive social change. Researchers and managers do not seem to agree on what constitutes (or not) a social issue, and there is even less agreement on how to measure social performance.

While some still contest the idea of firms having a social responsibility, there is no question that business organizations experience increasing internal and external pressure to fulfil broader social goals (Davies, 2003;

Freeman *et al.*, 2001; Logsdon and Wood, 2002; Windsor, 2004). These come from the various stakeholder groups driven by a range of instrumental, relational and moral motives. However, like individuals, corporations are self-interested beings. Given the cost of some "socially responsible" initiatives and the obligation for managers to justify their resource allocation choices to shareholders, there must be a good reason for a business organization to buy into a social responsibility philosophy. Even though a number of studies clearly show a positive relationship between implementing socially-sensitive strategies and the firm's financial performance (Margolis and Walsh, 2003; Roman, Hayibor and Alge, 1999), the notion of corporate social responsibility remains poorly understood. This is partly because it is a multifaceted term covering a wide range of issues relating to the ethical rights and duties existing between the business world and society. Much has been written on the subject but the debate over what the term really means is far from being closed. Votaw (1973, p. 11) notes that

> the term is a brilliant one; it means something, but not always the same thing, to everybody. To some it conveys the idea of legal responsibility or liability; to others it means socially responsible behavior in an ethical sense; to still others, the meaning transmitted is that of "responsible for", in a causal mode; many simply equate it with a charitable contribution.

The difficulty in defining social responsibility starts with the lack of consensus on the purpose or *raison d'être* of a business organization in modern society. It is not at all obvious to everyone that a firm should pursue any objectives beyond generating profit or creating wealth for its shareholders. The answer to this question largely depends on one's ideology and adherence to a particular economic paradigm. Neoclassical economists (Friedman, 1962), are known for drawing a strict line between social and economic issues and strongly advocating the idea that "the business of business is business", leaving social affairs to governmental institutions and non-business organizations (Henderson, 2001).

Those managers who view the relationship between business and society as an implicit "social contract" and who admit the importance of building social responsibility into their company strategy continue to have a difficult time deciding whether a particular issue is one with which a firm should be particularly concerned. This is not surprising considering that what is generally considered to be a social or ethical matter may include a wide range of complex issues from pollution to poverty, racial discrimination, hiring, employer–employee relationships, product safety and training or health hazards. In addition, the definition of what is or what is not important in terms of social responsibility also depends on one's hierarchical and functional position in a firm.

Davis (1973), for example, defines corporate social responsibility as "the firm's considerations of, and response to, issues beyond the narrow economic, technical, and legal requirements of the firm to accomplish social benefits along with the traditional economic gains which the firm seeks" (p. 312). Almost thirty years later, for Henderson (2001), economic performance should be achieved "in close conjunction with an array of different 'stakeholders', so as to promote the goal of 'sustainable development'. This goal supposedly has three dimensions, 'economic', 'environmental' and 'social' " (p. 15). Waddock and Bodwell's even more recent definition (2004) does not clarify the issue any further. Their definition focuses on the stakeholders; corporate social responsibility is seen "as the way in which a company's operating practices (policies, processes, and procedures) affect its stakeholders and the natural environment" (p. 24). Whatever the emphasis may be, the vagueness of these definitions suggests their limited use for building efficient theoretical models. In other terms, it remains problematic to make the concept of corporate social responsibility operational in order to construct measures of firms' corporate social performance (Ullmann, 1985). As a result, it is often easier to note *ex-post* socially "irresponsible" behaviour rather than to improve the diagnosis and strategy formulation *ex-ante*.

8.3 TOWARD A MULTI-LEVEL PROCESS-ORIENTED STAKEHOLDER-BASED MODEL OF CORPORATE SOCIAL PERFORMANCE

The notion of corporate social responsiveness, first proposed by Sethi (1975), offered an alternative, more prescriptive perspective to social responsibility. The general idea was to evaluate corporate social performance on the basis of types of corporate behaviour in response to social pressures.

The idea of corporate responsiveness was integrated into the first comprehensive model of corporate social performance, proposed by Carroll (1979) and further developed by Wartick and Cochran (1985). It integrates the following dimensions: categories of social responsibility (economic, legal, ethical and discretionary), a philosophy of social responsiveness or types of behaviour adopted when confronted with social issues (reaction, defence, accommodation, pro-action), and a range of social issues addressed by all firms (consumerism, environment, discrimination, product safety, occupational safety, shareholders).

The main contribution of this three-dimensional construct has been to reconcile what had been considered as separate definitions of social responsibility, into a general framework of corporate social performance. The model has also clarified the idea that social responsibility and economic performance are in no way mutually exclusive, while suggesting that social responsiveness is the action phase of management in response to social issues.

In spite of its unquestionable contribution, Carroll's model has been criticized for being complex and difficult to test empirically. Indeed, apart from evaluating firms' profitability from publicly available sources and searching for evidence of illegal corporate behaviour, it is extremely difficult to assess the ethical or discretionary responsibilities a firm claims to assume.

The process-oriented stakeholder-based model of corporate social performance (Clarkson, 1995; Wood, 1991) partly resolves this problem. It focuses on the complex interactions and relationships between managers and the different interest groups. According to Clarkson (1995), the notion of responsibility can make sense to managers only within the context of their functional activities, such as marketing, production, human resources or finance. Managers can therefore be accountable for their actions only within the scope of their managerial domains and in relation to specific stakeholder groups such as shareholders, public institutions, suppliers, customers or employees. The implicit hypotheses are that managers manage their relationships with their stakeholders and not with society as a whole and that the economic and social purpose of the corporation is to create and distribute increased wealth and value to all its primary stakeholder groups.

The so-called "stakeholder management" model offers an actionable framework giving a better indication of the primary and secondary stakeholders of an organization, and enabling evaluation of corporate performance on the reactive, defensive, accommodative and proactive scale (RDAP). Its strength resides in helping managers define priorities regarding the expectations of various stakeholder groups. However, the ongoing process of globalization highlights another aspect of the increasing phenomenon of corporate engagement in social responsibility. This is because firms are embedded in a complex web of interdependencies among a number of sector-specific, national and international systems; these in turn involve different actors, who are driven by a variety of motives to expect more social responsibility.

8.4 CORPORATE SOCIAL PERFORMANCE IN THE POST-TRANSITION CONTEXT

The choice of "shock therapy" as a means to transform a centrally-planned economy into a modern market-based system in Poland has been supported by most Western analysts. However, this mode of transition results in members of a society losing many of their bearings, and its success depends, among other things, on that society's perception of social justice on societal, organizational and individual levels. Needless to say, such analysis is beyond the scope of this chapter, but it is important to note that (in Poland) from the societal perspective, after the initial generalized support for reforms, the feeling of social injustice rapidly became prominent. The reasons for this were factors such as: observable contrasts between "rich" and "poor", numerous and spectacular corruption scandals involving successive governments, inefficiency (and indeed corruption) of the judicial system and the absence of transparency of privatization programmes.

On the corporate level, inefficient public administration and complex business legislation have encouraged opportunistic, short-term quick-profit oriented business strategies. Most of the time businesses conduct their affairs at the edge of legal frontiers. Social dialogue seems to be practically non-existent for at least three reasons: a rather negative perception of the market economy, the general indifference to ethical and moral issues of employees, entrepreneurs and capital owners, and finally a lack of business education (Rok, 2004).

Corporate ethics and social responsibility are still rarely on the agenda of managers, whose priority is the very survival of their firms. Even the "window dressing" actions centred on improving the firm's image have been superficial and short-lived. For example, contrary to what the world has learned from the well known Tylenol case (in which, subsequent to doubts about its role in the death of several patients, Johnson & Johnson did not hesitate to remove the medication immediately from the market), in 2006 a Polish drug maker, Jalfa, took a few months before disclosing information about the faulty batch of Corhydron manufactured in June 2005 (PMR Ltd, 2006). Even if the production of Corhydron was resumed in December 2006, many questions remain unanswered. According to the public prosecutor's office, the report of the Main Pharmaceutical Inspectorate did not indicate clearly where the mistake could have occurred; neither did it describe the 2005 production process.

Although this case illustrates a clear misconception of what corporate responsibility towards consumers means, and demonstrates reactive behaviour, this attitude seems to be changing. The massive exodus of young Polish professionals finding jobs in other European countries and frequently coming back home with extensive experience of corporate life, and the increasing presence of multinational corporations implanted in Poland, serve as vehicles for importing socially responsible practices. Also, academic and other newly created non-business organizations of different status and nature (such as the Chambers of Commerce, The Institute of Research on Democracy and Private Enterprise, and The Centre for Business Ethics at the Leon Kozminski Academy of Management and Entrepreneurship) promote the idea that "doing well by doing good" is not a myth but a necessity for a modern society. Such bodies organize conferences, forums and educational programmes; they also sponsor research and different types of competitions to enhance learning and sharing of best practices.

8.5 WHAT DO WE LEARN ABOUT CSR IN POLISH FIRMS FROM THE "BEST PRACTICES IN HUMAN RESOURCES MANAGEMENT" COMPETITION?

The "Best Practices in Human Resources Management" national competition has been organized annually since the year 2000 by the Polish Institute of Labour and Social Studies. In 2005, corporate social responsibility issues were taken into consideration for the first time. The results were reported in Urbaniak and Bohdziewicz (2005).

The competition is organized in two phases. The first phase consists of a questionnaire on human resources management (HRM) practices, which is often used by the participant firms as a self-evaluation tool. There is no particular selection for taking part in this phase. The committee, comprising academics and practitioners, evaluates the organizational practices of the different companies and selects a number of them for the second phase. During the latter all firms are audited to verify whether the declared practices correspond to reality. Finally, three prizes are awarded to those who demonstrate the best HRM practices. Additional awards may be given to companies which have developed innovative practices in certain HRM domains such as recruitment or training.

In 2005, 21 companies qualified for the second phase of the competition, representing a diversity of:

- sectors: 19 per cent traditional services, 43 per cent knowledge-intensive services, 19 per cent traditional production, 19 per cent advanced technology-based production; and
- ownership structures: 33 per cent with exclusively Polish capital, 38 per cent with foreign capital and 29 per cent public entities.

Corporate social responsibility was evaluated by taking into account the following issues:

- the mission statement highlighting the values emphasized by the firm as important in its everyday business operations and the degree to which the company takes account of the interests of its diverse stakeholders;
- the existence of a corporate code of conduct;
- promotion of corporate social responsibility in the external environment;
- other specific actions taken considered as part of corporate social responsibility.

The evaluating committee examined the 21 mission statements, to find an example of the aspects of corporate social responsibility listed in Tables 8.1 and 8.2. Tables 8.3 and 8.4 summarize these findings in relation to the existence of a corporate code of conduct by sector and ownership structure. Data concerning the actions aimed at the promotion of corporate social responsibility is presented in Figures 8.1 and 8.2.

Table 8.1   Aspects of CSR mentioned in the mission statement by sector

Aspects of Corporate Social Responsibility	Sector				Firms in general	
	Production		Services		Number	%
	Advanced technology-based	Traditional	Knowledge-based	Traditional		
Ethical values	1	3	5	3	12	57.1
Cultural diversity	1	1	3	–	5	23.8
Local community needs	2	2	3	4	11	52.4
Natural environment protection	3	4	2	1	10	47.6
Customer satisfaction	4	3	9	4	20	95.2
Employee needs	4	2	7	4	17	80.9
Other shareholder expectations	1	2	1	–	4	19
Quality	3	4	8	4	19	90.5
Cost reduction	1	3	2	1	7	33.3
Profit	1	3	3	2	9	42.8

Source: Urbaniak and Bohdziewicz (2005), p. 146.

*Table 8.2   Aspects of CSR mentioned in the mission statement by
              ownership type*

Aspects of Corporate Social Responsibility	Firms accordingly to ownership type			Firms in general	
	Public entities	Firms with Polish capital	Firms with foreign capital	Number	%
Ethical values	4	4	4	12	57.1
Cultural diversity	1	1	3	5	23.8
Local community needs	3	4	4	11	52.4
Natural environment protection	3	5	2	10	47.6
Customer satisfaction	6	6	8	20	95.2
Employee needs	4	5	8	17	80.9
Other shareholder expectations	–	2	2	4	19
Quality	6	5	8	19	90.5
Cost reduction	1	3	3	7	33.3
Profit	1	4	4	9	42.8

Source: Urbaniak and Bohdziewicz (2005), p. 146.

Table 8.3   Existence of a corporate code of conduct by sector

Corporate code of conduct	Firms by sector				Firms in general	
	Production		Services		Number	%
	Advanced technology-based	Traditional	Knowledge-based	Traditional		
Rules codified in formal documents	4	–	6	1	11	52.4
Use of informal rules	–	4	2	1	7	33.3
No rules	–	–	1	2	3	14.3

Source: Urbaniak and Bohdziewicz (2005), p. 148.

The final aspect of the competition concerned specific actions taken by the firms which they considered to be an important element in the corporate social responsibility philosophy. In response to an open question, the companies declared that they were active in the following domains:

Table 8.4   Existence of a corporate code of conduct by ownership structure

Corporate code of conduct	Firms by ownership structure			Firms in general	
	Public entities	Firms with Polish capital	Firms with foreign capital	Number	%
Rules codified in formal documents	4	1	6	11	52.4
Use of informal rules	2	5	–	7	33.3
No rules	–	1	2	3	14.3

Source: Urbaniak and Bohdziewicz (2005), p. 148.

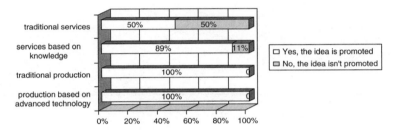

Source: Urbaniak and Bohdziewicz (2005), p. 148.

Figure 8.1   Promotion of social responsibility by sector

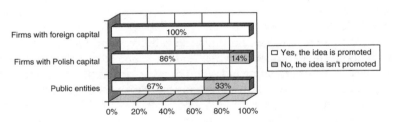

Source: Urbaniak and Bohdziewich (2005), p. 149.

Figure 8.2   Promotion of social responsibility by ownership structure

- communicating the need to adopt socially responsible attitudes – 47.6 per cent of companies;
- support of R&D activities – 57.1 per cent of companies;
- support for entrepreneurship – 52.4 per cent of companies;

Table 8.5   Specific actions by sector

	Firms according to sector of operations				Firms in general	
	Production		Services		Number	%
	Advanced technology-based	Traditional	Knowledge-based	Traditional		
Promotion of corporate social responsibility	3	2	3	2	10	47.6
Support for R&D activities	4	2	5	1	12	57.1
Support for entrepreneurship	3	2	5	1	11	52.4
Environmental conservation	3	3	2	2	10	47.6
Improvement of social climate	4	4	7	4	19	90.5

Source: Urbaniak and Bohdziewicz (2005), p. 151.

- environmental conservation – 47.6 per cent of companies;
- improvement of social welfare – 90.5 per cent of companies.

These activities can be also analysed by activity sector and form of ownership (Tables 8.5 and 8.6).

Even if these results have no statistical validity, some conclusions can be drawn about the nature of activities and the scope of social responsibility awareness of firms operating in Poland. It appears that the most frequently cited aspects of corporate social responsibility mentioned in mission statements are customer satisfaction (95.2 per cent), quality (90.5 per cent) and employee needs (80.9 per cent) followed by ethical values (57.1 per cent), local community needs (52.4 per cent) and natural environment protection (47.6 per cent). Also, firms with foreign capital seem to manifest more interest in social responsibility issues than firms with Polish capital and state-owned entities.

Concerning the existence of a corporate code of conduct, 52.4 per cent of companies declared that they possessed formal codified ethical rules and 33.3 per cent stated that the rules were not explicit. The remaining 14.3 per cent admitted that they were not at all concerned with ethical rules. It is

Table 8.6 Specific actions by ownership type

	Firms by ownership type			Firms in general	
	Public entities	Firms with majority of Polish capital	Firms with majority of foreign capital	Number	%
Promotion of corporate social responsibility	2	4	4	10	47.6
Support of R&D activities	4	3	5	12	57.1
Support for entrepreneurship	3	3	5	11	52.4
Environmental conservation	4	4	2	10	47.6
Improvement of social climate	5	7	7	19	90.5

Source: Urbaniak and Bohdziewicz (2005), p. 152.

important to note that the existence of a corporate code of conduct shows that the company is aware of the importance of behaving in an ethical manner. However, it says nothing about how the code is implemented. Firms with foreign capital were the ones in which rules were explicit and codified. Firms with Polish capital seemed to operate more often on the basis of implicit, informal rules.

Production firms using both traditional and advanced technology all declared that they promoted the idea of social responsibility as opposed to only half of traditional service firms. Interestingly, all foreign capital firms promoted social responsibility in comparison to only 67 per cent of public organizations.

The last open question dealt with what Carroll (1979) calls a discretionary category of social responsibility. In decreasing order of importance, managers cited: improvement of a company's social climate, support of R&D activities, support for entrepreneurship and environmental protection and the necessity to promote ethics in business. Knowledge-based service organizations considered improvement of social climate to be the most important and environmental protection to be the least important. They also emphasized the importance of supporting R&D and entrepreneurship.

8.6   CONCLUSION

It seems that the most important inspiration for Polish companies comes from international firms such as, for example, The Coca-Cola Company, PepsiCo, IBM or Marriott Corporation operating in Poland (Szyszka, 2000). Polish firms still have much to learn about the role of corporate social responsibility and stakeholder management in building the positive perception of their activities necessary for sustaining competitive advantage. Even if all large Polish corporations engage in some form of socially responsible activities, (most often charity donations), they declare that they are not convinced that social responsibility is necessarily profitable in the long run (Rok, 2004). They are even less convinced that social responsibility may be a beneficial factor in modern strategic management, helping in recruitment and retention, managing risk by building a genuine culture of "doing the right thing" or building a reputation for integrity and best practice.

Even though managers in Poland have become increasingly aware of the strategic character of corporate social performance, they rarely reach beyond the economic and legal dimensions. Also, contrary to what might have been expected intuitively, public organizations are less proactive in promoting business ethics and corporate social responsibility than are organizations in the private sector. The reluctance to accept corporate social responsibility characteristic of public organizations may be a result of forty years of a centrally planned economy in which initiative and private entrepreneurship were highly discouraged (if not forbidden and punished). In a context where all aspects of political, economic and social life were strictly regulated and controlled, the sense of individual and collective responsibility disappeared and this is now difficult to reconstruct. Also, the decline of moral authority in contemporary Polish society significantly slows down the societal transformation process. Even the Catholic Church, traditionally the most widely respected institution in the country, has a long history of breaking the "official" law during the communist times. During this period the entire Polish society functioned and survived by constantly breaking the rules. This attitude still remains anchored in the value system of many Polish citizens. These values are particularly ill-adapted to the market-based knowledge economy (Gasparski, 2004; Stachowicz-Stanusch, 2004).

In firms with foreign capital, diverse stakeholder groups, including employees at different hierarchical levels, have a significant influence on the choice of socially responsible actions undertaken by their firm, particularly through fundraising activities or community volunteering. In Polish public organizations, these kinds of decisions are made in a centralized manner, almost exclusively by top management, usually the CEO (Porter and

Kramer, 2003). Most of the time, the latter arbitrarily chooses to sponsor well-known sports or cultural events, clearly with a simple personal marketing objective. It is no surprise then that state-owned firms score the lowest on the corporate social performance.

The results of the "Best Practices in Human Resources Management" national competition indicate that there is a pressing need to create more awareness concerning the importance of developing good business practices. Training future managers to be sensitive to the impact the business world has on the different stakeholder groups and on the natural environment appears to be extremely important (Jędrzejczak, 2004) along with developing the awareness of these issues among all members of the society, ranging from human rights to environmental concerns to conflict. While research to date has helped us better understand processes and motivations related to corporate social performance in mature market economies, we hope to have elucidated at least some aspects of the specificity of the post-transition context; in this context, it appears that the economic advantage achieved through CSR strategies is more likely than "ethical" reasons to influence companies operating in new market economies to implement such measures.

REFERENCES

Carroll A.B. (1979) A Three-Dimensional Conceptual Model of Corporate Performance, *Academy of Management Review*, 4(4), 497–505.

Clarkson M.B.E. (1995) A Stakeholder Framework for Analyzing and Evaluating Corporate Social Performance, *Academy of Management Review*, 20(1), 92–117.

Davies R. (2003) The Business Community: Social Responsibility and Corporate Values. In: J.H. Dunning (ed.), *Making Globalization Good: The Moral Challenges of Global Capitalism*, Oxford University Press, New York.

Davis K. (1973) The Case For and Against the Business Assumption of Social Responsibilities, *Academy of Management Journal*, 16, 312–323.

Freeman B., Pica M. and Camponovo C. (2001) A New Approach to Corporate Responsibility: The Voluntary Principles on Security and Human Rights, *Hastings International and Comparative Law Review*, 24, 423–449.

Friedman M. (1962) *Capitalism and Freedom*, Chicago University Press, Chicago.

Gasparski W. (2004) On the Need for Knowledge about the Axiological Context of Economic Activity. In: W. Gasparski and J. Dabrowski (eds), *Creating Knowledge-based Economy: Infrastructure-Organizations-Individuals*, Publishing House of the Leon Kozminsky Academy of Entrepreneurship and Management, Warsaw.

Henderson D. (2001) *Misguided Virtue: False Notions of Corporate Social Responsibility*, Institute of Economic Affairs, London.

Jędrzejczak A. (2004) The Role of Training in Corporate Human Capital Development. In: W. Gasparski and J. Dabrowski (eds), *Creating Knowledge-based Economy: Infrastructure-Organizations-Individuals*, Publishing House of the Leon Kozminsky Academy of Entrepreneurship and Management, Warsaw.

Logsdon J. and Wood D.J. (2002) Business Citizenship: From Domestic to Global Level Analysis, *Business Ethics Quarterly*, **12**, 155–188.

Maignan I. and Raltson D.A. (2002) Corporate Social Responsibility in Europe and the US: Insights from Businesses' Self-Presentations, *Journal of International Business Studies*, 3rd Quarter, **33**(3), 497.

Margolis J.D. and Walsh J.P. (2003) Misery Loves Companies: Rethinking Social Initiatives by Business, *Administrative Science Quarterly*, **48**, 655–689.

PMR Ltd (2006) *Jelfa Permitted to Restart Corhydron Manufacture*, www.pharmapoland.com/search.php?caseid=show_article&id=44459vq=jelfa%-permitted [Accessed 14 December 2006].

Porter M.E. and Kramer M.R. (2003) Filantropia przedsiębiorstwa jako źródło przewagi konkurencyjnej, *Harvard Business Review Polska*, **7**, 34–45.

Rok B. (2004) Biznes w społeczeństwie – oczekiwania i ich realizacja. In: L. Kolarska-Bobińska (ed.), *Świadomość ekonomiczna społeczeństwa i wizerunek biznesu*, Instytut Spraw Publicznych, Warsaw.

Roman R.M., Hayibor S. and Alge B.R. (1999) The Relationship Between Social and Financial Performance: Repainting a Portrait, *Business and Society*, **38**, 109–125.

Sethi S.P. (1975) Dimensions of Corporate Social Performance: An Analytical Framework, *California Management Review*, Spring, **17**(3).

Stachowicz-Stanusch A. (2004) The Role of Core Values in the Process of Development Brain-Rich Companies Based on Hewlett-Packard/Compaq Merger Case Study. In: W. Gasparski and J. Dabrowski (eds), *Creating Knowledge-based Economy: Infrastructure-Organizations-Individuals*, Publishing House of the Leon Kozminsky Academy of Entrepreneurship and Management, Warsaw.

Szyszka B. (2000) Basic Ethical Aspects of American Companies Operating in Poland, in Ryan, R.V. (ed.), *Business Students Focus on Ethics: Praxiology: The International Annual of Practical Philosophy and Methodology*, **8**, Transaction Publishers, Piscataway, NJ, 61–72.

Ullmann A. (1985) Data in Search of a Theory: A Critical Examination of the Relationship among Social Performance, Social Disclosure, and Economic Performance, *Academy of Management Review*, **10**, 540–577.

Urbaniak B. and Bohdziewicz P. (2005) *Human Resources Management: Creating Modernity*, Institute of Labour and Social Studies, Warsaw.

Votaw D. (1973) Genius Becomes Rare. In: D. Votaw and S.P. Sethi (eds), *The Corporate Dilemma: Traditional Values versus Contemporary Problems*, Prentice Hall, Englewood Cliffs, NJ.

Waddock S. and Bodwell C. (2004) Managing Responsibility: What Can Be Learned from the Quality Movement, *California Management Review*, **47**, 25–38.

Wartick S.L. and Cochran P.L. (1985) The Evolution of the Corporate Social Performance Model, *Academy of Management Review*, **4**, 758–769.

Windsor D. (2004) Global Corporate Social Responsibility: International Regimes and the Constellation of Corruption, Poverty, and Violence. In: J. Hooker and P. Madsen (eds), *International Corporate Responsibility: Exploring the Issues*, Carnegie Mellon University Press, Pittsburgh, PA.

Wood D.J. (1991) Corporate Social Performance Revisited, *Academy of Management Review*, **16**, 671–691.

9. The sustainable peace roles of international extractive industries

Duane Windsor

9.1 INTRODUCTION

Conflict and violence, both intra-state and inter-state, are globally wide-spread conditions in which businesses, both domestic and foreign, must frequently operate. These conditions are most pronounced in some developing countries in which international extractive industries are especially prominent activities. The broad rubric of conflict and violence includes violent crime (for example, kidnappings of foreign oil workers in the Niger Delta of Nigeria), inter-group conflicts (for example, the Tutsi and the Hutu in the Rwanda genocide of 1994 or the disintegration of the former Yugoslavia), civil wars and insurgencies (for example, the current situations in Iraq, Somalia and Sudan) and cross-border wars (for example, the continuing conflict between Ethiopia and Eritrea and the persistent risk of war between India and Pakistan). In the post-09/11 era, terrorism of several varieties is a rising phenomenon.

Sometimes, businesses are targets of violence or threats of violence (for example, the Chiquita scandal in Colombia, which is described below, and foreign oil companies in Nigeria). Sometimes, businesses may be, however inadvertently, causes or promoters of conflict and violence (for example, allegations made against Rio Tinto on Bougainville Island).[1] The issue addressed in this volume is the potential role of businesses in respecting human rights and encouraging sustainable peace and conflict prevention both through direct business activities and indirectly through the often positive relationship between business profit and community benefit. International businesses especially may be able to operate as change agents promoting peace and harmony through adopting a focused approach to corporate social responsibility through emphases on human rights and corporate citizenship.[2]

Sustainable peace and conflict prevention activities are becoming increasingly important opportunities for and responsibilities of multinational enterprises (MNEs). An enterprise engages in buying and selling in markets. A multinational enterprise has headquarters (that is, is chartered and organized) in one country and operates in at least one other host country. Most reasonably significant MNEs operate in multiple host countries. An MNE can be privately owned and operated as a business for profit or state owned and operated for profit or for national interest more broadly defined. Private ownership can mean privately held or publicly held. State ownership may be full or partial interest. In the oil industry worldwide, for example, state-owned (or influenced) enterprises control substantially more natural resources than privately-owned businesses do.

This chapter is a case study focused at the industry level. It examines industries that share characteristics of extracting natural resources in developing (as well as advanced) countries. International extractive industries can play very important sustainable peace and conflict prevention roles around the world. Leading examples of such industries are forest products, mining (including diamonds, metals and minerals as well as coal), oil and gas, and water resources development. The key connection among these industries is that they involve extraction and export of natural resources from developing countries (that is, the South) to advanced countries (that is, the North) by MNEs typically headquartered in the latter. Generally speaking, the extractive industries are crucial to the economies of the advanced countries. Some of these natural resources are in theory renewable (forests and water); some are non-renewable (hydrocarbons, metals and minerals). Generally, this chapter will exclude fisheries and agriculture. Fisheries involve specialized issues of international waters as distinct from national jurisdictions. Agriculture is a broad array of products, and land is the key, and immobile, resource.

Drawing on case illustrations of international extractive industries, this chapter will address the issue of whether international business activity accelerates crisis or peace. Then the chapter will investigate how multinational corporations can serve as positive change agents and corporate citizens in these conditions. Fort and Schipani (2004) present the general case for how businesses can foster more peaceful societies. They argue that businesses should promote economic development (which itself may exacerbate conflict), permit external evaluation of corporate affairs and work on building a sense of community in host areas. We know relatively little yet about the practice of multinational companies working as peace builders to engage host communities through conflict resolution efforts (Ralph and Tyler, 2006). A growing literature addresses the mediation role in conflict resolution (Jones, 2003; Ramarajan *et al.*, 2002; Schroeter and Vyrastekova, 2003). But there is some evidence to suggest that mediation tactics are not the important issue (Mareshal, 2005). We might expect an evolutionary process along the lines of what Mirvis and Googins (2006) characterize as stages of corporate citizenship. Those authors argue that the sequence of challenges encountered by a firm determines the specific pace of development of its citizenship perspectives and activities. The reaction of Shell to the Brent Spar incident in the North Sea and difficulties in Nigeria illustrate this evolutionary process.

The remainder of the chapter is organized as follows. The second section provides information and data about international extractive industries and their vital economic role. The third section outlines the range of conflict and violence conditions in developing countries confronting these industries. The fourth section develops a viewpoint concerning the corporate social responsibilities of such industries, with emphasis on potential roles in sustainable peace and conflict prevention activities. This viewpoint is illustrated with several case instances. The concluding section summarizes the findings and prescriptions of the chapter concerning international extractive industries.

9.2 INTERNATIONAL EXTRACTIVE INDUSTRIES

The international extractive industries are key linkages between advanced and developing societies. There are no readily available statistical data for aggregating together production and trade information for the international extractive industries as defined here. The core of the trade, however, involves fuels and mining products, for which World Trade Organization (WTO) data are available.[3] In 2005, world exports of merchandise amounted to $10.159 trillion and of commercial services to another $2.415 trillion. Merchandise comprised $7.312 trillion in manufactures and $852 billion in agricultural products (which are thus relatively minor in market value). Fuels and mining products comprised $1.748 trillion, or about 17.2 per cent of total merchandise exports. (Commercial services are greater in export value.) Fuels and mining products comprised about 67.2 per cent of exports of primary products.

The importance of such extractive exports is much more dramatic on a regional basis. For the Middle East, mining products comprised 70.9 per cent of merchandise exports (measured on a market value basis); for Africa 65.2 per cent; for the Commonwealth of Independent States (CIS) 60.1 per cent; for South and Central America 37.1 per cent. In terms of share of primary products exports, for the Middle East fuels and mining products comprised 96.9 per cent; for Africa 85.7 per cent; for the CIS 88.5 per cent; for South and Central America 58.4 per cent. It is in these regions, together with the developing countries of Asia (which includes Japan as well as China and India), that conflict and violence (other than terrorism) are most endemic. While Asia's share of its total merchandise exports was only 9.1 per cent, the share of its primary products exports was 62.1 per cent. Asia had the highest proportion of mining products as a share of total merchandise imports, at 22.9 per cent (versus a 9.1 per cent share of its exports). In general, extractive exports tend to flow from developing countries to advanced countries. For North America, 16.5 per cent of its merchandise imports are mining products; for Europe the proportion is 14.7 per cent.

9.2.1 Oil and Gas Industries

The economically most important extractive industries concern oil and natural gas. As noted earlier, these resources are already largely controlled by governments rather than private enterprises. A national oil company (NOC) is one fully owned or substantially controlled by a national government. Well-known examples include Saudi Aramco, Pemex (Mexico) and Petróleos de Venezuela. Oil-rich countries (roughly the twelve members of the Organization of the Petroleum Exporting Countries, OPEC, plus some other countries such as Russia and Mexico, which are not OPEC members) reportedly control over 90 per cent of the world's oil reserves (*Economist*, 2006).[4] Frequently, these oil-rich countries operate through NOCs. Of the world's 20 largest enterprises measured in terms of oil and gas reserves, reportedly 16 are NOCs. The other four are the privately-owned businesses Exxon Mobil, Chevron, British Petroleum and Royal Dutch Shell. While Exxon Mobil ranked in 2006 as the world's largest market capitalization at an estimated \$412 billion, in terms of reserves it was 14th (*Economist*, 2006). The thirteen larger enterprises, measured in reserves, were NOCs. Saudi Aramco in 2006 reportedly had over ten times the reserves of Exxon Mobil (*Economist*, 2006). Based on *Petroleum Intelligence Weekly* (PIW) information, the Baker Institute (2007) estimated that state monopolies were the top ten reserve holders, while the large privately-owned companies (Exxon Mobil, Royal Dutch Shell, BP and ChevronTexaco in roughly that order) had relatively larger production shares and dramatically higher returns on capital.

World proven oil and natural gas reserves are geographically distributed very unevenly – and largely in "developing" countries and Russia. In 2006 (OPEC, 2006, p. 18), about 62.2 per cent of oil reserves were in the Middle East, 10.8 per cent in Eastern Europe (especially Russia), 10.3 per cent in Latin America, 9.8 per cent in Africa (especially Nigeria). The balance (perhaps 7 per cent in total) was located in Asia and the Pacific (especially Indonesia), North America and Western Europe in that order. The Middle East had a smaller proportion of gas reserves (40 per cent) in relation to Eastern Europe (32.6 per cent), especially Russia (OPEC, 2006, p. 20).

Africa and Asia-Pacific had 7.8 per cent and 8.2 per cent respectively. The balance (perhaps 11 per cent) was located in Latin America, North America and Western Europe in that order.

9.2.2 Conflict Diamonds

World diamond production concentrates in Africa, Russia and Australia.[5] As a very rough estimate, from 1870 to 2005, the total present-day value of diamond production in the top 27 producing countries is about $285 billion, to which the estimate adds about 10 per cent illicit production, for a total value of about $315 billion.[6] The top six producers in 2005 were Congo-Zaire, Australia, Russia, South Africa, Botswana and Angola (in that order). In 2005, Southern Africa accounted for 29 per cent of production, Central Africa for 29 per cent and West Africa for 5 per cent – aggregating to about 63 per cent of the year's production. Australia accounted for 17 per cent and Russia for 16 per cent. One significant component of illicit diamond production is so-called conflict diamonds (or blood diamonds), which are mined in war zones and then sold clandestinely for war financing (Campbell, 2002). The most significant locations have been Angola, the Congo region, Ivory Coast, Liberia and Sierra Leone. The UN has taken formal recognition of the problem. The diamond industry eventually established the voluntary Kimberley Process Certification Scheme supported by the UN. The KPCS presently comprises 45 participants, including the European Community, controlling about 99.8 per cent of the world's rough diamond production.[7]

9.2.3 Deforestation

Wood production, together with population pressures, may be leading to world deforestation, especially of the tropical rainforests (Wallace, 2007). One estimate is that some 57 915 square miles of forest are destroyed by commercial activities including logging and ranching (Kuli, 2007, citing Rainforest Foundation website). A World Wildlife Fund report concluded that loss of forest habitat is reducing the endangered population of pygmy elephants found only on Borneo Island (Joshi, 2007). One approach for addressing the problem is voluntary forest certification (Meidinger *et al.*, 2003). In 2004, according to U.S. Department of Agriculture data,[8] world exports of all wood products aggregated to $65.7 billion in value (in U.S. dollars). Of this value, the top three exporters (excluding intra-EU trade) were Canada ($17.3 billion, or 26.3 per cent), the EU-25 ($10.4 billion, or 15.8 per cent), and the U.S. ($6.2 billion, or 9.4 per cent). The next largest seven exporters in terms of dollar value were China, Russia, Malaysia,

Indonesia, Brazil, Chile and New Zealand. Important tropical rainforests are located in Southeast Asia and Brazil. For hardwood logs, of $2.1 billion in export value, the U.S. ranked first ($603 million, or 28.7 per cent) and Malaysia second ($525 million, or 25 per cent), followed by Russia ($483 million, or 23 per cent).

9.3   HOST COUNTRY CONDITIONS

International extractive industries play particularly important roles in developing countries, where important natural resources are located. The host countries are sometimes afflicted by bribery, crisis and governmental incapacity, as well as conflict, violence and sometimes terrorism. There are two key reasons for addressing the responsibility and citizenship obligations of MNEs engaged in international extractive industries.

One reason is that extraction, by its very nature, involves marked alteration of the natural ecology and society. Even if more difficult conditions are not present, extraction alone is likely to generate social conflict. Oil operations in Sudan occur in the middle of a long-term civil war between the Arab population in the north and the black population in the south. Darfur, the region of Sudan on the border with Chad, is now widely known for the refugee population residing there. A particular problem is that natural resources sometimes are located in areas occupied by indigenous populations. Peruvian indigenous leaders visited Houston to request that ConocoPhillips not drill in their forest areas (Fowler, 2006). Occidental Petroleum earlier in the same month of December 2006 had announced that it was giving up its long-standing oil concessions in the region. It has been noted that much of the world's tropical hardwoods occur in geographically remote areas in which reside indigenous populations (Klare, 2001, p. 193).

The second reason is that extraction often occurs in developing countries where bribery, conflict, crisis and terrorism are widespread (Amman and Duraiappah, 2001; Mazzuca and Robinson, 2006). Examples are Chad and Sudan, which share a border in Africa. There has been a recent spate of kidnappings of foreign oil workers in Nigeria. There have been bribery prosecutions involving multinational enterprises operating in Kazakhstan and the Lesotho highlands water development project.

Sustainable development with a growing world population will unavoidably place greater pressures on host communities and responsibilities for corporate citizenship on international business operations. Extractive industries are often at the forefront of this constellation of environmental and social issues. Bribery, conflict, crisis, and terrorism occur in different communities in different forms (Chua, 2003). There may or may not be a "clash of civilizations" (Huntington, 1993, 1996), but there appears to be evidence of rising international anarchy (Kaplan, 1994, 2000).[9] Klare (2001, p. 213) predicts that resource wars will be coming in the future – over water and other necessities (see Billon, 2005). Multinational extractive companies make large royalty payments to governments that can come under criticism (Doward, 2000).

9.3.1 Corruption

Corruption is endemic in many of the developing and transition countries in which international extractive industries operate. Transparency International's Corruption Perception Index results for 2006 include 163 countries, including advanced as well as developing and transition countries.[10] The index ranges from a high of 10 (highly clean) to a low of 0 (highly corrupt). The three cleanest countries were Finland, Iceland and New Zealand, at the 9.6 level (ignoring confidence ranges). The most corrupt countries reported were Haiti, ranked 163 at 1.8 and Myanmar, ranked 160 at 1.9 (scores reported as well for Iraq and Guinea). Among OPEC members, UAE ranked 31 (at 6.2) and Qatar 32 (at 6.0), both above Italy at 45 (at 4.9), while Kuwait was 46 (at 4.8). Some countries share rankings – the Czech Republic and Lithuania also rank at 46. Most OPEC members ranked even worse. Saudi Arabia at 70 (3.3) ranked on a par with Mexico and Brazil, China and India. Indonesia ranked 130 (at 2.4), Venezuela 138 (at 2.3), and Nigeria 142 (at 2.2). Among diamond-producing countries, Botswana ranked 37 (at 5.6), South Africa 51 (at 4.6), Namibia 55 (at 4.1), the Congo Republic and Sierra Leone 142 (at 2.2), Ivory Coast 151 (at 2.1) and the Democratic Republic of the Congo 156 (at 2.0). Russia, a major exporter of fuel sources, diamonds and forest products, ranked 121 (at 2.5).

9.3.2 Social Inequity and Poverty

Population distribution does not correspond particularly to geographic distribution of natural resources. Consider as an example the mismatch between energy resources and population. The world's population in 2005 was estimated at just below 6.5 billion according to UN data (UN, Economic and Social Affairs, 2005). The two largest countries are China at 1.3 billion and India at 1.1 billion – together about 37 per cent of world population. The U.S. must import much of its resources. The U.S. is third largest at 298 million, and with immigration still growing, is heading toward 395 million in 2050. Indonesia is next largest at 222 million, followed by Brazil at 186 million, Pakistan at 160 million, Russia at 143 million, Bangladesh at 142 million, Nigeria at 132 million, Japan at 128 million and Mexico at 107 million. The next largest country, the Philippines, has about 83 million. Some countries listed have major energy resources; others do not, and Japan must import most of its resources. Most countries in fact have relatively small populations. Iran has a population of about 69.5 million. Saudi Arabia, holding a large proportion of the world's oil, has a population of about 25 million. Assuming some decline in current fertility rates (the basis of the UN medium estimate), world population will reach an estimated figure of just under 9.1 billion in 2050.

Some countries in which international extractive industries operate are very poor. The measure reported here is gross domestic product per capita for 2005, as estimated by the UN, in current prices and US dollars. Among diamond-producing countries, the figure for the Democratic Republic of the Congo is $125, Liberia is $171 and Sierra Leone is $210. The Ivory Coast is higher at $925. Among oil-producing countries, Nigeria is $863 and Indonesia is $1263.

9.3.3 Inadequate Water and Sanitation Infrastructure

There are many developing countries where there is inadequate access to improved water supply, due partly to lack of infrastructure. For example, according to WTO data (using the same website address cited in note 3 earlier), in Ethiopia and Somalia less than one-third of the population has such access in the whole area. In Afghanistan and Papua New Guinea, the proportion is estimated at 39 per cent. These conditions are generally worst in parts of Africa and Asia. Rural areas are typically worse than urban areas. In Ethiopia, the worst case reported, perhaps 11 per cent of the rural population has access; the proportion for Romania, the next worst case reported, is 16 per cent. UN Secretary-General Kofi Annan reported in 2003 that one in six persons (something over one billion people) lacks regular access to safe drinking water and double that number (about 2.4 billion people) lack access to adequate sanitation (Mayell, 2003). About one-third of the world's population faces moderate-to-high water stress conditions; the proportion facing severe water stress is 90 per cent in West Asia (Mayell, 2003). Only 2.5 per cent of the world's water is fresh and only 0.3 per cent is surface water; about 75 per cent is locked in glaciers and permanent snow cover (for the moment), while the rest is in underground aquifers (Mayell, 2003). More than 80 countries, with about 40 per cent of the world's population, face serious water shortages already (Mayell, 2003).

9.4   SUSTAINABLE PEACE AND CONFLICT PREVENTION ROLES

Schipani and Fort (2003, p. 415) identify four contributions that businesses can make to sustainable peace and conflict prevention. First, businesses can foster economic development, especially for marginalized population groups. Second, businesses can support the rule of law and external evaluation of their operations for transparency. Third, businesses can nourish a sense of community in which they are "citizens". Fourth, businesses can attempt to mediate among conflicting parties and attempt to direct those parties toward some common goal, such as business profit linked to community benefit.

9.4.1   Sustainable Peace as a Business Objective

An MNE operating in an extractive industry has three basic reasons for making sustainable peace and conflict prevention a business objective. One reason is enlightened self-interest. There may be multiple opportunities for business profit and community benefits to coincide (Margolis and Walsh, 2003). Especially in international extractive industries, MNEs ultimately have relatively limited options. Manufacturing and commercial services may be relatively footloose geographically. One may contract for materials and labor going into athletic shoes from a number of locations. The Panguna mine on Bougainville closed in the midst of civil conflict partly because copper occurs elsewhere. There are only so many locations, mostly sharing adverse conditions for business operations, for diamonds, hydrocarbons, fresh water, metals and minerals. Under these circumstances, businesses may face limited choices for exit and may have to address conditions as they are in particular locations.

A second reason is corporate social responsibility. Democracy and reform may have significant positive effects on economic growth (Persson and Tabellini, 2007). Every business (that is, its chief executive and its directors) must make a fundamental decision about identity. A business seeks to make profit only, or seeks to link profit and community benefit. That conception of community benefit must be one of broad appreciation for the interdependence of society, government and economy. Barber (1995), cited by Schipani and Fort (2003, p. 386), argues that democracy depends upon civil society. Barber regards both "Jihad" (that is, broadly parochial reactions against globalization) and "McWorld" (that is, broadly market self-interest pursued through globalization) as dangers to democracy and civil society. A business must decide whether its identity includes corporate citizenship or not. Citizenship suggests partnering with society (Adler, 2006).[11]

A third reason is good business ethics. For present purposes, ethics concerns how one treats other people. Generally, one does not harm others, lie, steal, cheat, discriminate, abuse and so forth. These rules of conduct apply to businesses just as much as (or arguably even more then) they do to individuals. A business should be a good neighbor, as well as a corporate citizenship, because neighborly conduct is the right course of action. The increasingly important debate for business ethics concerns human rights around the world and how to define those rights.

9.4.2 Evolution toward Responsibility and Citizenship

A corporation is more likely to evolve or adapt toward responsibility and citizenship through a sequence of events and experiences. Mirvis and Googins (2006) and Zadek (2004) develop somewhat different phase models of how this evolution or adaptation can work. In the final analysis, however, responsible business practices can reshape markets and then societies or communities (Zadek, 2001, 2006).

9.4.3 Illustrative Case Studies

The brief case studies below suggest a path of evolution or adaptation from business profit as a sole objective toward responsibility and citizenship definable in terms of sustainable peace and conflict prevention roles. The case studies involve, directly or tangentially, resource extraction activities by MNEs.

An initial posture is to treat host country conditions as simply undesirable constraints on the profit objective to be sidestepped as expeditiously as possible. The illustration here involves agricultural production for export. In March 2007, Chiquita Brands International – a major producer of bananas in the Americas – pleaded guilty in the U.S. federal court to charges that it had provided money to a terrorist organization in Colombia (O'Carroll, 2007). The confession was that Chiquita had paid $1.7 million to the United Self-Defense Forces of Colombia (AUC), declared a terrorist organization in September 2001 by the U.S. government. The alleged purpose of the payment was to avoid threat of action against Chiquita assets and personnel by the AUC. Chiquita agreed to pay a $25 million fine over five years. As part of the plea agreement, the U.S. government agreed not to reveal the names of eight Chiquita personnel involved in the scheme. The Colombian government indicated that it might seek extradition of the unnamed individuals for criminal prosecution. The payments had occurred from 1997 forward through Banadex, Chiquita's subsidiary in Colombia. The Organization of American States (OAS) also charged that Banadex had helped deliver weapons and ammunition to the AUC. Chiquita sold Banadex to a Colombian buyer in June 2004. Subsequently, civil lawsuits concerning the matter were filed against Chiquita seeking damages (Gold, 2007; Leonnig, 2007).

A subsequent posture is MNE corruption of the host country government or its officials. Lesotho (formerly Basutoland) is a small, landlocked country located on the eastern side of South Africa, by which it is entirely surrounded. A geographic feature is that the whole country is located at a relatively high and thus well-watered elevation. The Lesotho Highlands Water Scheme, begun in 1986, partly funded by the World Bank and other international institutions, was one of the world's largest construction projects (*Africa News*, 2006). The intention was to pipe water from the Orange River system to South Africa for its industrial needs. Water is one of the few resources available to the Basotho people of the country. More than a dozen international construction firms have been charged with bribery (*Africa News*, 2006). A lengthy trial began in 1999 (*Africa News*, 2003). The former chief executive of the water project was sentenced to 15 years in prison for receiving bribes. In 2002, a Canadian company was convicted; in 2003, a German company was convicted. French companies and an Italian company, among others, also face prosecution.

In June 2003, J. Bryan Williams, formerly a senior executive with Mobil Oil, pleaded guilty in a federal district court to two felony counts of income tax evasion on more than $7 million in unreported income (U.S. Attorney, 2003). In 1996, Mobil paid $1 billion for a share in a Kazakhstan field. Williams represented the Mobil chairman in a visit to the country. Of $41 million paid by Mobil to a New York merchant bank representing Kazakhstan, Williams received a kickback of $2 million. There was no finding that Mobil itself had knowledge or involvement. The defendant received a sentence of three years and 10 months. He had to pay a fine of $25 000 and make restitution to the IRS of $3.5 million plus penalties and interest. Williams maintained during the years 1993–2000 a secret bank account in Switzerland into which he deposited some $7 million, reflecting various bribes and on which he earned some $1 million in non-reported interest.

A subsequent position is to recognize that a business may have to engage the governmental authorities in the host country legal system. In the state of Kerala, located in southern India, a lengthy controversy erupted over operations of Coca-Cola Co. and PepsiCo, Inc. At Plachimada, Hindustan Coca-Cola Beverages Pvt. Ltd operated a bottling plant. The local community persistently sought to prevent operation and close the plant on grounds that the plant was taking its ground water. The state government intervened, arguing that Coca-Cola had failed to implement a required wastewater treatment plant (*The Hindu*, 2005b). In August 2006, the state government banned sale or manufacture following an independent research report of high levels of pesticide residue (*Wall Street Journal*, 2006). Generally the Indian courts have supported the companies (*The Hindu*, 2005a; Johnson, 2006).

Further progress would be investment to generate community benefits and sustainable peace. Farouk Shami (2007), founder of a Houston-based beauty products company (of about $400 million revenues annually and 10 000 U.S. employees) and an immigrant (1964) from Palestine, emphasized that peace requires both economic development and justice. Shami called for changes in U.S. and Israeli policies to help facilitate a more investment-friendly environment in Palestine. He indicated a desire to establish a factory in Palestine.

A subsequent posture is partnership among MNEs, international institutions and host governments for sustainable development to foster thereby sustainable peace and conflict prevention. An illustration is the Chad–Cameroon pipeline project. Chad is landlocked, with a shrinking Lake Chad. It has been wracked by invasions from Libya, military coups and refugee problems on its eastern border with Darfur (Sudan). Chad's one resource is oil, located in southern Chad at Doba. The World Bank helped fund a more than 1000-kilometer pipeline from Doba through neighboring Cameroon to that country's Atlantic coast (Esty, 2001). The production field and pipeline involve a joint venture of ExxonMobil, Petronas of Malaysia and ChevronTexaco. The pipeline, buried to minimize environmental and social impacts, runs through deserts and forests, under rivers and through areas of indigenous populations and black rhinos. Because of the corruption in Chad and Cameroon, special controls and monitoring devices were imposed so that the revenues would not be diverted to military purposes or corrupt officials. Amnesty International (2005) issued a report highly critical of the World Bank and the joint venture in terms of its conduct and impacts on Chad and Cameroon (Kemp, 2007). The chief argument of the critical report is that the arrangements effectively undermine governmental willingness and capacity to protect human rights and effectively relieve participating companies from accountability for such rights. Negative effects of the pipeline might offset positive effects. Furthermore, the Chad government itself has attempted to get more revenues from the pipeline, and will probably start its own NOC. China is now engaged in oil operations in Chad (Pearmain, 2007a, 2007b).

9.5   CONCLUSION

This chapter has assessed the potential roles of international extractive industries in promoting sustainable peace and conflict prevention in developing countries. Frequently, such countries have difficult problems of conflict, violence, corruption, poverty, injustice, governmental incapacity, and sometimes terrorism. Extractive industries most particularly must operate in adverse environments where natural resources, demanded by the advanced economies, are located. In addition to the problems noted above, such resources often occur in remote areas inhabited by indigenous population groups. This circumstance imposes special obligations on MNEs in extractive industries. MNEs should work to promote economic development in host countries on the basis of community benefit generated in connection with business profit. In addition, as argued by Schipani and Fort (2003), MNEs should attempt to foster respect for law and transparency, foster community by good citizenship and neighborly conduct, and mediate among conflicting parties to the degree possible. These approaches are, of course, more easily stated than implemented. It will, however, not prove feasible in the long run for MNEs to avoid these obligations. They come organically with the relationship between international extractive industries and host developing countries.

NOTES

1. The island of Bougainville is, with certain other neighboring islands, the autonomous North Solomons Province of Papua New Guinea (PNG). Rio Tinto partly owned (with the PNG government) and operated a copper and gold mine (subsequently abandoned) at Panguna. There was a long secession war, ended by a peace agreement creating an Autonomous Bougainville Government. In 2000, residents of Bougainville filed suit (Sarei v. Rio Tinto) in a U.S. federal district court under the Alien Tort Claims Act (ATCA) of 1789. The suit alleges complicity in war crimes, environmental impacts and racial discrimination against black workers. While the district court dismissed the suit in 2002, a U.S. court of appeals subsequently reinstated the suit (confirmed *en banc* as of April 2007). The U.S. Department of State expressed to the district court by "statement of interest" that the suit might harm the peace process on Bougainville and diplomatic relationships between Papua New Guinea and the United States. As with any other companies mentioned in this chapter, what is reported is publicly disclosed allegations on which the author takes no factual position and offers no specific opinion.
2. For example, there are reports of human rights abuses in gas-rich Turkmenistan, which inaugurated a new president in February 2007 following the natural death in November 2006 of the country's long-time dictator (Harvey, 2007).
3. www.wto.org/english/res_e/statis_e/statis_e.htm. Accessed 17 January 2008.
4. The Organization of Petroleum Exporting Countries (OPEC), established 1960, presently comprises twelve "developing" countries: Algeria, Angola, Indonesia, Iran, Iraq, Kuwait, Libya, Nigeria, Qatar, Saudi Arabia, the United Arab Emirates (UAE) and Venezuela. In 2006, OPEC estimated its proportion of world proven crude oil reserves at about 77.2 per cent (OPEC, 2006, p. 18). In 2006, OPEC estimated its proportion of world proven natural gas reserves at about 49.3 per cent (OPEC, 2006, p. 20). In 1976, OPEC created a Fund for International Development for aid assistance activities.
5. Data are taken from Janse (2007).
6. Activists critical of the Kimberley Process as a largely symbolic commitment without sufficient insight argue that 20 per cent of diamonds are controversial flows, defined in

terms of smuggling and abusive labor conditions in addition to conflict diamonds. The UN maintains a strict distinction. The flow of conflict diamonds may have been slowed to a trickle (Duke, 2006).

7. The KPCS maintains a website, www.kimberleyprocess.com, accessed 17 August 2007. The website reports statistical data on production and trade.

8. USDA, www.fas.usda.gov/ffpd/wood_products_presentations/wood_presentations.htm, for Wood Exporters.pdf. Data subsequent to 2004 are maintained by FAOSTAT, available at http://faostat.org. Both accessed 17 January 2008.

9. The scenario depicted by Kaplan has been questioned (Serwer, 1994), and the critique applies to Chua and Huntington as well.

10. www.transparency.org/layout/set/print/layout/set/print/policy_research/surveys_indices/cpi/2006, accessed 17 August 2007. Because there has been great unhappiness among developing country officials and others concerning the CPI results, in 2002, TI issued a corresponding Bribe Payers' Index (BPI). The BPI reports indices for 30 major exporting countries. Scores of the advanced countries tend to be lower than on the CPI. The top country Switzerland ranked at the 7.81 level. The UAE ranked 14 (at 6.62), again well above Italy at 20 (at 5.94). However, the bottom ranks continue to be developing and transition countries: Saudi Arabia 22 (at 5.83), Brazil 23 (at 5.65), South Africa 24 (at 5.61), Malaysia – a major wood exporter – 25 (at 5.69), Taiwan 26 (at 5.41) and Turkey 27 (at 5.23). The last three countries are (28 through 30) Russia (5.16), China (4.94) and India (4.62).

11. Dean (2003) argues that any partnership is impossible.

REFERENCES

Adler, N. J. (2006) Corporate Global Citizenship: Successfully Partnering with the World. In G. G. S. Suder (ed.), *Corporate Strategies under International Terrorism and Adversity*, Edward Elgar, Cheltenham, UK and Northampton, MA, pp. 177–195.

Africa News (2003) Lesotho: Lesotho Judge Convicts German Firm of Bribery on Water Project, Wednesday 18 June.

Africa News (2006) Lesotho; Lesotho Corruption Case a Watershed, Monday 11 September.

Amman, H. M. and Duraiappah, A. (2001) *Land Tenure and Conflict Resolution: A Game Theoretic Approach in the Narok District in Kenya*, CREED Working Paper No. 37 (May), http://ssrn.com/abstract=279170. Accessed 17 January 2008.

Amnesty International UK (2005) *Contracting Out of Human Rights: The Chad-Cameroon Pipeline Project*. Amnesty International UK, London, September.

Baker Institute Energy Forum (2007) The Changing Role of National Oil Companies in International Energy Markets. www.rice.edu/energy/research/nationaloil/index.html. Accessed 18 August 2007.

Barber, B. R. (1995) *Jihad vs. McWorld: How Globalization and Tribalism Are Reshaping the World*, Time Books (Random House), New York.

Billon, Philippe Le (2005) *Fuelling War: Natural Resources and Armed Conflicts*. Routledge for the International Institute for Strategic Studies, Abingdon and New York.

Campbell, G. (2002) *Blood Diamonds: Tracing the Deadly Path of the World's Most Precious Stones*, Westview Press, Boulder CO.

Chua, A. (2003) *World on Fire: How Exporting Free Market Democracy Breeds Ethnic Hatred and Global Instability*, Doubleday, New York.

Dean, K. (2003) *Capitalism and Citizenship: The Impossible Partnership*, Routledge, London and New York.

Doward, J. (2000) Mineral Riches Fuel War. Not the Poor, *The Observer*, 18 June, Business Pages, p. 4, http://www.guardian.co.uk/business/2000/jun/18/the observer.observerbusiness 6.

Duke, L. (2006) Blood Diamonds: Stream or Drop? The numbers Given for Stones off the Market also in Conflict, *Houston Chronicle*, **106**(79), Sunday 31 December, E5 (Outlook).

Economist (2006) National Oil Companies: Really Big Oil – Sluggish behemoths Control Virtually all the World's Oil; They Should be Privatised. 10 August www.economist.com/opinion/displaystory.cfm?story_id=7276986. Accessed 17 January 2008.

Esty, B. C. (2001) *The Chad-Cameroon Petroleum Development and Pipeline Project (A and B)*, Harvard Business School Cases, 9-202-010 and 9-202-012.

Fort, T. L. and Schipani, C. A. (2004) *The Role of Business in Fostering Peaceful Societies*, Cambridge University Press, New York.

Fowler, T. (2006) Thanks but No Thanks: Indigenous Leaders Come to Houston to Request that ConocoPhillips not Drill in their Areas of Peru, *Houston Chronicle*, **106**(67), Tuesday 19 December, D1, D6 (Business).

Gold, J. (2007) *Lawsuit Accuses Chiquita of Funding Terrorism Groups*, Associated Press Worldstream, 19 July, International News.

Harvey, B. (2007) A Tale of Terror in Turkmenistan: Resident Reveals an Array of Human Rights Abuses in Gas-Rich Nation, *Houston Chronicle*, **106**(135), Sunday 25 February, A27.

The Hindu (2005a) Coca-Cola Case: Kerala Moves Supreme Court, 15 September.

The Hindu (2005b) Coke Plant Will Not Be Allowed to Function, 25 October.

Huntington, S. P. (1993) The Clash of Civilizations? *Foreign Affairs*, **72**(3) Summer, 22–49.

Huntington, S. P. (1996) *The Clash of Civilizations and the Remaking of World Order*, Simon and Schuster, New York.

Janse, A. J. A. (2007) Global Rough Diamond Production from 1870 to 2005, *Gems and Gemology* **43**(2), Summer, pp. 98–119.

Johnson, J. (2006) Kerala lifts Pepsi and Coke Drinks Ban, *Financial Times* (London), Saturday 23 September, Edition 1, Asia-Pacific, 7.

Jones, G. T. (2003) *Toward an Integrated Practice of Behavioral Conflict Management*, http://ssrn.com/abstract=399622.

Joshi, V. (2007) Logging Threatens Pygmy Elephants: Satellite Tracking Shows the Loss of Habitat has Led to Drop in Numbers in Malaysian Forests, *Houston Chronicle*, **106**(300), Thursday 9 August, A12.

Kaplan, R. D. (1994) The Coming Anarchy: How Scarcity, Crime, Overpopulation, Tribalism, and Disease Are Rapidly Destroying the Social Fabric of Our Planet, *Atlantic Monthly*, February, pp. 44–75.

Kaplan, R. D. (2000) *The Coming Anarchy: Shattering the Dreams of the Post Cold War*, Random House, New York.

Kemp, P. (2007) Exxon Rapped on Chad-Cameroon Pipeline, *International Oil Daily*, 25 July, Feature Stories.

Klare, M. T. (2001) *Resource Wars: The New Landscape of Global Conflict*, Metropolitan Books (Henry Holt and Co.), New York.

Kuli, A. (2007) Peru Moves to Protect its Forests: Nation Marks off Areas to Combat Illegal Logging, *Houston Chronicle*, **106**(301), Friday 10 August, D6 (Business).

Leonnig, C. D. (2007) In Terrorism-Law Case, Chiquita Points to U.S.; Firm Says It Awaited Justice Dept. Advice, *Washington Post*, Thursday 2 August, Met 2 Edition, A01 (A-Section).

Mareshal, P. M. (2005) What Makes Mediation Work? Mediators' Perspectives on Resolving Disputes, *Industrial Relations*, **44**(3) July, 509–517.

Margolis, J. D. and Walsh, J. P. (2003) Misery Loves Companies: Rethinking Social Initiatives by Business, *Administrative Science Quarterly*, **48**(2) June, 268–305.

Mayell, H. (2003) UN Highlights World Water Crisis, *National Geographic News*, 5 June, http://news.nationalgeographic.com/news/2003/06/0605_030605_water crisis.html. Accessed 17 January 2008.

Mazzuca, S. and Robinson, J. A. (2006) *Political Conflict and Power-Sharing in the Origins of Modern Colombia*, Centre for Economic Policy Research Discussion Paper No. 5606 (April), http://ssrn.com/abstract=913053. Accessed 17 January 2008.

Meidinger, E., Elliott, C. and Oesten, G., eds (2003) *Social and Political Dimensions of Forest Certification*, Remagen-Oberwinter, Kessel.

Mirvis, P. and Googins, B. (2006) Stages of Corporate Citizenship, *California Management Review*, **48**(2) Winter, 104–126.

O'Carroll, E. (2007) Colombia Seeks Eight in Chiquita Terrorist Scandal: The Banana Conglomerate has Confessed to Paying Right-Wing Paramilitaries, *Christian Science Monitor*, 22 March, www.csmonitor.com/2007/0322/p99s01-duts.html.

Organization of the Petroleum Exporting Countries (OPEC) (2006) *Annual Statistical Bulletin*, OPEC, Vienna.

Pearmain, T. (2007a) Chad Signs New Hydrocarbons Law; Aims to Launch NOC in 2007, World Markets Research Centre, *Global Insight*, Main Story, 25 July.

Pearmain, T. (2007b) China Strikes Oil in Chad; Five Percent Committee Disbanded, World Markets Research Centre, *Global Insight*, Main Story, 31 July.

Persson, T. and Tabellini, G. (2007) *The Growth Effect of Democracy: Is it Heterogeneous and how can it be Estimated?* Center for Economic Studies and Ifo Institute for Economic Research (CESifo) Working Paper Series No. 2016, http://ssrn.com/abstract=994810. Accessed 17 January 2008.

Ralph, N. and Tyler, M. C. (2006) *Companies as Peacebuilders: Engaging Communities Through Conflict Resolution*, University of Melbourne Legal Studies Research Paper No. 196, http://ssrn.com/abstract=946849. Accessed 17 January 2008.

Ramarajan, L., Bezrukova, K., Jehn, K. A., Euwema, M. and Kop, N. (2002) *Successful Conflict Resolution Between Peacekeepers and NGOs: The Role of Training and Preparation in International Peacekeeping in Bosnia*, http://ssrn.com/abstract=305206. Accessed 17 January 2008.

Schipani, C. A. and Fort, T. L. (2003) Adapting Corporate Governance for Sustainable Peace, *Vanderbilt Journal of Transnational Law*, **36**, March, 377–426.

Schroeter, K. and Vyrastekova, J. (2003) *Does it Take Three to Make Two Happy? An Experimental Study on Bargaining with Mediation*, CentER Discussion Paper No. 2003-60, http://ssrn.com/abstract=556088. Accessed 17 January 2008.

Serwer, A. E. (1994) The End of the World is Nigh – Or Is It? *Fortune*, **129**(9), 2 May, 123–124.

Shami, F. (2007) Let's Show that we Mean Business with Palestine: Break Through Restrictions that Hold Back Prosperity, *Houston Chronicle*, **106**(309), Saturday 18 August, B9 (City and State).

UN, Economic and Social Affairs, Population Division (2005) *World Population Prospects: The 2004 Revision: Highlights*, ESA/P/WP.193, www.un.org/esa/population/publications/WPP2004/2004Highlights_finalrevised.pdf.   Accessed 17 January 2008.

U.S. Attorney, Southern District of New York (2003) *Former Mobil Executive Sentenced on Tax Evasion Charges in Connection with Kazakhstan Oil Transactions*, Public Information Office, 17 September, www.usdoj.gov/usao/nys/pressreleases/September 03/williamsjbryansentencingpr.pdf. Accessed 17 January 2008.

Wall Street Journal (2006) World Watch – Asia/Pacific: Indian State Bans Sale or Manufacture of Coke, Pepsi Sodas, Thursday 10 August, Section A, Column 1, 5.

Wallace, S. (2007) Last of the Amazon, *National Geographic*, **211**(1) January, 40–71.

Zadek, S. (2001) *The Civil Corporation*, Earthscan, London.

Zadek, S. (2004) The Path to Corporate Responsibility, *Harvard Business Review*, **82**(12) December, 125–132.

Zadek, S. (2006) Responsible Competitiveness: Reshaping Global Markets Through Responsible Business Practices, *Corporate Governance* (Bradford), **6**(4), 334–348.

PART IV

The big picture – tool kits

10. Sustainable enterprise and sustainable futures

Malcolm McIntosh

This chapter argues that it is time for the corporate social responsibility (CSR) movement to assess its successes over the last decade and more, and now to move on. The imperative of rapid adaptation to the global scientific consensus on climate change, the implementation of internationally agreed sustainable development policy and the delivery of the Millennium Development Goals, not forgetting terrorism, mean that all our economic institutions, not just corporations, must step up to the mark and seize the challenges and opportunities that are presented for humanity in the twenty-first century. Hence the call for "Sustainable Enterprise and Sustainable Futures".

10.1 A NEW CAPITALISM: SUSTAINABLE ENTERPRISE

Stuart Hart is among many when he says that "Capitalism [is] At The Crossroads" (Hart: 2005). Some political, business and civil society leaders have recognised this and are attempting to operate within a new paradigm, while other leaders are deliberately capitalising on tensions, inequities and global governance gaps to abuse the Earth's resources and profit from social inequity.

It can be argued that the corporate social responsibility movement has been an attempt to bring the current model of capitalism, and its progeny the global corporation, down to earth and realign the creation of value with the sustenance of sustainable values. There is no necessary linkage between sustainable *value* and sustainable *values*, but that is where a new model of capitalism must be heading if the world is to face the challenges of climate change, sustainable development, terrorism and the Millennium Development Goals. The emerging human security agenda provides a transdisciplinary framework which brings together disparate components of the global social development project. In 2003 the UN Commission on

Human Security argued that the world needed "a new security framework that centers directly on people". Human security, they argued, "focuses on shielding people from critical and pervasive threats and empowering them to take charge of their lives". The Commission sought to develop a global framework focussed on "survival, dignity and livelihood; freedom from fear; and freedom from want". A 1994 UN Development Programme Report had said: "For most people today a feeling of insecurity arises more from worries about daily life than the dread of a cataclysmic world event. Job security, income security, health security, environmental security, and security from crime – these are emerging concerns of human security all over the world".

Sadako Ogata and Amartya Sen argued in their 2003 report on human security, *Human Security Now*, that "existing institutions and policies [are] unable to cope with weakening multilateralism and global responsibilities . . . the state has the primary responsibility for security, but the security challenge is complex and various new actors attempt to play a role . . . so we need a shift in paradigm". That new shift in paradigm means global corporations and all enterprises accepting their social, political and economic responsibilities. In 1998 and 2003 we argued that if CSR meant anything it was a call for all enterprises to know themselves: to be able to articulate their role, scope and purpose to the wider world (McIntosh *et al.*, 1998, 2003).

So it is that the growing human security agenda offers an integrated view of social development and provides a framework for local communities and global society to recognise the imperatives, challenges and opportunities that the global scientific consensus on climate change presents, that enables the implementation of internationally agreed sustainable development policy and leads towards the delivery of the Millennium Development Goals.

Sustainable enterprise is the next step for the CSR movement and should be at the heart of the human security agenda. If enterprise, in all its shapes and forms, can adopt sustainability as its template then we have a new capitalism, one geared to making life on earth not only a quality objective for all humans but perhaps enabling humans to continue to live on planet home.

The new sustainable capitalism gears production, consumption and efficiency to finding innovative and profitable solutions to issues of clean energy, the conservation of biological resources, increasing transparency and accountability of organisations, and decision making and finding leaders for the common good. The divorced, dispassionate, amoral third party investor will become a thing of the past as investors in whatever form they come are connected, accountable, knowledgeable and transparent in their financial dealings.

The new economy of sustainable enterprise is not just about business. It is inclusive of all enterprise and organisations because the challenge is for all institutions to change the way they relate to local and global environmental and social issues. This means government departments rethinking the way they work, community organisations and local government reorganising themselves, global corporations aligning their mission, purpose and practices with the realities of climate change and sustainable development and individuals making this happen by actively participating in the change.

Over the years, capitalism has adapted to social change and environmental resource restraints and there is no doubt that the great leap that is now necessary is possible, plausible and necessary. At various points in the past, accountability and governance checks have been introduced to enable society to oversee and regulate all manner of social institutions from the global corporate to the community charity.

In the late twentieth century and early twenty-first, a number of specific initiatives have compelled private and public enterprises to move from the back to the front foot on issues of eco-efficiency, human rights, accountability, stakeholder communication and understanding relatively complicated systems such as global supply chains. Some leaders may have taken on board the concept of accounting for sustainability, where financial profitability, ecological integrity and social equity are balanced, but the transition has not been made by society as a whole as to how we might make all enterprise account in an integrated manner for its various impacts. We are on the way but there is much work to be done. For example, in September 2000 the UN adopted the Millennium Development Goals (MDGs), which commit member states to collectively achieving significant improvements in a range of social and environmental target areas. The year before, in 1999, the UN launched the Global Compact (UNGC), which asked enterprises to commit to implementing nine, and later ten, principles on human rights, labour standards, environmental protection and anticorruption. The sustainable enterprise economy marries goals such as the MDGs with principles such as those in the UN Global Compact. This synergistic action makes all enterprises mindful of, and bound to be part of, the delivery of sustainable development through the incorporation of internationally agreed principles on social and environmental issues.

To date the evidence is that most large global corporations understand the imperative but do not know how to deliver it. Most CEOs know that in order to deliver on their commitment to such sets of principles they must re-manage their supply chains, promote human rights and incorporate better governance mechanisms, but they are still tending to rely on traditional media spin and counter-bluff to ward off their critics.

The development of the sustainable enterprise economy puts all enterprise on the same footing. The issues that confront global corporations confront all organisations and all of us individually.

First came environmental management, then came the incorporation of social issues into the corporate citizenship agenda. The last few years have seen a wide range of enterprises adopting new management systems and becoming signatories to an increasing number of sets of sustainability principles, agreements and initiatives. The sustainable enterprise economy is the next step, or second generation sustainability, which puts all enterprise on the same footing.

In envisioning the sustainable enterprise economy it is useful to recognise that there is a great deal of new or changed practice around the world that shows the way forward and how we might proceed. The power of positive change often comes from seeing the future in action and at this time of great change and uncertainty we need first to recognise the challenge and then articulate the opportunities for new enterprise, for new business, for new ways of living, for new wealth creation and for tackling head on the climate change prognosis and the current inequitable economic system. The sustainable enterprise economy is a way forward.

10.2   THE CSR MOVEMENT

How far has the corporate social responsibility and corporate citizenship movement traveled in the last decade or so? The transition to a sustainable enterprise economy will build on the work that some business, government and civil leaders have been engaged in around the world. There is much to be celebrated; there are many examples of positive change and there are many models of "what works". But, first it is necessary to see how we got to this place in the CSR movement.

The period from 1995 to 2005 has been significant for corporate social responsibility. 1995 was Shell's *annus horribilis*, involving its debacle over the disposal of the Brent Spar oil rig in the North Sea and its implication in the death of Ken Saro-Wiwa, a Nigerian human rights activist who was murdered by his government for protesting about the distribution of revenues from what was perceived to be Shell's damaging extraction of oil from the Ogoni region of Nigeria. The following decade saw the flowering of the Global Reporting Initiative, out of the CERES Principles, the development of SA8000, the birth of AccountAbility and AA1000S out of the Institute for Social and Ethical Accountability, and the first five years of the UN Global Compact.

Most pertinent to this is the ongoing debate concerning the links between business profitability and global social progress. While the business benefits of corporate social responsibility (CSR) is a topic much debated and written about, it needs to be reiterated over and over again that business operates for the benefit of society, not vice versa. There can never be a sole business benefit to CSR, only ever a social and ecological benefit. If a minority gains net material wealth in the short term at the gross expense of society and the planet in the short, medium or long term, what benefit is that? The only reason to argue the case for the business benefits of CSR is to make the case for business being more socially and ecologically responsible if we are to create a more just and equitable world that uses and shares resources for the benefit of this and future generations.

While good progress has been made on a number of corporate responsibility initiatives over the last decade, they have not been as successful as they might have been because we have failed to understand that in the modern global corporation we have created a being over which we have less control than we would like to think. It is recognised that many of its agents (who work within its portals) have the best of intentions, but, because the corporation itself has a life of its own, they have less control than is sometimes recognised. The current rules of incorporation tend to steer the organisation away from necessarily delivering social progress and protecting our planetary home. Here, then, in this chapter, is a prescription for the profitable, human-scale sustainable enterprise that operates in tune with social progress and in harmony with planetary boundaries by connecting with all stakeholders.

The corporate social responsibility agenda has been described as "a desire and a necessity to humanize the globalization process; to build social and environmental pillars in the global temple of commerce" (McIntosh *et al.*, 2004, p. 13). John Ruggie, former Assistant Secretary-General of the UN and now Director of the Centre for Business and Government at Harvard University and, since 2005, special adviser to the UN Secretary-General on CSR, has pointed out that "Business created the single global economic space; business can and must help sustain it. And corporate social responsibility offers one viable and vital approach" (Ruggie, 2004, p. 41).

The CSR movement has been resurgent over the last ten years and multi-stakeholder engagement between business, government and civil society has resulted in a significant number of global voluntary corporate citizenship initiatives. Non-governmental public action, or civil society activism, has been at the heart of the development of a number of these initiatives. The field of corporate social responsibility and corporate citizenship has developed significantly (Andriof and McIntosh, 2001; Waddock, 2002). There are those who argue that voluntary mechanisms have replaced or prevented regulatory initiatives and therefore set back real corporate responsibility. Examples of significant global voluntary corporate citizenship initiatives include ethical workplace management systems certification (SA8000), sustainability management systems assurance (AA1000S), learning platforms based on international conventions on human rights, labor standards, environmental protection and anti-corruption (UN Global Compact), and the standardisation of reporting on corporate financial, social and environmental reporting (Global Reporting Initiative). These have been referred to as four of the "Global Eight" (McIntosh, 2003; pp. 86–123).

10.3   CAPITALISM AND SOCIAL PROGRESS?

The promise of the CSR rhetoric is that it will civilise corporate behavior so that there is an alignment between capitalism and social progress. While recognising that some companies were making great efforts in this direction, UN Secretary-General Kofi Annan also said when addressing global business leaders meeting in New York in July 2004 to discuss progress on the UN Global Compact: "Symbolism is good, but substance is even better" (Annan, 2004).

In September 2004, the World Bank issued a report on just this issue which said:

> The growing integration of societies and economies has helped reduce poverty in many countries. Between 1990 and 2000 the number of people living on less than $1 a day declined by about 137 million. Although global integration is a powerful force in reducing poverty, more needs to be done, and 2 billion people are in danger of becoming marginal to the world economy.

So, some progress is being made, perhaps because of new global corporate citizenship initiatives like the UN Global Compact, which asks companies to: "embrace, support and enact, within their sphere of influence, a set of core values in the areas of human rights, labour standards, the environment, and anti-corruption" (UN Global Compact, n.d.).

10.4   CHANGE ISSUES

But is the CSR movement asking companies to lead social change on social and environmental issues? Recent research on behavior change in the UK related to sustainable development published by the UK Government shows an alarming failure to educate people on these issues. In 2006 only one-third of the UK population had heard of sustainable development, and only 8 per cent were able or willing to explain it. If companies are being called upon to embed, for instance, the ten principles of the UN Global Compact on human rights, labor standards and environmental protection in their workforce, are we asking them to do what government has failed to do across wider society? (DEFRA UK, 2005). Similar findings can be found across Europe.

So how is business progressing on these issues? According to the international Association of Certified Chartered Accountants (ACCA) in September 2004:

> Businesses worldwide are failing to produce enough sustainability reports, while governments are doing little to encourage such reporting. There are still only 1,500 to 2,000 companies producing reports worldwide. The majority of companies still have to recognise the business case for reporting and starting to engage their stakeholders. (ACCA, 2004)

In July 2007 the total number of global signatories to the UN Global Compact was just 4000. Perhaps this is because the challenge of sustainable development, human rights and labor standards are not uppermost in the minds of CEOs? Also in September 2004, the US Conference Board reported that a global survey of CEOs showed that they had four challenges, none of which included the CSR agenda. They were: sustained growth; speed, flexibility, adaptability to change; customer loyalty and retention; and stimulating innovation and creativity, and enabling entrepreneurship (www.conference-board.org).

A clear differentiation occurs between those companies that are proactive on CSR and others. The proactive groups have tended, until this point, to be global and have similar characteristics. The exception to this is a proportion of the UN Global Compact signatory companies, 60 per cent of which now come from non-OECD countries and are not the usual supporters of CSR initiatives. But apart from the proactive group there are three other groups of corporate "citizens": those from the informal and illegal sectors that actively avoid paying taxes, compliance and incorporation; the vast majority of the SME sector, which try hard to comply with the law and establish good relations with their local customers; and then there is a group of discretionary companies that are in compliance with all aspects of the law but have also chosen to be proactive in one or more areas of CSR, such as the environment or human rights (McIntosh *et al.*, 2004). These categories are not necessarily exclusive and there are some companies that have been radically proactive on CSR issues, such as Enron, Parmalat and Shell, which have subsequently been found wanting on issues of transparency and integrity in the boardroom.

It is this lack of integration and contextualization that is most worrying. First, some companies are happy to perform on human rights while forgetting their environmental impact, and second, where is the specific (and solid research) linkage between CSR initiatives such as the UN Global Compact and social development platforms such as the MDGs? Economist Kenneth Galbraith said in 1978: "Nothing disguises the reality of economic life more than that there is a single theory of the firm . . . There is also confusion between the market and the corporation, they are not the same . . . they are all parts of the political economy" (Galbraith and Salinger 1978, p. 37). More recently, in 2004, Klaus Leisinger from the Novartis Foundation, when writing of the links between business and human rights, said that it was:

> a feature of modern society to differentiate into a variety of functionally specialized subsystems, such as economy, law, politics, religion, science, and education . . . The quality of cooperation of the different subsystems determines the degree of possible synergies and allows for the whole (society) being more than the sum of its parts (subsystems). (Leisinger, 2004)

10.5   THE NEW RESPONSIBILITY AGENDA?

To summarise: we need human-scale organisations, that have at their heart planetary imperatives; that are servant leaders (where the corporation serves society rather than vice versa); that marry sustainable value *and* sustainable values; that put integrity and trust, as described earlier, at the heart of the decision-making processes. This means that instrumentally there needs to be a greater emphasis on accountability and assurance, and a rewriting of the rules of incorporation; but first there must be an emphasis on learning and education in business and across society as a whole. As Nobel Prize winner Amartya Sen says: "To build a country first build a school" (Sen, 2004). The same applies to our global corporations.

The sustainable human-scale corporation is founded on specific conditions: low ecological footprint, enhanced social equity and extended sense of futurity. Sustainable incorporation therefore involves long-term life and appropriate size (rather than immortality and unlimited size), and a balance of power between (and accountability to) a range of stakeholders. We must be aware that currently we fail to see the corporation in the whole, which means that very often one hand of the corporation takes away what the other promises. As President Lula of Brazil said at the UN Global Compact Leaders Summit in New York on 24 June 2004: "Business must refrain from taking away by its lobbying activities what it offers through corporate responsibility and philanthropy" (Lula, 2004).

10.6 THE SUSTAINABLE ENTERPRISE ECONOMY

Sustainable enterprise, like sustainable development and corporate citizenship, is a contested term. In this chapter the term sustainable enterprise is used more inclusively than in other contents, where it only refers to business, particularly in business and management literature in the USA. In this chapter, and in our use of the term, a sustainable enterprise economy is an economy where *any* enterprise – corporate, social or individual – aims to have as little impact on the environment as possible and is mindful of its social impact. In an enterprise economy the spirit of the community is geared to innovation, creativity, problem solving, entrepreneurialism and enthusiasm for life. A sustainable enterprise economy produces wealth, preserves the natural environmental and nurtures social capital. The sustainable enterprise economy recognises that the greatest threat to human security comes from our ability (or *in*ability) to tackle climate change and to bring about sustainable development. All enterprises have a part to play, but our largest organisations and economic institutions have a greater responsibility to accept the challenge and seize the opportunities.

Enterprise, innovation and creativity, like conversation, caring and sharing, are part of what it means to be human, and this century needs to recognise and reward these human characteristics more than any before if we are to make the transition to a sustainable future on earth.

The sustainable enterprise economy creates wealth for people and communities in terms of financial prosperity, ecological integrity and social equity. Financial prosperity must satisfy the conditions of observing ecological integrity and increasing social equity, while ensuring that all enterprises are financially sound. The sustainable enterprise economy includes private, public and civil society, and social enterprise. It is based on the benefits of collectivism and wealth creation, whether organised publicly or privately. A sustainable enterprise economy also recognises that individuals, communities and investors must gain from the fruits of their labors.

Bringing together the principles of sustainable development, which include eco-efficiency and social justice, with the principle of allowing enterprise and innovation to blossom, provides the best possible milieu for a wholly new model of capitalism to be born out of the current wasteful and inequitable model of wealth creation.

The sustainable enterprise economy requires a better understanding of complex dynamics and systems, particularly fragile earth eco-systems, but also an increasingly continuously connected and boundary-less social world. Both transcend traditional territorial boundaries and established institutional social mechanisms. Our current way of thinking and seeing the world has created global warming and global terrorism. We must now use our new-found knowledge to create a paradigm shift to a more equitable global socio-ecological situation.

In the transition to new systems thinking we need to recognise new models that make the difference, build new policies that make the change, and develop strategies to make the new reality come alive. One of the greatest challenges is not that we may recognise that this change in our attitude to life on earth is necessary but that we will find it impossible to take collective responsibility for the common good. In a multi-polar world of competing stakeholder interests, who will stand for people and planet above all else? Vested interest groups will naturally tend to work for their own interests, even while acknowledging the common good. New constitutions, arrangements and governance systems that recognise this hard reality will prove the success of the new sustainable enterprise economy.

Is it possible to nurture different interests (private, public and civil society, social and individual) within a sustainable enterprise economy while also creating clear, stable and transparent mechanisms that force different entities to work seamlessly together for the common good in partnerships and other social arrangements?

ACKNOWLEDGEMENTS

This chapter develops ideas from two sources: McIntosh (2007) and Roundtables on Sustainable Enterprise held in London, Cape Town, Toronto, Brussels and Geneva in 2007 which culminated in a conference *A Conversation About The Future: Sustainable Enterprise*, with The Eden Project, Boston College and the UN Global Compact in October 2007.

REFERENCES

ACCA (2004) *Towards Transparency: Progress on Global Sustainability Reporting*. 9 September. www.accaglobal.com/pdfs/environment/towards_trans_2004_pdf, accessed 17 January 2008.

Andriof, J. and McIntosh, M. (eds) (2001) *Perspectives On Corporate Citizenship*. Sheffield: Greenleaf .

Annan, K. (2004) *UN Secretary-General's Address to Global Compact Leaders Summit* 24 June, UN, New York.

DEFRA UK (2005) www.sustainable-development.gov.uk/taking-it-on/background.

Galbraith, J.K. and Salinger, N. (1978) *Almost Everyone's Guide to Economics*. New York: Bantam.

Global Reporting Initiative (2007). www.globalreporting.org, accessed 17 January 2008.

Hart, S. (2005) *Capitalism At The Crossroads*. Philadelphia, PA: Wharton Publishing.

Leisinger, K. (2004) "Business and Human Rights" referring to Niklas Luhmann, in McIntosh, Malcolm, Waddock, Sandra and Kell, Georg (eds) *Learning to Talk: Corporate Citizenship and the Development of the UN Global Compact.* Sheffield: Greenleaf, pp. 72–100.

Lula, L.I. (2004) *Speech to UN Global Compact Leaders Summit*, UN, New York, 24 July 2004.

McIntosh, M. (2003) *Raising a Ladder to the Moon: The Complexities of Corporate Social Responsibility.* London: Routledge.

McIntosh, M. (2007) *Progressing from Corporate Social Responsibility to Brand Integrity*, in May, S.K., Cheney, G. and Roper, J. (eds) *The Debate over Corporate Social Responsibility.* Oxford: Oxford University Press.

McIntosh, M., Leipziger, D., Jones, K. and Coleman, G. (1998) *Corporate Citizenship.* London: FT Pitman.

McIntosh, M., Thomas, R., Leipziger, D. and Coleman, G. (2003) *Living Corporate Citizenship.* London: FT Pitman.

McIntosh, M., Waddock, S. and Kell, G. (eds) (2004) *Learning to Talk: Corporate Citizenship and the Development of the UN Global Compact.* Sheffield: Greenleaf.

Ogata, S. and Sen, A. (2003) *Human Security Now.* New York: Commission On Human Security.

Ruggie, J. (2004). The Theory and Practice of Learning Networks, in McIntosh, M., Waddock, S. and Kell, G. (eds) *Learning to Talk: Corporate Citizenship and the Development of the UN Global Compact.* Sheffield: Greenleaf.

Sen, A. (2004) *Time for School.* www.pbs.org/wnet/wideangle/shows/school/ transcript.html.

UN Global Compact (n.d.) The Ten Principles. www.globalcompact.org/About TheGC/TheTen Principles/index.html, accessed 17 January 2008.

UN Development Programme (1994) www.undp.org/reports/global/1994

Waddock, S. (2002) *Leading Corporate Citizens.* Boston MA: McGraw-Hill Irwin.

11. Corporate social responsibility as a new orientation in response to crisis management of sea changes and navigational dead reckoning

Ihsen Ketata and John R. McIntyre

11.1 INTRODUCTION

Given the characteristics of the 21st century, with terrorist attacks a tangible reality at any time in heretofore relatively immune geographic areas, climate change as a multi-level threat, and business corruption increasingly a common occurrence, international business is struggling to find a compass to navigate through successive crises. The threat and advent of terrorist attacks (as well as the perception of such threats and their objective assessment) have weakened the world economy in both tangible and intangible ways, while consumers are increasingly asking for life-cycle sustainable and safer products with minimal ecological and health untoward impacts, that is, using less energy, reducing environmental damage and enhancing health and security conditions. Companies should respond creatively and forthrightly to these concerns, which, unaddressed, could have the unfortunate result of lasting boycotts of specific goods or services (Grimpe *et al.* 2007). Against the background of rising global risks and uncertainty, multinational companies must navigate a more complex, faster shifting environment, in which crisis management is a required component of global operations with varied impacts on all stakeholders. Increased pressures on all phases of decision making and strategic choices by corporations are the most pressing result.

In this chapter, we have selected three overarching and salient issue areas from the multiplicity of challenges, threats and risks that the new century has brought to the forefront of international actors' agendas and those of their top executive teams. Buttressing our analysis on these three issue areas – which pose specific challenges for a proper and long-term response to corporate actors operating across boundaries – we propose a reconceptualized orientation premised on peaceful resolution of conflict, corporate social responsibility and intergenerational environmental stewardship and equity to position the multinational firm at the fulcrum of global policy solutions. This orientation is focused on anticipating and preventing the occurrence and diffusion of corruption, terrorism and climate change by adopting a corporate socially responsible behavior. In this context, international organizations and NGOs are placing heightened pressures on multinational companies to make conscious choices towards what is perceived as peace-inducing moves and the survival of future generations. New strategies covering the multiple aspects of the sustainable development domain have been suggested. However not all the multinational corporations (MNCs) have been equally or greatly concerned by these policies and looming "sea changes" in the broad policy environment. In fact, while some companies are working on improving their products with a view to environmental neutrality or even benefits as well as energy consumption savings, others are strategizing in some developing countries to reflect countries' lack of concern in their own corporate choices and policies.

We believe that this chapter may help 1) identify some of the salient drivers of what can be viewed as a crisis in global corporate management; 2) achieve a better grasp of how multinational companies' actions may contribute to improving or to damaging the environment; 3) determine how seemingly unrelated components of a global corporate crisis partake of the same dynamic, at a given point in history, and are organically related, requiring "holistic" approaches by global corporations in their individual and industry-sector strategy and action; and finally, 4) derive some normative solutions and policy recommendations which may allow international business corporate actors better to describe, understand, predict and manage the multiple intertwined looming crises. In short, how do multinational corporate entities navigate in unknown waters and in the "rough" seas of the crisis-plagued early twenty-first century?

11.2 CRISIS AND NAVIGATION

Several causal and interactive drivers have allied in aggravating present-day international business dynamics and led to a climate of pervasive crisis; these include, inter alia, the recent terrorist attacks, the threats associated with patterns of global warming, and the rising lack of transparency and corruption practices displayed in numerous markets. A crisis could be defined as "any situation that is threatening or could threaten to harm people or property, seriously interrupt business, damage reputation and/ or negatively impact share value" (Bernstein, 1996). To understand the requirements and the contours of sound crisis management, it is critical to analyze it and to identify its drivers.

Crisis management with a view to the future is often best analogized to a process of navigation in uncharted seas. Corporations scan, monitor and assess their operating environment for both threats and opportunities as a function of their strengths and weaknesses. The ensuing process of analysis is called strategy, or to carry on with the analogy, plotting a course for the corporate entity as it seeks to survive and grow. Given the "plotting" errors (always defined a posteriori) made by major governments in the post-World War II era regarding "tectonic" shifts in the world's political economy (from the fall of the Berlin Wall to the rise of the regime of Ayatollahs in Iran to the advent of a world economy gradually dominated by emerging economies, for example), one cannot express great surprise that large-scale corporations are hard put to forecast with precision the occurrence of shifts in their own operating environment.

At the end of the fifteenth century, celestial navigation was barely in its beginning stages in Europe. Prior to its development, sailors navigated by "deduced" (or "dead") reckoning of their positions in open high seas. Indeed, this method was used by Christopher Columbus, among other contemporaries, with unpredictable results and happenstance discoveries. The West Indies remained Asia for a long while before this plotting error in course charting became obvious. In so-called "dead-reckoning", navigators plot their position by measuring the course and distance they have sailed from some known point. For such a method of successive measurements to work, the sailor needs a measurement instrument to determine time and speed. This can be viewed as highly dependent on past history with a view to the future. What is missing are rates of changes in the flows of currents, winds and other forces which might deviate the ship from its target destination. An overreliance and static dependence on past history yields the predictable results of repeated charting errors. While past positions (or "history") are essential, the critical aspect is using this knowledge and adjusting it to a data stream in dynamic evolution. This is the proper way to chart a course in fast-changing seas or uncharted waters.

Without detailing such navigational methods, suffice it to say that governments and corporations have not evolved to a point of accuracy and precision close to celestial navigation in monitoring and forecasting the broad political, social, economic, technological and cultural forces that buffet them. At best, the crude instrumentation of pre-fifteenth century dead reckoning characterize the reliability and predictability of corporate forecasting of the untractable issue areas we are reviewing. Long-term planning, forecasting and strategies abound with models, stochastic or deterministic, but the complexity of the topic has not yielded the precision of computerized navigation.

11.2.1   Corruption

"There is always somebody who pays, and international business is generally the main source of corruption" (Soros 1998). Corruption has become one of the major policy and practical issues facing the broad range of international organizations. According to a survey conducted by Control Risks and Simmons and Simmons (2006), corruption constitutes a significant impediment to the smooth growth trajectory of international business. Even though new legislative frameworks were introduced against bribery, dishonest competitors are still resorting to what is best described as unfair trade and business practices to capture market share and drive out legitimate competition in third-country markets. In addition, many countries are still known for their explicit or implicit tolerance of various levels of corruption, which has the effect of driving out investment by reputable businesses.

Corruption has indeed led to multiple and often unanticipated effects on government, society, economy and community. One of the effects that it can have is an unexpected and steady rise in the cost of services and a retardation effect on the process of economic development, which disproportionately hurt bottom of the pyramid actors (Hawley, 2000). The late Prime Minister of India, Rajiv Gandhi, claimed that 85 per cent of aid money does not reach its intended beneficiaries and that corruption leads the poor to get poorer (Mehta, 2004). In fact, by buying the influence, corruption takes away the process of decision making from the poor and makes them lose the opportunity of improving services and the basic standards of their life. Corruption is known to impact on external debt levels of developing countries (sovereign or more traditional forms of debt, largely owed to external actors). Indeed, many governments, especially developing countries governments, borrow capital to finance long-term projects. Knowing that corruption leads to increased project costs, external debt is often the default source of funds for such practices. The accounting practices governing the use of external aid funds are problematic and lacking in the usual transparency, making for ready identification of misappropriation or deviation from the mandate. Moreover, countries that are known for their high level of corruption discourage honest business and dissuade them from investing in their economy (Control Risks and Simmons and Simmons survey, 2006).

One can also argue that corruption, though harmful to a country's long-term interest and reputation (its national brand as it were), may indeed be clearly beneficial for a corporate entity keen on rapid entry and penetration but lacking a longer-term perspective. Moreover, corruption practices can work around regulations, often leading to outright destruction of the wilderness environment, as is reputed to be the case in the Amazon basin of Brazil, or it can create the opportunity to inject illicit arms sales in certain regional conflicts. Further to Hawley (2000), several companies have resorted to outright bribes to get around regulatory frameworks with ease in relation to environmental guidelines and requirements. In fact, the Nicaraguan government showed in its 1999 audit that Greenstone Resources, a mining company from Canada, had made a $20 000 donation to then President Aleman and other donations to certain persons in his Liberal Party. It also provided bribes to several officials located in the mining area Greenstone operated in defiance of ecological guidelines. As a result, this company was able to escape extant ecological laws and regulations and eventually to receive a positive compliance assessment from the Nicaraguan officials of the time.

Thus there is an interconnection between ecological disregard and lack of transparency of business processes. Forecasting the nature of the risk that the interaction of the two can engender for a corporate entity is far from easy. Maneuvering around these shoals is equally difficulty as companies seek to balance market entry and penetration with transparency and equitable practices.

11.2.2   Climate Change

The heightened awareness of climate change risks and ensuing fears have made ecological risk assessment and mitigation policies important drivers of the global management crisis for corporate actors operating across borders upstream and downstream in the life cycle of their products. Consequently, climate change is receiving far more attention from customers, international organizations and companies themselves. Corporate actors have achieved a new awareness of the issue and its impact on their global "brand", "image", and reputation and consequently their competitiveness and survival as corporate actors. In this context, many multinational companies are experiencing acute pressures from their stakeholders to respond to these challenges with creative and image-enhancing environmental strategies. According to Sir David King, adviser to former United Kingdom Prime Minister Tony Blair, climate change constitutes a larger threat to the planet than terrorism (Little, 2006). The awarding of the Nobel Peace Prize to former U.S. Vice President Albert Gore, in October 2007, is another indication of the level of concern felt at all levels of global civil society and the sense of the imminence of the threat posed by unmanaged economic and industrial growth to our sea, air and earth resources, the great "commons" of the globe.

The range of climate change impacts is not incontrovertible and various lines of argumentation and data remain in controversy in some policy and even a few remaining scientific circles. Reports prepared for the Intergovernmental Panel on Climate Change have shown the impending and potentially catastrophic consequences of this challenge if unaddressed with the immediacy of a global threat. One of these implications is the rise of sea levels, which increases the number of people at risk of flooding (BBC News 1997). Moreover, even if scientists do not expect crop production (increasingly managed through pesticides and chemical enrichment techniques) to change, they anticipate that climate change would have a broad-spectrum regional effect. It would affect the population dependent on isolated agricultural structures in dry or semi-dry land areas. This part of the population would experience food shortages, bordering on famine, the likes of which have been unknown in the past generation. Climate change has the potential of also affecting the population living in dry areas such as Sub-Saharan Africa, parts of South-east Asia, and some of the tropical areas in Latin America. Furthermore, disease morbidity and mortality could flow from climate change, such as malaria, dengue fever and asthma. Indeed, the extension of the seasons in itself could exacerbate malaria, dengue fever and yellow fever. Pollution and global warming could further accentuate the incidence of asthma and severe respiratory diseases.

Finally, some species' composition could be altered and desertification could accelerate, while certain forests and glaciers could gradually diminish in response to global warming. In short, the word extinction, for better or for worse, is on many minds in the scientific and policy communities. The corporate world has not fully come to grips with the perceptual implications of this ongoing debate and the governmental responses it is about to engender. Hence, the management crisis is twofold: the objective scientific one and the public policy one. The more the two dimensions can be addressed jointly and simultaneously, the better corporate actors will be able to grasp this evolving crisis and the mix of appropriate policy choices and outcomes. Linking corporate social responsibility and sustainable development practices and policies to such macro events is problematic at best and is asserted as self-evident, but requires more research and demonstration projects. One can point to the practices of a global cement and construction company, Lafarge, which has developed micro-practices in the immediate surroundings of its operations sites which integrate health, ecological and educational policies.

11.2.3 Terrorism

Terrorism has become a pressing driver of the present global international crisis. It has focused corporate attention on the role of terrorists as global actors. Terrorism could be subjectively defined as Lars Mammen has in his speech of 13 September 2005: "The expression 'terrorism' and 'terrorist' have always had different meanings in different connotations. The well-known saying 'one's man terrorist is another man's freedom fighter' shows that its definition also depends on the political point of view of the relevant party to the conflict." However, a report of the United Nations High-Level Panel on Threats, Challenges and Changes from December 2004 has defined terrorism objectively as: "any action . . . that is intended to cause death or serious bodily harm to civilians or non-combatants, when the purpose of such act, by its nature or context, is to do or to abstain from doing any act" (Hill, 2005). Terrorism has numerous effects, both direct and indirect. Even though the direct effects are easier to assess and measure, the indirect effects should also be evaluated. Direct terrorism effects essentially constitute victims and material damage. They generally occur in the immediate short term, following a terrorism attack (Looney, 2002). Mammen (2005) estimated in his speech the direct effects of the 9/11 terrorism attack. He claimed that basically the life cost damage of this attack was incalculable using acturial science. On the other hand, he gave an approximate evaluation of the material loss. The physical assets damage was estimated at $10 billion. In addition, about $11 billion were spent on the process of cleaning destroyed urban sites. The Manhattan area lost about 25 per cent of its corporate space, several small businesses stopped their activities, and some 200 000 job positions were damaged or relocated.

While the direct effects are obvious and occur in a short time span, the indirect effects are hidden and extend on various timescales. These latter effects include macro-economic and financial crises. The indirect effects of the 9/11 attack were not as significant as anticipated at first. Mammen gave the example of the gross national product, which rebounded in the last quarter of 2001 following the attacks. He added that the immediate effects of the Madrid and London terrorist attacks (2004 and 2005) were relatively weak and that the evaluation of the overall global terrorism economic effect requires that a distinction be made between short, medium, and long terms. Several years in the wake of the 9/11 attacks, most of the impacted economic sectors have recovered, but some negative effects persist, such as an increase in security and insurance costs. Some sectors were acutely affected by the 9/11 attack, because of their exposure as easy targets, such as the airline, insurance and tourism sectors, while others were positively affected, such as the security and information technology sectors (McIntyre and Travis, 2006).

11.3   APPROACH TO RESOLVE THE CRISIS

A crisis can be interpreted as a challenge that requires a response. Most often corporations will conceive of it as this, even if refraining from a proactive course. To deal with an international crisis, assess and protect against its likely occurrence, implies an analytical effort grounded in expert knowledge of its causes and an understanding of the position of the industry sector and corporate exposure.

11.3.1   Crisis Causes

Having argued in the previous section that the corporate global crisis is most exemplified by corruption, climate change and terrorism, this section focuses on explaining some of the most likely drivers for each cluster.

Corruption drivers
Economic shifts in regulation, competition and government can lead to increased corruption. Privatization in emerging and developing markets, for example, has often been escorted by corruption. The top executive of the World Bank's Asia-Pacific section, Jean-Michel Severino, has argued that privatizations in the region turned into a "horror story" with a "high level of corruption". Both the International Monetary Fund and the World Bank imposed tight deadlines for the privatization of public services, which made it difficult to set up a regulatory framework for this process. Lack of time is not the only problem. In fact, even with flexible deadlines, it remains unlikely that legislative change alone will stem the tide (Hawley, 2000). Moreover, the World Bank also notes that economic liberalization can provoke a wave of corruption, confirmed by a 1996 research report holding that liberalization "has contributed to a more generalized process of political decay. This reduces the incentives for probity on the part of officials and politicians, and creates a widespread social alienation from the political process." Hawley (2000) highlighted that liberalization creates opportunities for corruption. Since money transfers can be conducted without providing any economic justification, it is easier to circulate and transfer money and capital. Attendant decentralization can provide further incentives for corrupt business practices. Severino claimed that "decentralization will lead to less governance and more corruption spread around the country, disruption of public service and a fiscal burden" (Hawley, 2000). Grassroots research in rural villages in Uganda concluded that decentralization was responsible for the amplification of corruption. In short, privatization, economic

liberalization and decentralization are often drivers of corruption when they are introduced without "preparing the ground" as the saying goes (Bardhan and Dilip, 2005). They all require an adjustment in values, attitudes and proper mechanisms to reduce incentives.

Climate change drivers

Climate change is clearly not a unicausal phenomenon and its evident complexity in scale and scope often leaves global corporate actors with a sense of powerlessness. Hence, a corporate actor needs to define how its operations and practices intersect with various aspects of this "intractable" process of climate change and define how it can impact, at what level, on what scale, with what scope. One of the factors that has helped accelerate the climate change is modifications to the earth's orbit. For example, variations in the earth's orbit, tilt and precession have increased the amount of sunlight toward the earth. Changes in the sun's intensity have also led to climate changes. Indeed, the changes within the sun could have influenced its intensity. Moreover, volcanoes could have had an impact on the climate since they could be responsible for aerosol and carbon dioxide emissions. Furthermore, the change of the earth's surface temperature could have modified the concentration of greenhouse gases and the currents of the ocean, which can accelerate climactic changes (National Research Council, 2001).

Beyond these natural drivers, in which corporate actors can at best have a supporting role in the scientific enterprise, climate change is also the tangible results of companies' production and therefore pollution through effluents and the like. For decades, consumers accorded companies' environmental strategies little importance. They were principally attracted by product price, brand and quality and sought no information about how companies acted towards the environment. Environmental strategies were at best perceived as a luxury or a supplementary option that did not impact product choice. In addition, regulatory systems sanctioned companies acting harmfully towards the environment, implicitly or in some cases explicitly. Consequently, most companies did not perceive environmental strategies as a priority. In a short span of years, this trend has reversed. Industrialized countries' regulatory systems are paying more attention to corporate environmental strategies and a multilateral treaty and other frameworks for coordinated policies are being considered. Developing and emerging countries, very much in the catch-up frame of policy, are still struggling with an inadequate regulation system, which creates incentives for some multinational firms to consider this policy gap a locational advantage. International treaties, protocols and guidelines have the potential of harmonizing a very uneven environmental policy landscape.

Terrorism drivers

Many authors have sought explanatory frameworks for terrorism. The empirical evidence as to causes is lacking. Dave Clarke (2005) considers terrorism an act of choice resulting from conditions of societal and individual despair. In multiple case studies, conditions of anomie or various psychopathologies, at the individual level, have been shown to be fertile grounds for terrorism (Victoroff, 2005). Michael Radu considers that "poverty", "injustice", "exploitation", and "frustration" are the "root causes of terrorism" (2002). Societal factors range from conditions of colonial oppression to systemic poverty, including patterns of corruption and eco-system failure. However one analyzes such acts, corporations seeking to understand the phenomenon should not be precluded from taking preventive measures by a lack of theoretical framework regarding causation. Plotting errors are tolerable if they can prevent loss and deflect chaos. The threat and potential risks themselves justify action. The option is to remain paralyzed by the lack of empirical evidence to grasp and predict a protean phenomenon, subject to historical cycles (that is, long wave theories such as Kondratieff cycles or similar). This is a further demonstration of how complex the dynamic environment has become to navigate for global corporate actors as much as governments themselves. Global corporations cannot rely only on the wisdom and policies of national governments given the transnational nature of the terrorism threat, and they have therefore been challenged to come up with damage-mitigation and prevention strategies for their global value chains.

11.3.2   The Position of International Businesses

Flowing out of the global threat clusters of corruption, climate change and terrorism, a global management crisis for multinational companies has emerged and is defining itself more sharply in the first decade of the twenty-first century. Pressures from corporate stakeholders, including governments themselves, are incentivizing companies to adopt a more anticipatory and responsible behavior while conforming to minimum ethical norms still in a process of definition (Christmann and Taylor, 2002; Hartman and Stafford, 2006). Multinational companies are struggling to meet the expectations of their stakeholders while retaining competitiveness. Global operations add a level of complexity to the adoption of corporate responsible behavior flowing from the diversity of cultures, norms, values, employees and stakeholders involved. A salient issue related to adopting common and predictable responsible and ethical behavior guidelines at an international level is the divergence among national regulatory systems (Davies, 2002). Diversity of law may be the stuff of conflict, but it does not make easy crisis management. The evident lack of an effective international regulatory system could be seen by some multinational actors as a temptation to behave opportunistically, especially in emergent and developing countries where governments are seeking and competing for job-creating foreign direct investment. According to Chudnovsky and Lopez (2003), many multinational companies seek a locational advantage in developing countries to avoid overly burdensome domestic requirements adding costs and unpredictability to their value chain.

Corporate actors may thus profit from the relatively cheaper local labor unit costs while using less demanding and potentially environmentally damaging technologies. Nike, for instance, ignored a pattern by its Asian subcontractors of using a much too young workforce. NGOs have been building up campaigns for greater corporate social responsibility on the global scene. Greenpeace, for instance, opposed the use of hydrochlorofluorocarbons (HCFCs) by The Coca-Cola Company in Australia during the 2000 Olympics, as using these chemicals has been shown to accelerate climate change. In response to these pressures, The Coca-Cola Company promised to stop buying HCFCs, to increase its research into other refrigerants, and to ask its suppliers to cease the use of HCFCs by 2004. It posited a target of decreasing its production energy use by 40 per cent before 2010 (Hartman and Stafford, 2006). Greenpeace also protested the British Shell Company's decision to sink the platform, Brent Spar, in the North Atlantic in early 1995. Consequently, German customers decided to boycott Shell gas stations, so that sales at German Shell dropped by approximately 11 per cent in June 1995, leading to the reversal of the Shell subsidiary's decision to dump the platform (Christmann and Taylor, 2002). Customers could react aggressively, when provided with information in regard of any firm's lack of social responsibility. Stakeholders' pressures and particularly NGOs' pressures are now taken seriously by multinational firms. Their reputation on the global stage is increasingly a subject of careful management and a "backdoor" to effective crisis management. Pressures from global non-corporate actors can be understood as an important driver of enhanced corporate social responsibility on the world stage.

Stakeholders' pressures are clearly not the sole motivation leading multinationals to adopt responsible behavior. This decision is also motivated by competitive advantage gains, economic opportunities and internal responses to the company's own ethical values. Studies about business and environmental performance have distinguished different drivers for ecological conduct: stakeholders' pressures, competitive advantage, legislation, economical opportunities and moral concerns (Dillon and Fischer, 1992; Lampe *et al.*, 1991; Lawrence and Morell, 1995; Vredenburg and Westley, 1993; Winn, 1995). By implementing corporate social responsible strategies, multinationals can enhance their image and capture the attention and imagination of green consumers. Reputational gains are hard to quantify but are clearly appreciated by shareholders and top management. In addition, multinationals with corporate social responsible policies can reduce wasteful energy consumption and as a result increase their revenue streams. Multinationals can be driven by various factors simultaneously. Bansal and Roth (2000) have argued that companies can decide to adopt ecological behavior with the intention of responding to mixed and dominant motivations (Ketata and McIntyre, 2006). In short, understanding a company's approach to crisis management is also a question of understanding how it perceives its ethical stakes.

According to Berry and Rondinelli (1998), companies are switching their position from regulatory obedience to responsible proactiveness. This change in companies' strategies was made in three steps: in the 1960s and the 1970s, companies were making an effort to handle environmental damage and deal with dishonest competitors. During the 1980s, companies started to follow environmental and ethical regulations, which were quickly evolving, and to control the costs of their adjustment. During the 1990s, the companies started approving a proactive strategy. With such strategies, companies are expected to predict the environmental impacts of their activities, attempting to reduce their waste of energy and limit their pollution, broadly acting ethically and responsibly towards their stakeholders. Today, corporate socially responsible strategies are most often a part of the global companies' management and culture.

Adopting such proactive strategies constitutes a new way of thinking that dominates the twenty-first century. Companies are becoming more conscious of the importance of adapting this behavior in order to attract more customers. Intergovernmental organizations have become a force pushing forth the values making up corporate social responsibility. The United Nations, the World Bank and the OECD, as exemplars among several other international organizations, have become active in this respect. The socially responsible investment movement is the focus of increasing attention in Europe and America (Davies, 2002). The most challenging aspect for a company today perhaps is to make decisions which consider a complex range of impacts beyond financial and economic ones (Hart and Milstein, 2003). While the mechanics of triple bottom line accounting remain largely an academic topic, it remains salient in the mind of corporate boards and management leaderships of global companies.

There is clear evidence that the global public has changed its attitude and shifted from passive to active actor; it seems now more interested in values and more open to confront corruption. This new orientation is evident especially in advanced industrial countries, where governments are more conscious than ever of the saliency of promoting corporate socially responsible practices in their resident firms. More progress needs to be made among developing countries' governments to stem unethical business practices while working on preserving the environment and the human rights of their workforce.

Several reports about globalization have criticized the uneven nature of business regulations and strong hurdles in the way of development that weigh heavily on poorer nations (Davies, 2002). In this sense, one can conclude that it remains unclear whether international business actors are accelerating a process of conflict resolution or accentuating a situation of crisis. Still, it is obvious that the crisis has provided the seeds of resolution and that it is the reason why customers and other stakeholders have placed change-inducing pressures on multinational firms in the first place. The question now is how to motivate all multinational corporate actors to build on this process of change and press forward in the adoption of binding responsible and ethical behavior codes.

11.4   RECOMMENDATIONS

The distance between intent and action is great in the effective management and prevention of patterns of global corruption and climate change-inducing practices, and the development of terrorism-reducing strategies. These actions of necessity involve governments as well as international communities, along with global companies and civil society. The opportunity for corporate actors to lead this process of reform is great, under the broad rubric of corporate social responsibility, and can turn the risks and threats into opportunities for a growth-friendly and safe economic environment.

11.4.1   Governments

First, developing countries need to reform their regulatory systems and introduce effective sanctions against multinationals that are involved in corrupt practices or whose practices are harmful to the environment. In essence, removing a market distortion due to differential regulatory frameworks is what is involved in the foreign direct investment landscape. According to the Commonwealth Report of 1998 on corruption: "Action programs need to be designed to meet the expectations of citizens . . . Effective action to fight corruption is most likely through programs which are nationally owned, designed to meet national circumstances and built on the foundation of popular empowerment" (Hawley, 2000). Governments should inform their citizenry about national policies pursued not only against corrupt or environmentally harmful companies which are international, but also those with domestic roots. National treatment ought to be extended in this regard to all corporate actors.

Second, developing countries' governments that are competing to attract multinational firms' equity and portfolio investment are unwilling to bring their standards to world levels for fear of losing such opportunities. Convincing governments that the costs and risks associated with non-action are greater than the working out of reasonable standards for even implementation is worth the attention of globally responsible companies. By implementing fair and predictable laws, developing countries will attract honest and reputable multinational firms with a long-term perspective on their investments in these societies. Governments must set a high standard of behavior for their agencies and personnel as a first and essential step in seeking to discourage companies tempted by corrupt practices as a way to bypass socially responsible frameworks. Stemming terrorism may provide a model of transnational government cooperation for the other crisis management clusters.

11.4.2 The International Community

Observers have claimed that developing countries can hardly introduce an efficient regulatory system against large multinational firms since they are often corrupt. The anti-bribery convention of the OECD (1997) had the goal of reducing bribery by sanctioning corrupt companies located in the OECD member states. This was a first step pointing in a hopeful direction. In this context, the leaders of the World Bank, the African Development Bank, the Asian Development Bank, the European Bank for Reconstruction and Development and the International Finance Corporation decided to conduct anti-corruption programs specific to a country's needs and to prepare the ground for structural reforms sector by sector, to support transparency and fair competition. These programs constitute important measures. They provide global corporations with guidelines and models. Companies should seek to be involved in the international organization community, and this should impact on their policies and insure their relevance and feasibility.

Second, as a corollary, true progress must be made in the construction of international regimes governing these three threat clusters beyond merely guidelines established willy-nilly by corporate actors sharing a similar worldview. In short, conventions and treaties of a binding nature must be crafted, negotiated and ratified to further strengthen the national regulatory systems and reduce their dissonance through a process of construction of a *jus gentium* for the new millennium (Gluck and Doyle, 2004). The Kyoto Protocol standstill is an indication of the complexity of the challenge. It also demonstrates the insufficient advancement in the construction of a world system to address transborder issues, in the wake of the modest achievements of the post-World War II Bretton Woods regime. A high degree of policy coordination among governments, particularly among developing countries' governments, will therefore be the essential precondition. It implies a willingness to adjust the claims of national sovereignty to the demands of a changing and seemingly unmanageable environment. That the United Nations has a critical part to play is obvious but that new institutions need to be constructed is also evident.

11.4.3   Civil Groups

"There is no question that the world needs peace to prosper and prosperity to have peace" (Alder, 2006, p. 191). Such lofty words require all society's actors' involvement in fighting the triad of terrorism, pollution and corruption. The population should, first, have the courage and the ability to reform governmental processes. Building a strong civil society with effective intermediary institutions is clearly a precondition. Civil society groups should encourage and reward companies that are adopting sustainable development strategies and are producing green products.

11.4.4   Companies

Companies should be rewarded by customers and host governments alike, as well as civil society, for adopting corporate socially responsible behaviors in dealing with environmental challenges and corrupt practices, and enhancing the safety of their operations. Governments can introduce tax policies that reflect such value loadings. A pattern of fiscal incentives can be devised, seeking relative trade-competitive and fiscal neutrality, to incentivize corporate behavior with benchmarked outcomes. Corporate stakeholders must also be encouraged and rewarded for eschewing the short-term bottom line perspective at all costs for a longer if not medium-term view of their profitability in which a values-driven agenda can find its proper place as a tool for competitiveness. Reputation and image associated with environmental and ethical behaviors have become a key success factor for performance and growth in the 21st century (Ketata and McIntyre, 2006). Insuring that all management layers understand how to implement such an approach remains a training and values challenge. Companies have a full agenda in educating their various stakeholders, retraining their workforces and in explaining why corporate socially responsible behaviors in a globally independent economy is the way to growth and profitability.

But the authors find that the notion of "co-opetition" has not been put to good use nor given the attention of top managements in encouraging broad-spectrum collaborative efforts and systems among corporations to deal with the identified and shared global threat clusters. Co-opetition best describes cooperative competition. While cartels are the best known examples of companies working together to limit competition, companies can also work together to establish common regimes, with the cooperation of international institutions, to deal with common transborder threats. Defining precisely the boundary between competition and collaboration in this regard is no easy task, but the process has barely begun (Arnott *et al.*, 2003).

11.5 CONCLUSION

Corruption, climate change and terrorism-related issues are weakening our economic fabric. Global corporate actors have been slow in changing their strategies and in adopting a new orientation based on ethical principles. But clear trends have emerged, further accelerated by an analysis of the threat levels and the limited window of opportunity. Adopting requisite strategies is clearly beneficial to future generations and to the growth and survival of corporate entities. Increasingly, mergers and acquisitions result in a requirement for the rapid adoption of values-driven principles of corporate behavior. Global corporate actors have the opportunity to diffuse such reforms into their practices in developing countries, thereby encouraging changes in the very host governments through which they do business. A surprising reversal of role in this globally interdependent world!

While the tools made available to corporate entities for monitoring, assessing and anticipating the evolution of crises are imprecise and best analogized to a process of navigational "dead reckoning" in uncharted waters, the substantial resources available to them should mitigate conceptual boundaries and open the way for breakthroughs. Global corporate actors can show the way and define their own operating environment in which they will reduce the level of threats and manage the evolving crises we have identified.

REFERENCES

Alder, N. J. (2006). "Corporate Global Citizenship: Successfully Partnering with the World". In Suder, G. (ed.) *Corporate Strategies Under International Terrorism and Adversity*. Edward Elgar, Cheltenham, UK and Northampton, MA, USA.

Arnott, R., Greenwald, B., Kanbur, R. and Nalebuff, B. (eds) (2003). *Economics for an Imperfect World: Essays in Honor of Joseph E. Stiglitz*. MIT Press, Cambridge, MA, USA.

Bansal, P. and Roth, K. (2000). "Why companies go green: A model of ecological responsiveness". *Academy of Management Journal*, **43**(4), 717–736.

Bardhan, P. and Dilip, M. (2005). "Decentralization, Corruption and Government Accountability: An Overview", http://people.bu.edu/dilipm/publications/decorr. pdf, accessed 7 February 2008.

BBC News (1997). *"Special Report: Impact of Global Warming May be Severe and Wide-Ranging"*, 28 November, http://news.bbc.co.uk/1/hi/special_report/1997/ sci/tech/global_warming/32961.stm, accessed 17 January 2008.

Bernstein, J. (1996) The Ten Steps of Crisis Communications, www.bernsteincrisis-management.com/docs/10steps.html, accessed 17 January 2008.

Berry, M. A. and Rondinelli, D. A. (1998). "Proactive corporate environmental management: A new industrial revolution". *Academy of Management Executives*, **12**(2), 38–50.

Christmann, P. and Taylor, G. (2002). "Globalization and the environment: Strategies for international voluntary environmental initiatives". *Academy of Management Executives*, **16**(3), 121–135.

Chudnovsky, D. and Lopez, A. (2003). "Diffusion of Environmentally Friendly Technologies by Multinational Corporations in Developing Countries". *International Journal of Technology Management and Sustainable Development*, **2**(1), 5–18.

Clarke, D. (2005). *Terrorism: Opinion on its Causes and Cures*, www.geocities.com/ daveclarkecb/Terrorism.html, accessed 15 May 2007.

Control Risks and Simmons and Simmons (2006). "International business attitudes to corruption", http://www.control-risks.com/PDF/corruption_survey_2006_ v3.pdf, accessed 7 February 2008.

Davies, R. (2002). "The Business Community: Social Responsibility and Corporate Value". In Dunning, J. (ed.) *Making Globalization Good*. Oxford University Press, New York.

Dillon, P. W. and Fischer, K. (1992). *Environmental Management Incorporations*. Tufts University Center for Environmental Management, Medford, MA.

Gluck, E. C. and Doyle, M. W. (2004). *International Law and Organization: Closing the Compliance Gap*, Rowman and Littlefield, Lanham, MA.

Grimpe, C., Ketata, I. and Sofka, W. (2007). "Profiling Sustainable Innovators: Not Ready to Make Nice?" Paper presented at the *16th International Conference On Management of Technology*, 13–17 May, Miami.

Hart, S. L. and Milstein, M. B. (2003). "Creating sustainable value". *Academy of Management Executive*, **17**(2), 56–67.

Hartman, C. L. and Stafford, E. R. (2006). "Chilling with Greenpeace, from the inside out". *Stanford Social Innovation Review*, Summer.

Hawley, S. (2000). "Exporting Corruption Privatisation, Multinationals and Bribery", June, www.thecornerhouse.org.uk/item.shtml?x=51975, accessed 17 January 2008.

Hill, C. (2005). "How to save the United Nations (if we really have to), *Hoover Digest*, www.hoover.org/publications/digest/3001526.html, accessed 17 January 2008.

Ketata, I. and McIntyre, J. R. (2006). "Sustainable Development and Multinational Firm: Contrasting corporate approaches", paper presented at the *International Research Colloquium* organized by Georgia Tech, ICN-Nancy and GREFIFE-Lorraine, 19–20 October, Georgia Institute of Technology, Atlanta.

Lampe, M., Ellis, S. R. and Drummond, C.K. (1991). "What companies are doing to meet environmental protection responsibilities: Balancing legal, ethical, and profit concerns". *Proceedings of the International Association for Business and Society*, pp. 527–537.

Lawrence, A. T. and Morell, D. (1995). "Leading-Edge Environmental Management: Motivation, Opportunity, Resources, and Processes". In Collins, D. and Starick, M. (eds), *Research in Corporate Social Performance and Policy*. JAI Press, Greenwich, CT, pp. 99–126.

Little, A. G. (2006). The King and I, http://www.grist.org/news/maindish/2006/02/17/griscom-little/, accessed 7 February 2008.

Looney, R. (2002). "Economic Costs to the United States Stemming From the 9/11 Attacks", *Strategic Insights*, **1**(6).

Mammen, L. (2005). *Remembering the 4th Anniversary of 9-11: Economic and Legal Impacts of the Terrorist Attacks*; American–German Business Club, Duesseldorf, 11 September, www2.dias-online.org/direktorien/int_terr/050911_26, accessed 17 January 2008.

McIntyre, J. R. and Travis, E. F. (2006). "Global Supply Chain under Conditions of Uncertainty: Economic Impacts, Corporate Responses, Strategic Lessons". In Suder, G. (ed.), *Corporate Strategies Under International Terrorism and Adversity*. Edward Elgar, Cheltenham, UK and Northampton, MA, USA.

Mehta, V. (2004). "Letter: Heat and Dust of Political Reform", http://news.bbc.co.uk/2/hi/programmes/3911193.stm, 22 July, accessed 7 February 2008.

National Research Council (2001). Climate Change Science: An Analysis of Some Key Questions. National Academy Press, Washington, DC, http://www.nap.edu/html/climatechange/1.html, accessed 7 February 2008.

OCED (1997). "OCED Convention on Combating Bribery of Foreign Public Officials in International Business Transactions", Organization for Economic Cooperation and Development, http://www.oecd.org/document/21/0.3343.en_2649_201185_2017813_1_1_1_1.00.html#Text_of_the_Convention, accessed 8 February 2008.

Radu, M. (2002). *The Futile Search for Root Causes of Terrorism*, www.unc.edu/depts/diplomat/archives_roll/2002_07-09/radu_futile/radu_futile.html, accessed 17 January 2008.

Shah, A. (2007). *Climate Change and Global Warming*, www.globalissues.org/EnvIssues/GlobalWarming.asp, accessed 18 January 2008.

Soros, G. (1998). "Fund Management Guru Reveals Doubts", *Financial Times*, 8 December.

United States Institute of Peace, *Teaching Guide on International Terrorism: Definitions, Causes, and Responses*, www.usip.org/class/guides/terrorism.pdf, accessed 18 January 2008.

Victoroff, J. (2005). "The Mind of the Terrorist". *Journal of Conflict Resolution*, **49**(1), 3–42, http://jcr.sagepup.com/cgi/content/abstract/49/1/3, accessed 14 February 2008.

Vredenburg, H. and Westley, F. (1993). "Environmental Leadership in Three Contexts: Managing for Global Competitiveness". *Proceedings of the International Association of Business and Society*, pp. 495–500.

Winn, M. (1995). "Corporate Leadership and Policies for the Natural Environment". In Collins, D. and Starik, M. (eds), *Research in Corporate Social Performance and Policy*, supplement 1. JAI Press, Greenwich, CT, pp. 127–161.

12. Corporate responsibility in peace, conflict reduction and crisis prevention: human security for thriving markets – a tool kit

Gabriele G.S. Suder and Jonathan Lefevre

Thriving markets and human security go hand in hand. (Former United Nations Secretary General Kofi Annan)

12.1 INTERNATIONAL BUSINESS IN CRISIS ZONES: HOW CONFLICTS AFFECT BUSINESS

Conflict and crisis have been defined in many different ways, depending on the origin, culture and objectives of the interpreter. We understand by *conflict* any situation in which two or more cohabiting individuals or groups have (seemingly or real) incompatible short- and/or long-term goals or expectations. Globalization shortens the distance between these cohabitations and the time it takes for these relationships (nodes) to form, maintain or break. *Crisis* is the end stage of such conflict, for its actors and the community in relation or proximity to that conflict. Hence, conflicts entail a goal or object, whether tangible or not, with respect to which differing parties have different expectations, and employ a range of strategies to achieve their objectives. The worst-case scenario of conflict is violence, bloodshed and war, with war being defined as a prolonged conflict that has turned violent.

This chapter starts out by exploring the main conflict types and their causes; argues that in most cases any type of conflict is bad for business; illustrates the role that firms play (directly or indirectly) in conflict and in conflict reduction, demonstrating the responsibility that international business carries; and finally, focuses on the elaboration of corporate tools and mitigation vehicles that help solve such issues. It is meant to be a toolkit.

12.1.1 Conflict Defined

Conflict, as classified by Windsor in Chapter 9 mainly takes the shape of:

- Violent crime (for example kidnappings of foreign oil workers in the Niger delta, or of managers in Colombia; terrorism in all its guises);
- Inter-group conflicts (for example the Rwandan genocide of 1994, or the disintegration of the former Yugoslavia). Here we note, following Rummel's extensive research into the conflict helix, that exchange-based societies tend towards pluralistic conflict; authoritarian towards communal or traditional conflict; coercive towards elite repression and instability (Rummel 1976);
- Inter-state (cross-border) wars: state-to-state wars over territory and resources, unresolved boundary issues (often based on differing historical interpretations) or the artificial imposition of boundaries by outside forces. This last might be through modern or past colonialism, resulting in artificially united nations that experience civil wars or genocide, or artificially divided nations;
- Civil wars: conflict between groups within a state, or crossing state boundaries, along ethnic lines, or focused around a separatist movement (Northern Ireland, Afghanistan), and including terrorism associated with secessionism (as in the Basque region or Corsica). It is often associated with an instrumentalization of culture or religion for the social, political or economic aims of a minority group. It is also associated with irredentism: the desire to bring into the state all areas that were once part of it, and establish a new frontier.
- World wars: between blocs of states, often resulting from alliances formed according to politico-economic interests (Suder 2004).

A large number of United Nations reports clearly demonstrate that business concerns at times supersede security issues (for example, in the case of Congolese resources), and that "the trend of privatization of conflicts, including the business sector involving itself in conflict issues, needs to be arrested and reversed including by engaging the business sector, within the existing conflict prevention fora" (United Nations 2004).

In a 2001 report by Jason Switzer, some of the main ways in which businesses have become involved in conflict were enumerated:

- by causing conflict over control of resources or areas (uranium resources in Australia and Aborigines' rights);
- by claiming a right to participate in decision making and a share of benefits (forest communities in Ecuador versus mining activities of international firms);

- by financing (directly or indirectly) the repression of certain groups (energy company in Sudan allowing governmental air raids from its airstrip);
- by benefiting from conflict (Swedish company in Sudan profiting from a "scorched earth" campaign of fighting elements leading to infrastructure repairs that benefits their operations);
- by becoming a target of conflict for indirect access to decision-makers (oil companies in Nigeria) (UN 2001).

12.1.2   Conflict Theories

What are the causes of conflict? Samuel Huntington has repeatedly put forth the hypothesis of a clash of civilizations, described as clashes at the cultural or civilization level that occur between societies between which fundamental incompatibilities in terms of ideology, religion and/or culture exist (Huntington, 1993; 1997; 1998). In contrast, anti-dominance theory argues that while power is always a main causal factor in conflict (Rummel 1976), rebellion can happen as a reaction to dominance that is perceived as illegitimate, even when certain values of the dominant culture are accepted.

Theories that seek to explain war exist in a wide range of disciplines, from history to economics to psychology. Amongst them, as an element of demographic theories seeking to explain violence, youth bulge theory seeks to explain the rise of armed conflicts. It is argued that when a country experiences a large rise of the population aged 15–25 combined with conditions of economic stagnation, the level of conflict is typically high. According to Henrik Urdal, "youth bulges are believed to strain social institutions such as the labour market and the educational system, thereby causing grievances that may result in violent conflict" (Urdal 2004). The incompatibility gap between one's perceived condition and one's goal, becomes a significant identifier from which conflict arises in this context.

Reasons for youth engaging in violence at higher rates than older population groups are explained as being part of youth's greater propensity to rebel against tradition. Their perception of a difference between what they deserve and what they have makes them prone to activism. When combined with high unemployment and low education, youth bulges are more likely to be associated with violent conflict (Urdal 2004). Furthermore Urdal found a significant correlation between youth bulge violence and poor economic conditions, but no relation between youth bulge violence and political regime. He also found that emigration acts as a safety valve against violence, by allowing youth to access opportunities available in other countries.

In Chapter 5, Sachs and Dieleman have noted that minority groups show patterns of cohesion around home-country culture and traditions. They also noted that these allegiances held by minority groups are exploitable by authoritarian elements. The latter can be leaders of groups working towards political, social or geopolitical goals, on a state level or on a level that may comprise terrorism and warfare.

Taking a different perspective, the hegemony theory of war analyses violent conflict as a result of structural changes in the balance of power between nations. Typically, wars have occurred when there is a power balance shift among dominant powers. When a hegemonic power is challenged by the second greatest power, hegemonic wars arise. This is a theory that postulates that systemic changes arise when certain economic and technological conditions are met. The theory does not necessarily seek to determine the initiator of war, but rather the conditions that need to be met for war to arise (Gilpin 1988). The hegemonic theory of war does not, therefore, have any predictive power with respect to the initiation of war or its consequences. Rather, it is an analytic tool that helps understand what happened. This knowledge then serves in defining tools for conflict reduction and prevention. The hegemonic theory of conflict also provides a framework for consideration of the way in which corporate power may create new dominance patterns – for example in underdeveloped regions, when access to resources is granted by corrupt and/or totalitarian regimes that receive incentives.

In the case of terrorism-type conflict and crisis, Laqueur (2003) argues that conflict does not find its cause in poverty alone, but is rather caused by governmental incompetence and inequitable conditions. He notes that in the world's 50 poorest countries, little or no terrorism can be found (Laqueur 2004). Krueger and Maleckova's (2003) research indicates that terrorists tend not to be poor people, nor come from poor societies. The Harvard economist D. Rodrik (1998) demonstrated that economic growth is closely related to a society's ability to manage social crises connected to such conflict. However, 09/11-type terrorism is not location-dependent: it can make or break business opportunities on world markets and increase the exposure to risk of particular firms or industries, as well as alter consumer behaviour and perception of company identity and brand (Gillingham and Suder 2007). Moreover, 09/11- type terrorism, in terms of neo-realist theory of pro- and anti-globalization, constitutes a "geo-terrorism" (Thornton 2003) that adds to the toolbox of traditional conflict.

With 09/11, conflict has gained yet another, more global dimension, causing crisis on a large scale and in a great variety of sectors and activities. The theories highlighted above explore important phenomena of conflict. They need to be placed into the contemporary, highly globalized environment, in which not only societies but also businesses evolve and change in a non-linear manner. Brooks (1999) posits that the production structure of developed countries is so spread out and increasingly based on knowledge that the benefits of wars of conquest are significantly reduced. Hence, it is not worth it for a given country to attack another one whose economy is largely based on global supply chain business due to the non-locality of added value (as opposed to extractive industries that are largely dependent on given sites). The counter-argument points to the dependence of developed economies on international extractive industries, their (relatively scarce) resources and limited locations. The same goes for the dependence of advanced economies and their technology and construction sectors on being able to conquer new markets following the military sectors' interference in external relations.

Because the power of business has become significant vis-à-vis that of states and intergovernmental organizations, opportunities and threats of conflict have altered for all actors. For corporations, there are several factors that reduce the benefits of war:

- the global economy is increasingly based on knowledge;
- supply chains span the globe, thus dispersing production across great distances;
- inter-firm alliances are becoming a predominant feature of the global economy; and,
- the liberalization and expansion of capital markets has eased the flow of FDI, and its relative importance with respect to nation states is shifting.

This scenario, however, only remains true in poorer nations abundant in natural resources. For highly developed countries, governments' tendencies to "offshore" warfare is a phenomenon that keeps the worst form of conflict at a distance that is considered safe, and allows the pursuit of resource or political objectives to be legitimized through the tools available in democratic decision making (the main one being public opinion building). International peacekeeping efforts depend largely on the same tools and objectives. Goals in these circumstances need to be compatible with those of a maximum number of stakeholders (businesses, governmental or NGO actors) in order to be beneficial, or, at a minimum, to escape condemnation. In all cases, globalization (despite its benefits to some) is also the root of increased exposure of international business to conflict and conflict prevention issues. Interestingly, even global terrorism (causing cyclic states of fear in highly developed countries) results not only in risks for certain sectors (for example, tourism, finance), but also opportunities for others (for example, security equipment, videoconferencing) (Suder 2006).

Goal incompatibility between parties can arise from a different understanding of where power should emanate from (a hegemonic theory of war that can be transposed to powerful corporations) or a lack of vision of the future. In the case of violence against globalized supply chains, goal incompatibility will not tend to arise from a desire to capture resources. Friedman's Dell theory (Friedman 2005, p. 420) of conflict prevention hypothesises that if actors (nations, but also possibly corporations) cooperate economically, and are dependent upon each other for economic wealth and welfare (linking corporations and communities), then the opportunity for, and interest in conflict or harm will decrease at the same time as the others' capability of contributing to one's well-being increases. Global terrorism, as we know it since 09/11 however, appears to disprove this very concept.

12.2 HOW BUSINESS AFFECTS CONFLICT

To wilful men
The injuries that they themselves procure
Must be their schoolmasters.
(Shakespeare, King Lear II.iv)

The negative contributions of corporations to conflict, stirring them directly or indirectly, are particularly well documented, such as in studies of oil drilling (Swanson 2002), deforestation (Wallace 2007) and diamond harvesting (UN 2006). However, there is less literature dealing with corporate contributions made to reduce or prevent conflict. It is nevertheless reassuring to note the increasing literature on real-life cases of CSR – corporate philanthrophy and corporate citizenship initiatives in the battle against disease, poverty and environmental damage, as well as in relation to refugee issues. The UN is also a source of case studies (and initiatives) in which companies facilitate conflict resolution (for example, Lonhro in the Mozambique crisis of the early 1990s) (Switzer 2001).

12.2.1 Today, though much disputed, governmental and NGO pressure is rising; firms are observed, judged and perceived as conflict raisers or good citizens – affecting markets and performance

For business, realities and self-interest are catching up with pure philosophizing about their role in conflict and its impact. Today, though much disputed, governmental and NGO pressure is rising; firms are observed, judged and perceived as conflict raisers or good citizens. For example, a software tool introduced by US federal regulators has led to the exposure of international companies as "indirectly subsidising a terrorist state"; starting with the five countries of Cuba, Iran, North Korea, Sudan and Syria, and listing companies such as Unilever, Cadbury, Nokia, Siemens, Total, Syngenta and HSBC (Grant 2007, p. 1). Through a link on the Securities and Exchange Commission (SEC) website, it has become possible for investors and other stakeholders to identify companies that mentioned SEC-defined terrorism hotspots in their latest annual report.

McIntyre and Ketata, in Chapter 11, describe the 21st century as a time in which terrorist attacks are likely to happen anytime, climate change is a significant threat and corruption is commonplace. It is a rather uncomfortable and difficult time, in which globalized international corporations, civil society, governments and NGOs struggle with crisis. In this, conflict prevention seeks to reduce the risks that lead to crisis, because a crisis is the sequence of events that creates a high degree of risk of actual harm to specific individuals or organizations. In the worst case scenario, a risky situation or crisis ends in a disaster, leading to the cessation, destruction or interruption of organizational core systems. As Fort and Schipani (2004) have argued, it is important that business, in its own enlightened self-interest, should work for peace through the increase of economic development, transparency, and community-building in conflict-prone areas. Recent literature on the conduct of multinational enterprises (MNEs) as peace builders (Ralph and Tyler 2006; Switzer 2001), and their contribution to mediation (Jones 2003; Ramarajan *et al.* 2002; Schroeter and Vyrastekova 2003) and corporate citizenship (Suder and Nicolas 2007), points out the path to be taken.

For corporations, priorities in managers' daily activities often impede strategic planning in areas such as peace building that may gain margins in the long term. Corporate social responsibility (CSR) and conflict prevention can only become strategic in the partnership of companies, international communities, civil groups and governments for the benefit of all.

Suder (2004) provides a review of thinkers and an analysis of geopolitical turmoil, from Machiaveli's *Il Principe*, to Mackinder's (1904) pivot area theory that forecasts world dominance through self-sufficiency in Euroasia and Africa, to the multi-polarity theory in post-war Europe, and beyond. Each theory is anchored in its historic context, and attempts to understand the reasons for war and peace, for dominance or submission, for opportunities or threats for societies and for their economic systems.

> Modern mainstream geopolitics have complemented classical geopolitics with the notions that help us to understand the impact of geography, politics and history on international (business) relations, comparing different geographic approaches to geopolitics throughout the world, as well as mentalities and concepts. This presupposes the assessment and prioritising of international knowledge of social,

economic, political, cultural, and environmental forces, that analyses the relationships between locations and the global marketplace, taking into account (geographically speaking) location, distance, direction, diffusion, place and regions. (Suder 2004)

International businesses deal with a wide range of people, states and cultures, sometimes in areas of weak governance, and often without particular legal obligations concerning their social responsibilities. Therefore even though international corporations may not need to comply with mandatory standards of behaviour in the field of CSR and conflict prevention, market forces can motivate them to participate in global standard setting. De Jonge (Chapter 3) argues that clear international standards are capable of helping host countries to legislate without fear of investors leaving in favour of lower standards in other locations. Firms often deal with governments that are unable to respond to contemporary challenges that are transnational in nature. These are challenges impossible for nations to cope with alone, whether this concerns conflict or its underlying factors, such as poverty or the need for education and knowledge. Actors will engage in a quest for solutions and the application of tools only if goals are compatible amongst them.

12.2.2 Stakeholder Goal Incompatibility

Stakeholder goal incompatibility describes a situation in which different groups of stakeholders have conflicting agendas. We focus specifically on such conflicts that result in the worsening of the situation of an uninvolved third party (applying to global terrorism as much as traditional forms of conflict). In the case of the MNE, these types of situations can arise when a more powerful stakeholder enters into direct negotiations with the company due to increased leverage on the resources or shareholders of the firm. Or, in the case of donor organizations financing NGOs in poor countries, strict anti-terrorism laws may result in NGOs in southern countries losing access to finances or losing out to bigger structures that are in a position to pay the higher price of conforming to regulations.

Multi-stakeholder approaches such as that promoted by the UN Global Compact hold great promise, but are also fraught with difficulties. Indeed the simple "process of creating multi-stakeholder dialogue, and the dialogue itself, is a significant achievement in and of itself" (Haufler 2002, p. 4). The various constituencies that compose any multi-stakeholder meeting can be compared to those composing all the resource dependencies of a multinational corporation. The chances of shareholders, customers and suppliers having aligned interests with respect to corporations are very low. This phenomenon is very clearly illustrated by Schepers (2006) through the developed–undeveloped country NGO conflicts. Stakeholders from different countries can have differing political agendas that lead to power struggles between stakeholder constituencies. Generally, constituencies with more resources (that is, from developed nations), will tend to impose their views on those with lesser resources through fund or information flow deprivation or political pressure. That is, they tend to expand on values that are closer to theirs, and sometimes in contradiction to the values of stakeholders positioned or rooted in, and in possession of a better understanding of the need zones. Hence, when businesses try to interact in zones that are under stakeholder scrutiny, conflicting stakeholder agendas may lead to pressure for suboptimal corporate responses. The issue around child labour illustrates this point. While it is undeniably a situation in need of remedy, banning child labour does not necessarily lead to higher child, or country-wide welfare.

A "consensus gap" polarizes stakeholder understanding of the role of business in conflict prevention, and there appears to be a "participation gap" of stakeholders in developing countries in the issue (Switzer and Ward 2004, on the basis of a report prepared by DFAIT Canada). Nonetheless, tendencies in the private and public sector point to major developments in this field in the future. The legitimacy of any initiative comes from a multi-stakeholder approach that takes account of local and global expertise. The corporation's partnerships and network relations are important keys for success in any initiative, whether at a higher political level or grassroots led. This approach needs sound management, and a knowledge transfer between actors is crucial. Our research has collected and analysed a variety of case studies, initiatives and research from the three main stakeholders of the international business environment and the area of conflict prevention, and is reported below: on the basis of this work, we propose a tool kit for MNEs: the *modus vivendi* of conflict prevention and hierarchy balancing.

12.3   MITIGATION – HOW BUSINESS CAN MITIGATE THE NEGATIVE EFFECTS OF CONFLICTS

12.3.1   Mitigation Vehicles

Mitigation vehicle 1: diffusion

Dimaggio and Powell (1983) differentiate between three types of constraining processes, or isomorphisms through which institutional change occurs – coercive, mimetic and normative.

Coercive change occurs through formal and informal channels as well as cultural expectations of the society in which the organization functions.

These factors can be legal factors such as Sarbanes-Oxley[1], or business factors, such as changes in fund availability. Whatever the source of these pressures, the result is that organizations change due to external pressures.

Mimetic isomorphism happens when organizations adopt innovations due to environmental uncertainty. In this case organizations seek to imitate others that they see as more certain. This process of innovation is one in which the adopter innovates in what it sees as a legitimizing process, for example, the adoption of ISO management practices.

Normative isomorphism occurs through a professionalization process in which the human production factor of a knowledge-based industry or firm is homogenized. This type of isomorphism results from firms seeking employees with the same type of educational and/or occupational background. This happens to such an extent that when elements that have had a different socialization engage in a firm, the intra-firm socialization processes will tend to homogenize the human element of the firm.

Rogers (1995), Wejnert (2002) and others have also identified social networks as having a very strong effect on adoption decisions. According to them, social and geographical proximity strongly influence potential adopters through peer group pressures.

Multinational corporations are subject to all of the above pressures for change, and also impose all three pressures when they expand operations. That is, when corporations expand into foreign countries, they tend to require similar reporting, and employ or search for people with similar skills as those in their home country, and bring with them the same types of uncertainty faced at home.

Mitigation vehicle 2: social dominance theory
The clustering of people and technology into spatial and virtual locations also leads to a clustering of business in "urban regions and large towns improv[ing] the efficiency of the local economy and lead[ing] to higher productivity", which in turn leads to higher GDP per capita in urban regions (OECD 2007). Hence, the digital divide is accompanied by a wealth divide that is redefining how societies operate between one another and within themselves. Social dominance theory is the study of "why [and how] human societies tend to be organized as a group based hierarchy" (Sidanius *et al.*, 2004). Specifically, Social dominance theory is a systematic exploration of oppression that takes into consideration the institutional and individual nature of discrimination.

One of the precepts of this theory is that societies or social groups produce ideologies that legitimize or de-legitimize inequality, and that people within these groups will have a certain predisposition towards group-based dominance, known as a social dominance orientation (SDO).

The SDO of individuals can be either high or low, whereas social groups and institutions will tend to have an attenuating or enhancing effect on hierarchy. Generally speaking, individuals with a high SDO will seek to join hierarchy-enhancing groups, which will in turn tend to be more discriminatory of groups with hierarchy-attenuating structures and a low SDO. While it is argued that it is possible for individuals to adapt to the strength of hierarchy of their group, it is more likely that individuals will dis-identify from groups that do not share the same orientation as their own. Dis-identified individuals will seek to join groups with a similar orientation (compare the earlier analysis of Sachs and Dieleman of minority groups in Chapter 5). In terms of social conflict, Sidanius argues that hierarchy-attenuating and -enhancing institutions balance out to create stability in society, and when the balancing process loses legitimacy, social conflict arises.

Mitigation vehicle 3: resource dependency theory

Resource dependency theory states that organizations will tend to seek to satisfy the needs of those external actors on whom they most depend for resources, while at the same time trying to reduce their dependence on such actors. This dependence on external actors for acquiring resources reduces the discretion of management in company operations, which may interfere with the goals of the organization.

Taking a resource-dependency approach to business, the three main dependencies of any business are its need for resources, customers and finance:

- With respect to its need for resources, the business will either have to have no alternative source of resources, or have sufficient motivation to engage in a zone where gathering resources is good for its core business.
- With the customer, the business will have to convince him or her that its actions are really as responsible as it claims.
- In engaging in conflict prevention, the corporation will have to convince the financers that it is advantageous for them to invest in a corporation that puts emphasis on social responsibility by demonstrating that returns in this kind of business are superior or equal to that of other organizations, or by using moral leverage to get finance.

However, the problem with respect to consumers is that pressure groups exist for all types of wrongdoing, and it is extremely costly for business to focus on all social and environmental issues at the local as well as at the global level. In addition, the phenomenon of global terrorism has brought a level of conflict awareness to the general public that is unique because threats are close to every citizen, while citizens believe that responsibilities for the phenomenon are rooted in the abuse of powers by multiple actors in the international arena, including business.

12.3.2 Business as an Agent of Change in Conflict Zones

On the one hand, we can conclude that global business contributes to the homogenization of:

- its workforce through normative isomorphism;
- its supply chain through coercive isomorphism;
- competition through mimetic isomorphism.

On the other hand, however, business is coerced by its resource dependencies (natural resources, markets, human resources, capital), whose interests, balanced or not, must be stabilized for MNEs to be able to operate efficiently.

Obviously, tangible resource dependencies will tend to occur mostly in manufacturing, or in business segments that are highly dependent on commodities to function. However, in a knowledge-based industry in which the professional force is a highly homogenized resource, dependency will tend to operate through three channels, namely, talent, customers and shareholders. Whereas talent is undeniably an essential factor for success, talent retention is still in its infancy in terms of academic research and to date no best practice has arisen. Customer and shareholder dependencies, however, are well-understood and studied phenomena. Customers, on the one hand, will be motivated by price factors, ideological factors (as in the case of The Body Shop, fair-trade coffee and so on) (Storbacka *et al.* 1994), product exclusivity or a balance of these three factors. Shareholders, on the other hand, seek the highest utility margins within the risk range of their choice (according to the theory of shareholder value). Whereas there has been an undeniable rise in the number of ideologically motivated investment funds, these still do not have the same weight as the traditional value-seeking ones.

The resource dependencies of MNEs, the global span of their supply chain and their capacity to shape their local workforce, suppliers and competitors, inevitably leads to a shift in the power balance of host countries. These shifts can serve either as a legitimizing or de-legitimizing process in relation to the current social structure of a society. The legitimizing activities of MNEs will tend to stabilize societies, while the de-legitimizing ones will tend to enhance the possibility of conflict. The hierarchy imbalance that

MNEs can create for high SDO groups (in terms of the innovation diffusion they spread) may lead to an anti-dominance reaction in which unintegrated SDO group(s) will enter into conflict with influences seen as foreign and destructive of the social order that was to its or their advantage.

12.4   TOOL KIT FOR HIERARCHY BALANCING

While short-term risks exist for business when entering a market with a high probability of conflict, a long-term risk also exists for business that de-legitimizes a stable social regime and causes conflict (however much the MNE or MNE home country might not share the new market's values). Hence the importance of bi-directional risk assessment in strategic planning and strict, externally audited, "do no harm" policies adopted by multinationals upon entering a new market.

Below we propose a set of strategies that attempt to respond to the issues mentioned in this chapter. This is not meant to be an exhaustive analysis but rather an exemplification of courses of action that can be taken by MNEs.

12.4.1   Stakeholders

Multi-stakeholder initiatives
As mentioned earlier, aligning stakeholder interests facilitates MNE operations by limiting the constituencies with which the MNE has to interact. This allows for leveraged problem solving since the focus of the MNE is tighter. The United Nations Global Compact (GC) initiative is to date the most complete forum, allying the United Nations with business, NGOs, trade unions and local communities. It aims to identify key issues and provide a forum for the exchange of experience and best practice, in order to stimulate the role of all stakeholders in conflict reduction and prevention, and peace preservation. Multi-stakeholder initiatives already provide important experience in Northern Ireland, Croatia, Somalia and Azerbaijan.[2] Human rights, human security, the respect of local communities and stakeholders, and business security go hand in hand. Accountability and transparency of all actors can be fostered efficiently through business interventions, sometimes voluntary, sometimes forced by NGO pressures, and have the potential to benefit all through reduced uncertainty. This is the conclusion that can be reached from a growing number of CSR reports published by successful companies, from the existence of rankings such as the Dow Jones Sustainability Index, the Domini 400 Social Index or Eurosif and (by extension) from the example of inno-

vative initiatives that serve marketing and communication purposes too. Partnerships with UN and UNHCR projects and other initiatives are good starting points.

Certification
The certification of commodities is one mechanism that has been adopted by MNEs, governments and stakeholders to stem the flow of commodities that are extracted from conflict zones or in ways that conflict with stake-holder values (illegal logging for example, with the certification of wood). Certification, however, can be a source of conflict in itself. On the one hand, it is not always very easy to verify the source of the certified commodity. The Democratic Republic of Congo, for example, has an annual production of diamonds estimated at 55 000 carats, but exports over 5 million carats annually (Addison 2004). On the other hand, certification is intrinsically value laden. Nonetheless, despite these drawbacks, accurate certification is a significant source of transparency for stakeholders.

Partnerships with regional organizations or government
In regional conflict prevention, firms can engage in partnerships that help coordinate peace initiatives. They can:

- help run cultural, political or social network events that help conflicting communities communicate and understand each other better;
- help international organizations monitor efficiently and intervene in a timely fashion where necessary;
- sponsor peace-related events; or,
- assist with controlling the transfer of illegal material, information or capital.

Digitas Advertising Company, for example, has partnered with the Roots for Peace anti-landmining program. Through awareness-raising campaigns, they contribute to the education of the international community, and thus help to promote funding of prevention measures.

12.4.2 Diffusion

The importance of local knowledge
Understanding local knowledge and cultures can act as a source for reducing hierarchy de-legitimatization. Indeed, understanding local customs and knowledge can help to adapt business practices in a way more suitable to the destination country while reducing the probability of conflict. An

example is the adaptation of advertising to ethnic groups, or of offices to religious customs, in a way that contributes to successful cohabitation of traditionally conflicting groups. This much more profound, local knowledge is about politics, culture, needs and tendencies in the different strata of society. A thorough, non-ethnocentric understanding of these factors can help MNEs. Some of this is dealt with in political risk analysis, most often adopting an external perspective. However, local knowledge in this field serves as a market opener, as a cultural and geopolitical fusion with the market can be created. This fosters the " 'know your customer, know your supplier, know your community" principles that are well-recognized as relevant tools in risk reduction. Supporting local entrepreneurs and relevant future business partners in conflict areas (selected through criteria of core business relevance and peace building and peace keeping relevance) is also a sound approach to building the foundations for human security, market opportunities and social cohesion.

Partnerships in education and communication

MNEs may engage in partnerships that focus on improving communication and education in target countries. However, as is the case with certification, education is value laden and could have adverse effects in terms of social hierarchy stability. The importance of the education process and the need for approval by the local community should never be understated, and the effect of value diffusion should always be properly weighed against the possibility of non-integration. For example, Microsoft International's Unlimited Potential initiative "supports community technology learning centres with funding, training, equipment and software, and employee involvement . . . with over 100 partners, assisting unemployed youth and adults, people with disabilities, older people, women and refugees" (Courtois 2004). Intel is running its "Intel Teach to the Future Program" in Lebanon as part of its "Digital Transformation Initiative for the Middle East": a comprehensive, multi-year programme of economic, educational and technology-related support of the company throughout the Middle East and North Africa regions.

Launch and/or support of private and/or independent, not-for-profit security initiatives

The Russell Family Foundation is just one example of a global security initiative from the private sector. Its George F. Russell, Jr Fund supports nonprofits working globally to address critical issues that threaten peace and security, especially in Eastern Europe, Russia and the Asia-Pacific region. For think tanks, the EastWest Institute is one of many dealing with international political, economic and security issues. An example of an independent peace-building organization is International Alert, which aims for lasting peace and security in communities affected by violent conflict, and is active in more than 20 countries and territories around the world, working directly with people affected and at government, EU and UN levels.

Partnerships with governments

The South Africa Chamber of Business has indicated that crime and conflict pose a larger threat to business than economic turmoil (South African Chamber of Commerce and Industry 2007). In the area of crime, Business Against Crime South Africa, founded in 1996 by Nelson Mandela, aims to make South Africa a safer place through the partnership of business, government and citizens. Its toolbox contains public–private partnerships that allow for knowledge and skills transfer, and increased strategic capacity to counteract adversity. Examples in this field are the blacklisting of stolen cell phones, mentoring programmes, the improvement of data transfer and policing.[3]

Partnerships with international organizations

The European Union, Organisation for Economic Co-operation and Development (OECD), World Bank, various UN agencies and a number of governments have all acknowledged the critical role of economic factors in conflict through a number of key policy documents, and are beginning to recognize the potential of the private sector to contribute to peace building. There is a growing debate on the need for clearer international guidelines and constraints on companies operating in conflict-prone zones. Corporations can engage in early warning and preventive diplomacy, and contribute to preventive disarmament and post-conflict peace-building initiatives that are all interdependent. UNOPS (United Nations Office for Project Services) also arranges for staff exchanges to facilitate the transfer of skills and technology in the field of conflict prevention and rehabilitation. In addition, since October 2006, the United Nations has been striving for a global Arms Trade Treaty, and can be lobbied and informed about issues in that (and other) areas.

12.5 CONCLUSIONS: BEYOND A CONSTRAINING FACTOR

Conflicts are situations in which goal incompatibilities arise between parties. We have seen that violent conflict can be explained through youth bulges, as the consequence of communication failure or anti-hegemonic movements, or for power reasons, and finds its expression in violent crime, inter-group conflicts, civil wars and insurgencies or cross-border wars. Furthermore, we have seen that the causes for these conflicts can be incompatible claims over control of resources or areas, the desire of new claimants to participate directly in decision making and sharing of benefits, the financing by MNEs or governments of repression of groups, outsider interference in local decision making, the clash of civilizations or anti-dominance.

We have also seen that the global economy is increasingly knowledge based, with widely spread supply chains, and that the liberalization of capital markets and inter-firm alliances makes targeting firms or countries directly through activities in other countries very hard. Multinationals can delegate responsibility at any point in the supply chain and, conversely, can hardly be expected to take responsibility for the entire supply chain due to the diverse legal constituencies and traditions in which various parts of it are based. For example, a supply chain can span a set of countries and corporations with different legal traditions and governance, and significantly different levels of acceptance of corruption. Contracts made in one country might not be legally enforceable in another, and corruption might be a standard business practice in yet another country but not in the country of incorporation. Moreover, if an MNE decides to tackle a conflict seriously it will need to align the interests of its stakeholder constituency.

We have isolated three ways in which MNEs can affect conflict, namely through isomorphism, legitimization or de-legitimization of social hierarchy, and giving priority to some element of unaligned resource dependency interests, and we have developed mitigation vehicle and tool mechanisms than can help international firms tackle the issues arising directly or indirectly from conflict, and that respond to the moral responsibilities that automatically result from doing business in host communities (see Figure 12.1).

The increasing range of actors aware of the link between business and human security issues is adding pressure on the former to engage in the latter. The OECD (2006) publishes important guidelines for MNEs in conflict zones, termed "weak governance zones", that not only provide information and advice on risks and ethical dilemmas for firms that operate in these zones which is relevant to their managerial challenges, but also encourages contributions to the creation of a more peaceful society and responsible governance by "speaking out about wrongdoing".

Jean-Francois Rischard (2002), the European Vice-President of the World Bank, pointed out in his book *High Noon: 20 Years to Solve 20 Global Problems* that traditional governance is faltering or inadequate to address many of the fundamental contemporary problems in the world, especially poverty, conflict and environmental issues. The world changes continuously and with it, the opportunities and threats that affect societies

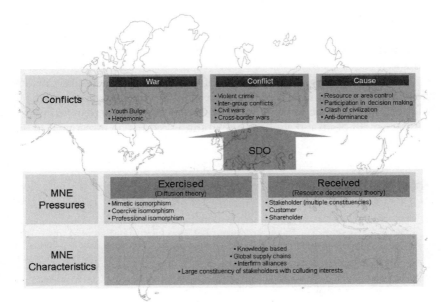

Figure 12.1 Social dominance orientation (SDO) map: the impact of MNE specificities in conflict

and businesses. For corporations, adaptation to an ever-changing marketplace and the ability to address infrastructural, financial and reputational risks is key. A contribution to conflict reduction and prevention does not always need to translate into corporate citizenship, CSR or philanthropy, though these may constitute part of the strategy. The 2007 World Wealth report by Merrill Lynch and Capgemini shows that in particular, ultra-high net worth individuals (with assets above $30m) tend to engage in socially responsible investments, and companies with high performance levels are particularly active in CSR (Suder and Nicolas 2006). The creation of change in society, the increase of influence and better returns on investment go along hand in hand with ethical considerations. This type of investment is supported and reinvigorated by sound returns on investment. For example, the Domini 400 Social Index (that includes 400 companies), monitoring environmental and social contributions, has returned 12.71 per cent annually since 1990 (the S&P 500 shows an 11.48 per cent return). Indeed, one can argue that true business interest in conflict prevention will thrive when returns on conflict prevention investments can be measured, or are perceived. It is an intangible asset, the know-how of top management.

Similar to other corporate citizenship or CSR initiatives, conflict prevention contributions are only considered appropriate for a corporation when they do not affect its core finance or core business, but rather take place at the margin of core activity and are in line with corporate strategy and performance aspirations, or are in its enlightened self-interest to pursue.

The most accessible starting point for corporate contributions in this field is the establishment of best practices, not by benchmarking on others, but by innovating the way in which corporate contributions can be made – for the benefit of all stakeholders and granting returns on investment in the long run.

NOTES

1. The Sarbanes–Oxley Act came into force in 2002 as a response to major corporate scandals including the fall of Enron, Worldcom and Tyco International, among others. The legislation established new rules for stock exchange-listed companies mainly focusing on external auditors, corporate responsibilities and financial reporting. In addition, it established the Public Accountancy Oversight Board to oversees public company auditors.
2. For case studies, see www.unglobalcompact.org/Issues (accessed 18 January 2008) for conflict-prevention and multi-stakeholder initiatives.
3. For more information, see www.bac.co.za/, accessed 18 January 2008.

REFERENCES

Addison, T. (2004) The global economy, conflict prevention and post conflict recovery, paper presented at the *DESA Expert Group Meeting on Conflict Prevention, Peacebuilding and Development*, New York, 15 November.

Brooks, S.G. (1999) The globalization of production and the changing benefits of conquest, *Journal of Conflict Resolution*, **43**(5), 646–670.

Courtois, J.P. (2004) Microsoft EMEA role of corporate responsibility and the OECD guidelines for multinational enterprises, paper presented at the *OECD Public Forum*, 11 May.

Dimaggio, P.J. and Powell, W.W. (1983) The iron cage revisited: institutional isomorphism and collective rationality in organizational fields, *American Sociological Review*, **48**(April), 147–160.

Fort, T.L. and Schipani, C.A. (2004) *The Role of Business in Fostering Peaceful Societies*, Cambridge University Press, New York.

Friedman, T.L. (2005) *The World is Flat: A Brief History of the Twenty-First Century*, Farrar, Straus and Giroux, New York.

Gillingham, D. and Suder, G. (2007) Corporate Strategies for Countering Security Risks, in: Merkidze, A (ed). *Terrorism Issues: Threat Assessment, Consequences and Prevention*. Novascience, New York.

Gilpin, R. (1988) The theory of hegemonic war, *Journal of Interdisciplinary History*, **18**(4), 591–613.

Grant, J. (2007) Outrage over SEC terrorism "blacklist", *Financial Times*, 29 June, p. 1.

Haufler, V. (ed.) (2002) *Case studies of Multistakeholder Partnerships: Policy Dialogue on Business in Zones of Conflict*, published on www.un globalcompact. org/docs/issues_doc/7.2.1/MultistakeholderInitiativesinZonesofConflict.pdf, accessed 18 January 2008.

Helmke, R. and Tessner, S. (2000) *Partnering with the Private Sector: The Return of the UN-Business Partnership*, UNOPS, Geneva and New York, www.nyu. edu/classes/UNcourse/fall00/additionalrdgs/speakernotes/foreignaffairswithbibl iooct30.doc, accessed August 2007.

Humphrey, M. (2003) *Economics and Violent Conflict*, Harvard University, published on www.preventconflict.org/portal/economics/Essay.pdf, accessed 18 January 2008.

Huntington, S.P. (1993) The clash of civilisations?, *Foreign Affairs*, **72**(3), 22–49.

Huntington, S.P. (1997) The erosion of American national interests, *Foreign Affairs*, 76(5), 38–40.

Huntington, S.P. (1998) *The Clash of Civilisations and the Remaking of the World Order*, Touchstone, New York.

Jones, G.T. (2003) Toward an Integrated Practice of Behavioral Conflict Management, paper presented at the *16th Annual IACM Conference* Melbourne, Australia, June, Social Science Research Network Working Paper Series, http://ssrn.com/abstract=399622.

Krueger, A.B. and Maleckova, J. (2003) Education, poverty and terrorism: is there a Causal Connection? *Journal of Economic Perspectives*, **17**(4), 119–144.

Laqueur, W. (2003) *No End to War: Terrorism in the Twenty-First Century*, Continuum International Publishers, New York.

Laqueur, W. (2004) The terrorism to come. *Policy Review*, August–September Issue.

Mackinder, H.J. (1904) Geographical pivot of history. *Geographical Journal*, 421–442.

OECD (2006) *OECD Risk Awareness Tool for Multinational Enterprises in Weak Zones*, OECD, Paris published on, www.oecd.org/dataoecd/26/21/36885821.pdf, accessed 18 January 2008.

OECD (2007) *Regions at a Glance 2007*. OECD, Paris, published on www.oecd.org/document/61/0,3343,en_2649_37439_38690301_1_1_1_37439,00. html, accessed August 2007.

Pfeffer, J. and Salancik, G.R. (1978) *The External Control of Organizations: A Resource Dependence Perspective*. Harper and Row, New York.

Ralph, N. and Tyler, M.C. (2006) *Companies as Peacebuilders: Engaging Communities Through Conflict Resolution*, University of Melbourne Legal Studies Research Paper No. 196, http://ssrn.com/abstract=946849, accessed 18 January 2008.

Ramarajan, L., Bezrukova, K., Jehn, K.A., Euwema, M. and Kop, N. (2002) *Successful Conflict Resolution Between Peacekeepers and NGOs: The Role of Training and Preparation in International Peacekeeping in Bosnia*, http://ssrn.com/abstract=305206, accessed 18 January 2008.

Rischard, J.-F. (2002) *High Noon: 20 years to Solve 20 Global Problems*, Basic Books, New York.

Rodrik, D. (1998) Globalisation, social conflict and economic growth, *The World Economy*, **21**(2),143–158.

Rogers, E. (1995) *Diffusion of Innovations*, Free Press, New York.

Rummel, R.J. (1976) *Understanding Conflict and War, Vol. 2: The Conflict Helix*, Sage Publications, Beverly Hills.

Schepers, D.H. (2006) The impact of NGO network conflict on the corporate social responsibility strategies of multinational corporations, *Business and Society*, **45** (3), 282–299.

Schroeter, K. and Vyrastekova, J. (2003) *Does it Take Three to Make Two Happy? An Experimental Study on Bargaining with Mediation*, CentER Discussion Paper No. 2003-60, http://ssrn.com/abstract=556088, accessed 18 January 2008.

Sidanius, J., Pratto, F., Laar, C.and Levin, S. (2004) Social dominance theory: its agenda and method, *Political Psychology*, **25**(6), 845–880.

South African Chamber of Commerce and Industry (2007) Business Confidence Index, September, http://www.sacob.co.2a/bci.htm, accessed December 2007.

Spector, D. (2000) Rational debate and one-dimensional conflict, *The Quarterly Journal of Economics*, **115**(1), February, 181–200.

Storbacka, K., Strandvik, T. and Grönroos, Ch. (1994) Managing customer relationships for profit: the dynamics of relationship quality, *International Journal of Service Industry Management*, **5**(5), 21–38.

Suder, G. (Ed.) (2004) The complexity of the geopolitics dimension in risk assessment for international business. In G. Suder (ed.), *Terrorism and the International Business Environment: The Security – Business Nexus*, Edward Elgar, Cheltenham, UK and Northampton, MA, pp. 58–81.

Suder, G. (ed.) (2006) *Corporate Strategies under International Terrorism and Adversity*, Edward Elgar, Cheltenham, UK and Northampton, MA.

Suder, G., Chailan, C. and Suder, D. (2007) Strategic Megabrand Management: does Global Uncertainty Affect Brand Value and Ranking? A Post-09/11 US/non-US Comparison of the 100 Biggest Brands, CERAM Working Paper and Competitive Paper presented at the *World Marketing Congress* 11–14 July, Verona.

Suder, G. and Czinkota, M. (2007) Understanding the valence of terrorism in international business, Multinational Business Review, **13**(3).

Suder, G. and Nicolas, N. (2007) Pro Bono Publico? Corporate Citizenship at Microsoft, paper presented at the *Academy of International Business World Conference*, Indianapolis, and *EABIS 6th Annual Colloquium*, Barcelona, 22 September.

Swanson, P. (2002) *Fuelling Conflict: the Oil Industry and Armed Conflict*, Fafo Report 378. Fafo Institute of Applied Social Science.

Switzer, J. (2001) *Conflicting Interests*, International Institute for Sustainable Development, www.iisd.org/pdf/2002/envsec_conflicting_interests.pdf, accessed 18 January 2008.

Switzer, J. and Ward, H. (2004) *Enabling Corporate Investment in Peace: An Assessment of Voluntary Initiatives Addressing Business and Violent Conflict, and a Framework for Policy Decision-Making*, Discussion Paper, prepared for the Department of Foreign Affairs and International Trade (DFAIT), Canada.

Thornton, W. (2003) Cold War II: Islamic terrorism as power politics, *Antipode*, **35**(2), 205–211.

United Nations (2004) *DESA Expert Group Meeting on Conflict Prevention, Peacebuilding and Development*, 15 November 2004, published on www.un.org/esa/peacebuilding/Action/DesaTaskForce/egm_20041115.html, accessed 18 January 2008.

United Nations (2006) *Conflict Diamonds: Sanctions and War*, UNDPI, New York, http://www.un.org/peace/africa/Diamond.html, accessed 19 February 2008.

Urdal, H. (2004) The devil in the demographics: the effect of youth bulges on domestic armed conflict 1950–2000, *Social Development Papers: Conflict and Reconstruction Paper*, Paper 14, July.

Wallace, S. (2007) Last of the Amazon, *National Geographic*, **211**(1), January, 40–71.

Wejnert, B. (2002) Integrating models of diffusion innovations: a conceptual framework, *Annual Review of Sociology*, **28**, 297–326.

Index

9/11 terrorist attack 156, 171

accountability 18–19, 20, 22, 25–6, 146
accounting 60, 65–8, 153
added value 50, 172
Adler, N.J. 4, 127
advanced countries 122, 158, 172, 176
advanced technology production sector
    110, 111, 112, 113, 114, 115
Africa 121–2, 123
    see also Cameroon; Chad; Lesotho;
        Nigeria; Sudan
agency problems 59
    see also expropriation of minority
        shareholders
aid funds 153
Alien Tort Claims Act (ACTA) (US)
    17–18, 26
Amnesty International 130
Annan, K. 4–5, 11, 126, 144
anti-Americanism 57–8
anti-bribery measures 163
anti-corruption 12, 81–2, 162–3
anti-discrimination, in employment
    12
anti-dominance theory of conflict 170
anti-theft tags 79–80, 81
APC 96–7
appeals, International Court of Justice
    (ICJ) 38–9
Aptech 98, 99
arbitration, mandatory 35
Asia and Asia–Pacific 121–2, 123, 160
    see also Cambodia; China–India
        nexus; India; Israel; Japan;
        Kazakhstan; Middle East;
        Myanmar; Palestine; Salim
        Group; Taiwan
Association of Certified Chartered
    Accountants (ACCA) 145
auditing 65–8, 82
Australia 100–101, 123, 169

authoritarian rulers 63, 171
automatic number plate registration 78

Baker Institute 122
Barber, B.R. 127
Becker, G.S. 60
Beijing University 98, 99
Berry, M.A. 161
best practices 10
"Best Practices in Human Resources
    Management" competition
    110–115, 117
bio-identity databases 79, 87
Birks, C. 83
Bodwell, C. 107
Bohdziewicz, P. 110–115
bonding social capital 61–2
bribery 124–5, 129, 154, 163
bridging social capital 61–2
Britain 10–11, 17, 144–5
Brooks, S.G. 171–2
Burma Campaign UK 17
business ethics
    and competitive advantage 160–161
    and non-violent societies 49–50
    peace and conflict prevention 54–5,
        128, 160–161, 164
    Poland 109, 111, 112, 114, 115, 117
business objectives 127–8
Butler, R. 87

Cambodia 16–17
Cameroon 130
Campbell, G. 123
Canada 123, 154
capital *see* capitalism; foreign capital;
    foreign direct investment (FDI);
    human capital; investment; social
    capital
capitalism 9, 57, 139–42, 144
    see also market economy
Carney, M. 59, 62, 63, 64

Carroll, A.B. 107, 115
CC-TV (Closed Circuit Television) 77–8, 81
Central America 121–2, 123, 154
certification 123, 181
Chad 124, 130
Chamber for Environmental Matters (ICJ) 36, 38
child labour 160, 176
child labour abolition 12, 32, 176
China *see* China–India nexus; Salim Group
China–India nexus
  business and trade relations 95–6, 101–2
  Chinese business interests in India 96–7
  Indian business interests in China 98–9
  international competition 94–5, 100
  international political relations 94, 101
  military relations 93–4, 100–101, 102
  national interests and international rivalry 93–4
  PPP (Purchasing Power Parity) 93
  third country business interests 96–7, 99–100
Chiquita Brands International 119, 128
Chudnovsky, D. 160
citizens 14, 28, 162, 179
  see also corporate citizenship; global corporate citizenship
civic republicanism 54
civil society groups 164
Clarke, D. 159
Clarkson, M.B.E. 108
clash of civilizations theory of conflict 170
Claude, R.P. 15
climate change 27, 154–5, 158, 163–4
Cmiel, K. 8
Coca Cola 129–30, 160
Cochran, P.L. 107
codes of conduct 26–7, 29, 112–13, 114–15, 180–181, 185
coercive change 176–7, 179
Coffee, J.C. Jr 59
collective bargaining rights 12
Colombia 119, 128–9

Commonwealth of Independent States (CIS) 121–2
communication 182
Communication on Progress 13, 16, 21, 27
communism 57
communities 5, 6, 50, 130
competition 84, 94–5, 100, 165, 179
competitive advantage 108, 117, 160–161
conflict
  defined 168, 169–70
  host countries of international extractive industries 124–5
  international business involvement 4, 169–70
  international extractive industries 119, 121–2, 169, 170
  and stakeholder goal incompatibility 175–6
  theories 170–173
  and weak governance 175, 184
conflict diamonds 123
conflict mitigation and prevention
  business as agent of change 179–80
  business profit and community benefit 5–6
  Global Compact 13–14
  by human rights NGOs 22
  international business involvement 4–5, 173–6
  international extractive industries, 127–31, 172
  mitigation vehicles 176–9
  MNEs 119–20, 127–8, 131, 172
  theories 173
  tool kit 180–183
consumers *see* customers
Control Risks and Simmons and Simmons 153
Convention on the Law of the Sea (UN) 38–9
cooperation 165, 173
Corhydron 109
corporate citizenship 57, 127, 128, 131, 142–4, 145, 173–5
corporate social responsibility (CSR)
  accountability by states 18–19, 20, 22
  change issues 144–6

and customers 109, 160, 178–9
definitional difficulties 105–7
and economic advantage 108, 117
and Global Compact (UN) (*see*
    Global Compact (UN))
governments and human rights
    10–11
and image and reputation of MNEs
    9, 160–161, 164, 185
models 107–8
new agenda 146
and NGOs 160, 173, 174, 180
peace and conflict prevention 127
performance of Poland, post-
    transition 109–10
proactive strategies 161–2
progress, since 1995 142–4
reporting 180–181
self-interest, economic 106, 127, 174,
    186
and stakeholders 106, 107, 108, 143,
    145, 146, 160, 164, 186
and sustainable enterprise economy
    140–142, 147–8
corruption
    causes 157–8
    effects 153–4
    of firms 22, 63–4, 157–8
    of governments and officials 61, 64,
        66–7, 74, 125, 129, 157–8
    see also anti-corruption; bribery;
        expropriation of minority
        shareholders
cost–benefit analysis of risk
    management 19
cost savings 83, 84, 161
costs 96–7, 98, 101–2, 153, 156, 160
courts *see* justice system
crisis 124–5, 151, 168
    see also climate change; conflict;
        corruption; crisis management;
        terrorism; violence; wars
crisis management 152–3, 159–65
"crony capitalism" 61
culture 61, 170
customers 109, 111, 112, 114, 160,
    178–9, 182

data security 85–6, 87
Davies, R. 159, 161, 162

Davis, K. 107
debt, external 153
decentralization 157–8
Decision Support Systems (DSS) 85
deforestation 123–4
Deva, S. 21
developed countries 122, 158, 172, 176
developing countries
    anti-corruption measures 162–3
    climate change 158
    conditions 119, 121–2, 124–6, 172
    corruption 153
    human rights abuses 22
    international extractive industries
        121–2, 172
    opportunism by MNEs 160
    promoting corporate social
        responsibility, need for 162–3,
        164
    and social capital 61
    stakeholder goal incompatibility 176
diamond industry 123, 125, 181
Dieleman, M. 59, 62, 64
diffusion 176–7, 181–2
Dimaggio, P.J. 176–7
direct procurement 83
directors, legal personhood and social
    responsibility 25, 26
disaster recovery plan (DRP) 87
Dispute Settlement Understanding
    (WTO) 38–9
dispute settlements 38–9
diversified conglomeration 63
DNA 79
Domini 400 Social Index 180–181,
    185
Dow Jones Sustainability Indexes 27,
    29, 180–181

e-commerce and e-procurement 81–4,
    87
ecological performance 160–161
ecological risk assessment 154
economic advantage 108, 117, 160–161
economic development 127, 130, 131
    see also sustainable development
economic growth 171
economic liberalization 157–8
economic performance 50, 174, 177,
    185–6

education 15, 22, 60, 146, 164, 182
  see also knowledge; learning;
    qualified staff, recruitment and
    retention of; skills; university
    research centres
efficiency 63–4, 82, 83
  see also inefficiency
Eliminating World Poverty (UK,
  Department for International
  Development) 10–11
emergency call taking and response 75,
  76, 77, 78
employees 74, 111, 112, 114, 177, 179
employment 12, 51
  see also child labour; child labour
    abolition; employees; forced
    labour abolition; human
    capital; human resources;
    labour costs; labour protection;
    labour relations
enforcement 13, 15, 16, 19, 26, 30–33,
  34–5
engagement 13, 55–6
entrepreneurship support 113, 114, 115
environmental problems 124, 154
  see also climate change;
    deforestation; environmental
    protection; pollution
environmental protection
  "Best Practices in Human Resources
    Management" competition 111,
    112, 114, 115
  and corporate citizenship 142
  and corporate social responsibility
    145, 146, 160–161
  and Global Compact (UN) 12, 13
  and governments 162, 163–4
  risk assessment 154
  and sustainable enterprise economy
    147, 148
  see also international environmental
    law
environmental responsibilities 12
environmentally-friendly technologies
  12
"Equator Principles" 32
ethics 57
  see also business ethics; corporate
    citizenship; corporate social
    responsibility (CSR)

ethnic minority groups 61, 62–3,
  170–171
Europe 77, 122, 123, 161
  see also France; Kazakhstan;
    Poland; Russia; UK
evidence 76, 77
exports 97, 121–2, 123–4
expropriation of minority shareholders
  59, 60, 64–5, 66, 68

facial recognition 78
family firms 59–60, 63–4, 65, 68
Ferguson, T. 95
Ferrary, M. 63
Field, A. 33
fingerprints 79
First Optional Protocol 28
Fitzmaurice, M. 35, 39
forced labour abolition 12, 32, 33
foreign capital 110, 112, 113, 114, 115,
  116
foreign direct investment (FDI) 95,
  163, 172
Formosa Plastics Group 16
Fort, T.L. 49–55, 127, 131, 174
France 57–8, 59, 68, 96–7
Frederick, W.C. 53
Friedman, T.L. 100, 173
FTSE4Good Index Series 27, 29
fuel products 121

Galbraith, J.K. 146
Galileo project 77
Gandhi, R. 153
geopolitics 4, 174–5
Gillingham, D. 171
Gilpin, R. 171
GIS (Geospatial Information Systems)
  77, 78, 79
Global Compact Office (UN) 13, 18, 21
Global Compact (UN)
  assessment of 18–21, 22–3
  Communication on Progress 13, 16,
    21, 27
  network and NGOs 13, 14–18, 21
  principles and process 11–14, 21,
    141, 144, 145, 180
  signatories 14, 145
  voluntary nature 13, 15–16, 19, 20,
    21, 26

global corporate citizenship 4, 5
Global Reporting Initiative (GRI)
 Sustainability Reporting
 Guidelines 26–7
global supply chains 172, 173, 179
global terrorism 3–4, 155–6, 171, 172,
 173, 179
globalization 9, 22, 168, 171–2
governments
 and accountability for corporate
  social responsibility 18–19, 20,
  22, 25–6
 conflict mitigation partnerships 181,
  183
 crisis management 161–3, 164
 and human rights and corporate
  social responsibility 10–11
 and MNE relationships 9
 promoting corporate social
  responsibility 161–2, 173–4
 and Salim Group 59–60, 63–4
 and social capital 61, 62, 63
 and terrorism, causes of 171
 see also local governments; weak
  governance
GPS (Global Positioning Systems) 77,
 79, 81
Greenstone Resources 154
group cohesion 61, 62, 63
*Guidelines for Multinational
 Enterprises* (OECD) 26, 27
Guillen, M. 63, 64
Guliani, S. 98

Haier 96, 97
Harris, D.J. 28, 34, 36
Hart, S. 139
Hawley, S. 153, 154, 157, 162
hegemony theory of war and conflict
 171, 173
Henderson, D. 106, 107
Howard-Hassmann, R.E. 9
human capital 60
human resources 110–115, 117
human rights 8, 9–11, 145, 146
 see also Global Compact (UN);
  human rights abuses; human
  rights NGOs; international
  human rights law; regional
  human rights bodies

human rights abuses 9, 16–17, 21–2
human rights NGOs 13, 14–15, 16–18,
 21
Human Rights Watch (HRW) 15,
 16–17
human security 139–40
Huntington, S.P. 170

IBM 96, 99–100
ICTs (information and communication
 technologies)
 education partnerships 182
 for international business support
  75, 81–7
 in police and public safety agencies
  75–81, 87–8
 see also internet; software and IT
  industries
identity 52–3
 see also bio-identity databases
image 9, 160–161, 164
imports 122
In Larger Freedom (Secretary General
 of the UN) 36
India 129–30
 see also China–India nexus
indigenous populations 32, 124, 130
indirect procurement 83
individual responsibility 25, 26, 28,
 33–4
Indonesia *see* Salim Group
inefficiency 76, 81
 see also efficiency
influence 9, 25
informal codes of conduct 112, 114,
 115
information *see* data security; evidence;
 ICTs (information and
 communication technologies);
 information sharing; intelligence
 data analysis; internet; knowledge;
 knowledge management; paper
 records, elimination of; sensitive
 data; software and IT industries
information management 75, 76–7,
 80–81
information sharing 15, 21, 76
institutional environments 59, 61, 62,
 63, 64, 175, 184
intelligence data analysis 75, 77, 79

Intergovernmental Panel on Climate
　　Change 155
International Auditing and Assurance
　　Standards Board 27
international community, crisis
　　management 163–4
international competition 94–5, 100
*International Convention on Civil
　　Liability for Oil Pollution Damage*
　　(UN) 28
International Court of Justice (ICJ)
　　35–6, 38–9
*International Covenant of Civil and
　　Political Rights* (ICCPR) 28
International Criminal Court 28, 33–4
international criminal law 33–4
international environmental law 35–9
international extractive industries
　　conflict and violence 119, 121–2,
　　　169, 170
　　deforestation 123–4
　　diamond industry 123, 125
　　host country conditions 119, 121–2,
　　　124–6
　　international trade 121–2
　　oil and natural gas industries 122–3,
　　　124
　　peace and conflict prevention by
　　　MNEs 127–31, 172
International Finance Corporation
　　(IFC) 31–2, 33, 162
international financial institutions
　　31–3, 162
international human rights law 17–18,
　　26, 30–34
international labour law 34–5
International Labour Organization
　　(ILO) 13, 26, 27, 34–5
international labour standards 34–5
international law and corporate social
　　responsibility
　　current status of private
　　　corporations 28–9
　　environmental law 35–9
　　human rights responsibilities
　　　enforcement 30–33
　　International Criminal Court
　　　33–4
　　international labour standards
　　　34–5

market sustainability 29
　　state litigation 25–6
International Monetary Fund 157
international organizations 162, 163,
　　183
　　see also individual organizations
international political relations,
　　China–India nexus 94, 101
international regulation 159–60
International Rights Advocates
　　(IRAdvocates) 17–18
international standards 26–7, 29, 34–5,
　　175, 177
　　see also Global Compact (UN);
　　　United Nations Universal
　　　Declaration of Human Rights
　　　(UDHR)
international trade 95–6, 97, 121–2,
　　123–4
international trade forums 32–3
internet 51, 77, 85
　　see also e-commerce and
　　　e-procurement; ICTs
　　　(information and
　　　communication technologies)
investment 38, 95, 163, 172, 178
　　see also foreign capital
isomorphisms 176–7, 179, 184
Israel 130
IT and software industries 94, 95,
　　96–7, 98–9, 100

Jalfa 109
Japan 96, 100–101
Johnson & Johnson 109
jus cogens 29, 35
justice system 26, 33–4, 35–6, 38–9, 76,
　　77

Kalakota, R. 82
Kang, D.C. 61
Kazakhstan 124, 129
Kell, G. 18
Ketata, I. 161, 164
Khanna, T. 63, 64, 96, 97
Kimberley Process Certification
　　Scheme 123
Kinley, D. 32
knowledge 4–5, 172, 181–2
knowledge-based industry 177, 179

knowledge-based services
  "Best Practices in Human Resources
    Management" competition 110,
    111, 112, 113, 114, 115
  in police and public safety agencies
    75, 76–7, 80–81
knowledge management 75, 76–7,
  80–81
Knudsen, D. 83
Kock, C. 63, 64
Krueger, A.B. 171
Krupp 33
Kyoto Protocol 163–4

La Porta, R. 59, 68
labour *see* child labour; child labour
    abolition; employees;
    employment; forced labour
    abolition; human capital; human
    resources; labour costs; labour
    protection; labour relations
labour costs 101–2, 160
labour protection 12
labour relations 26, 27, 35
Lal, R. 93–4
Laqueur, W. 171
law 15–16, 19, 177
  see also international criminal law;
    international environmental
    law; international human rights
    law; international labour law;
    international law and corporate
    social responsibility; legal
    personhood; litigation; rule of
    law; traffic law infringements
learning 109–10, 146
  see also education; knowledge;
    learning network; qualified
    staff, recruitment and retention
    of
learning network 18, 21
Leary, V. 34
legal personhood 25, 34, 35
legitimacy 64–5, 66, 68
Leisinger, K.M. 10, 18–19, 146
Lenovo 96
Lesotho 124, 129
Levin, D. 18
litigation 17–18, 22, 25–6
local community needs 111, 112, 114

local governments 22
local knowledge 181–2
Lopez, A. 160
Loscocco, P.A. 86
Lula, L.I. 146

Maleckova, J. 171
Mammen, L. 156
Mandatory Access Control (MAC)
  86
manufacturing industries 94, 95, 96,
  97, 98, 179
  see also production sector; wood
    production industry
market economy 105, 108–9
  see also capitalism
marketing, and religion 51
markets 29, 32, 35
Mayell, H. 126
McIntosh, M. 140, 143, 144, 145
McIntyre, J.R. 156, 161, 164
mediation 127, 130, 131
Meir, G. 4
Middle East 121–2, 125
military relations, China–India nexus
  93–4, 100–101, 102
Millennium Development Goals 140,
  141
mimetic isomorphism 177, 179
mineral resources 96
mining products 121
minority shareholders, expropriation
  see expropriation of minority
    shareholders
mission statements 111–12, 114
Mobil Oil 129
mobile telecommunications and data
  services 76–7, 78–9
monitoring 13, 15, 16–17, 19, 22, 26,
  32
Monshipouri, M. 19, 20
morals 15–16, 19, 160–161
  see also business ethics; corporate
    citizenship; corporate social
    responsibility (CSR)
multi-stakeholder initiatives 143, 146,
  148, 175, 180–181
  see also Global Compact (UN)
murder investigations 77
Myanmar 17, 125

national firms 110, 112, 113, 114, 115, 122
natural gas industries 122–3
natural resources 96, 172, 173
nepotism 66
networks 13, 14–18, 21
　see also cooperation; group cohesion; partnerships; social networks; World Economic Forum Global Risk Network
NGOs 38, 39, 160, 173, 174, 175, 176, 180
　see also human rights NGOs
Nicaragua 154
Nicolas, N. 174, 185
Nigeria 119, 121, 124, 170
NIIT 98–9
Nike 160
non-violent societies 49–50
normative isomorphism 177, 179
North America 122, 123, 161, 182–3
　see also anti-Americanism; Canada; US
not-for-profit security initiatives 182–3
nuclear weapons 35–6
Nuremburg Tribunal 33–4
Nye, J.S. Jr 95

OECD 26, 27, 161, 163, 177, 183, 184
Ogata, S. 140
oil industries 122–3, 124
oil pollution 28
opaqueness 64, 154
　see also transparency
OPEC (Organization of the Petroleum Exporting Countries) 122, 125
opportunism 160
organizations 109–10
　see also international organizations; regional human rights bodies; regional organizations; individual organizations
outsourced services 98, 100
ownership structures 110, 112, 113, 114, 115, 116

Palepu, K. 63, 64
Palestine 130
paper records, elimination of 76, 81
partnerships 13, 181, 182, 183

Pauchant, T.C. 52
peace 4, 13–14, 119–20, 127–31, 172
　see also peace, business and religious harmony; 'Peace Through Commerce'; public safety; wars
peace, business and religious harmony
　next steps and conclusion 55–6
　"Peace Through Commerce" 47, 49–50
　personal example 48–9
　religion: key points 50–55
　rock metaphor 55
Poland
　corporate social performance post-transition 109–10, 116–17
　"Best Practices in Human Resources Management" competition 110–115, 117
　social injustice 109
　transition to market economy 105, 108–9
　Tylenol case 109
policing 74–81, 87–8
Polish Institute of Labour and Social Studies 110–115, 117
politics 14, 15, 16, 21, 54
pollution 16–17, 28, 158
poverty 50, 126, 153, 159, 171
poverty reduction 10–11, 144
Powell, W.W. 176–7
power 9, 25, 30, 31, 171
primary products 121
privately-owned oil companies 122
privatization 157–8
proactive strategies 161
procurement, traditional 82, 83, 84
　see also e-commerce and e-procurement
production sector 110, 111, 112, 113, 114, 115
　see also fuel products; manufacturing industries; mining products; primary products; wood production industry
profits 5, 6, 9
promotion of corporate social responsibility 113, 114, 115, 162
public safety 74–81, 87–8
　see also security

publicly-owned firms 110, 112, 113, 114, 115, 116–17
purchasing 82, 84
  see also e-commerce and e-procurement; procurement, traditional
Purchasing Power Parity (PPP), China–India nexus 93

qualified staff, recruitment and retention of 74, 179
quality 111, 112, 114

Radu, M. 159
R&D support 113, 114, 115
regional human rights bodies 30, 31
regional organizations 30, 31, 181
regulation and regulations 154, 158, 159–60, 162, 163–4
Reilly, B. 37
"related party" 68
religion, peace and business 48–9, 50–56
remuneration, and social capital 65–8
reporting 15, 17, 21, 22, 26–7, 60, 145, 180–181
reputation 9, 19, 160, 161, 164, 178–80, 185
resources 16, 30, 31
  see also human resources; natural resources
respect, and right of religious expression 52
responsibility *see* corporate social responsibility (CSR); individual responsibility
RFID (Radio-Frequency Identification) 79–80, 81
right of religious expression 51–2
Rio Declaration on Environment and Development 36–7
Rischard, J.-F. 184–5
risk assessment and management 4, 5–6, 19, 87
Robinson, M. 82
Rodrik, D. 171
Rohleder, R. 84
Rok, B. 109, 116
Role-Based Access Control (RBAC) 86

Rome Statute (International Criminal Court) 28, 34
Rondinelli, D.A. 161
Roth, K. 16
Ruggie, J.G. 20, 143
rule of law 50, 127, 129–30, 131
Rummel, R.J. 169, 170
Russell Family Foundation 182
Russia 57, 122, 123, 125

Sachs, W.M. 59, 62, 64
Salim Group 59–60, 63–4
sanitation infrastructure 126
Schepers, D.H. 175–6
Schipani, C.A. 49–50, 127, 131, 174
Secretary General of the United Nations 4–5, 11, 13, 15, 36, 126, 144
sectors 110, 111
  see also international extractive industries; knowledge-based industry; manufacturing industries; production sector; services sector; software and IT industries
Securities and Exchange Commission (SEC) (US) 174
security 85–6, 87, 139–40, 182–3
  see also public safety
self-interest 106, 127, 173, 186
Sen, A. 140, 146
sensitive data 85–6
services sector 110, 111, 112, 113, 114, 115
  see also knowledge-based services
Sethi, S.P. 107
Shambaugh, D. 101
Shami, F. 130
shareholders 25, 179
Shaw, M. 84
Shell 160
"shell corporations" 25
Singh, M. 82, 83
Sisci, F. 94
skills 60
  see also education; knowledge; learning; qualified staff, recruitment and retention of
Smalley, S.D. 86
Soar, J. 75
social assets 66, 67

social capital 60–68
social climate 114, 115
"social contract" 106
social depreciation 67
social dividends 67
social dominance orientation (SDO)
    177–8, 180, 184, 185
social equity 67, 147, 148
social inequality 125–6, 171, 177, 178,
    180
social injustice 109, 159
social issues, and corporate citizenship
    142
social liabilities 66–7
social networks 59–60, 61, 62–3, 64–5,
    67, 177, 181
social policy, reporting 26, 27
social problems 124, 159
social progress, and capitalism 144
software and IT industries 94, 95,
    96–7, 98–9, 99, 100
South America 121–2, 123
spirituality 52–4
stakeholders
    in corporate social responsibility
        definitions 106, 107
    education 164
    engaging with 145
    goal incompatibility 148, 175–6
    in models of corporate social
        responsibility 108
    multi-stakeholder initiatives 143,
        146, 148, 175, 180–181
    pressure, and corporate social
        responsibility 160
    and sustainable enterprise economy
        148
standards 163
    see also international standards
states *see* governments
Stephens, T. 36
Subramaniam, C. 84
Sudan 124, 130, 170
Suder, G. 3–4, 169, 171, 174–5, 185
Suharto 59–60, 63–4
Suryanarayana, P.S. 101
sustainability reporting 145
sustainable development 144–5
    see also sustainable enterprise
        economy

sustainable enterprise economy
    139–42, 147–8
Switzer, J. 169–70, 173, 174, 176

Tadaki, J. 32
Taiwan 16–17
Talero, E. 84
technical expertise 16
technology *see* environmentally-
        friendly technologies; ICTs
        (information and communication
        technologies); software and IT
        industries
terrorism 57, 124–5, 128–9, 155–6, 159
    see also global terrorism
Thadani, V. 98
Thomson, T. 82, 83
toxic waste dumping 16–17
trading favours 62–3
traffic law infringements 75, 77, 78
traffic safety 75–6, 77
transitional economies 59
    see also Poland
transparency 65, 84
    see also opaqueness
Travis, E.F. 156
Tripartite Declaration (ILO) 26, 27,
    34
trust 53
Tylenol case 109

UK 10–11, 17, 144–5
United Nations 11, 28, 30–31, 38–9,
    50, 123, 140, 141, 161, 164, 169,
    170, 183
    see also Global Compact (UN);
        Secretary General of the United
        Nations; individual
        organizations
United Nations Commission on
    Human Security 139–40
United Nations Development
    Programme (UNDP) 13, 140
United Nations General Assembly
    30–31, 38
United Nations High-Level Panel on
    Threats, Challenges and Changes
    156
United Nations Human Rights
    Commission 28, 30, 31

United Nations Human Rights
  Council 31
United Nations Security Council 36–8
United Nations Universal Declaration
  of Human Rights (UDHR) 8,
  9–10, 11, 13, 15
universality, of human rights 9–10
university research centres 16, 22
Urbaniak, B. 110–115
Urdal, H. 170
US 17–18, 26, 96–7, 99–101, 123,
  173–4

Vaidya, K. 82–3
violence 4, 50, 119, 121–2, 169, 170,
  171
  see also non-violent societies;
    terrorism; wars
Voltaw, D. 106
voluntary codes of conduct 26–7, 29,
  112–13, 114–15, 180–181, 185
  see also Global Compact (UN)

Waddock, S. 107
wars 4, 169, 171, 172

Wartick, S.L. 107
water supply 126
weak governance 59, 61, 62, 63, 64,
  175, 184
wealth accumulation 9, 185
WHO Nuclear Weapons case (ICJ)
  35–6
Williams, J.B. 129
Woo, C. 49
wood production industry 123–4
World Bank 31–2, 33, 50, 129, 130,
  144, 157, 161, 163, 183
World Economic Forum (Davos,
  1999) 11
World Economic Forum Global Risk
  Network 5–6
World Summit on Sustainable
  Development (Johannesburg,
  2002) 36
World Trade Organization (WTO)
  32–3, 38–9, 121–2

Yeo, V. 99–100
youth bulge theory of conflict
  170